Process Mapping,
Process Improvement,
and Process Management

Process Mapping, Process Improvement, and Process Management

*A Practical Guide
for Enhancing Work and
Information Flow*

Dan Madison

Paton Professional
Chico, California

Most Paton Press books are available at quantity discounts when purchased in bulk. For more information, contact:

Paton Press LLC
P.O. Box 44
Chico, CA 95927-0044
Telephone: (530) 342-5480
Fax: (530) 342-5471
E-mail: *books@patonpress.com*
Web: *www.patonpress.com*

14 13 12 11 10   8 7 6 5 4

ISBN-13: 978-1-932828-04-7

Staff
Publisher: Scott M. Paton
Editor: Taran March
Book design: David Hurst

This book is for my father.
I always got captured by his dreams.

Contents

Acknowledgments

This book was significantly enhanced by the contribution of several people. First, I want to thank Jerry Talley, Ph.D., for co-sponsoring the research on the management of work in Chapter 1. We've used this material with numerous clients, and it consistently helps shed light on the types of change activities that each particular client situation requires. Jerry also contributed Chapter 14: Building Cross-Departmental Process Management, which correlates very nicely with the management of work. His own work on cross-departmental cooperation is state-of-the-art. Working across organizational boundaries presents unique challenges, and with Jerry's road map, these efforts can be smoothly negotiated.

Chapter 15, Using Dynamic Simulation in Business Process Management, was written by Vic Walling, Ph.D. Vic's understanding and use of software for process management is a great complement to the preceding material on process mapping and improvement. As he likes to say, "The process management software is like a piano: It can sit there and look nice, but you need a talented pianist to make music." Vic is that great musician for process management software. Today's organizations can significantly accelerate process performance with the use of these tools. Process simulation has multiple benefits that organizations are just now exploring.

In Chapter 2, the section on process controls was from the work Jim Vanetta has done at Crown Castle. Jim was generous enough to share some of the concepts and sample documents and control measure protocols that have been recognized as best-in-class from Crown Castle's accounting firms. The Sarbanes-Oxley Act of 2002 has forced public companies to be very rigorous in their controls, and this material provides the structure for that purpose.

I want to thank all of my clients from my sixteen-year consulting practice. See-ing the tools used to drive results is most satisfying. Also, I want to thank all of the participants in my executive education seminars for their questions, comments, and suggestions. Many of them found their way into this book.

Lastly, I want to express appreciation for my wife, who put up with me during this project. Her helpful comments and sage advice keep me from getting into too much trouble.

Chapter 1

The Importance of Process

Every day each one of us works in or interacts with a process. At work, we prepare documents, deliver reports, and attend meetings; away from work, we shop, plan vacations, and arrange meals. All of these activities are processes. Often we don't notice the process because it runs smoothly. However, when things don't go as planned, we want to know what happened, triggering the need for process analysis.

Processes are important because:

- They're a major component of organizations.
- A process-focused organization can use process analysis to diagnose all types of problems (e.g., structure, controls, people, and processes).
- Most organizational problems have their root cause in a process.
- Organizations can manage work much more effectively and efficiently through a process mindset.

Each of these concepts is discussed in more detail in the following sections.

WHAT ARE ORGANIZATIONS?

Organizations comprise four elements:

- People
- Processes
- Control mechanisms
- Structure

The *people* element refers to roles and responsibilities, skills, training, motivation, capability, and job fit. In many organizations when something goes wrong, people blame co-workers because they believe most problems are somehow people-related. But what about problems with the other organizational elements? Let's look at them each in turn.

What does a process mean, exactly? It can be defined it in three ways:

■ A group of activities that leads to some output or result.
■ The means by which work gets done.
■ A mechanism to create and deliver value to a customer.

The two main processes in any organization are workflow and information flow. In 1992 the American Productivity and Quality Center (APQC) compiled a proc-ess classification framework (PFC). It's exceedingly helpful in defining processes within organizations without having to be industry-specific. The APQC's PFC is included in Appendix B.

Control mechanisms exist for all processes. Sometimes they're quite visible; at other times, they're not. In manufacturing processes, controls generally are electrical, mechanical, and/or statistical in nature, such as gages and measurement devices. In service processes, controls are usually the people, or their supervisors, who work in the process. Included with these controls are the beliefs and assumptions of the key players.

Controls can include behavioral prods such as rewards for desirable actions or penalties for undesirable ones. Corporate policy and business rules are controls. In addition, software rules control activities and information flow. Finally, measurement and feedback systems are controls as well.

Control mechanisms are important in process management because any big change in a process will require a change to the existing controls. If they're not changed, the process will begin to revert back to how it was. Recall, for example, a time when you or a co-worker had a great idea for improving something only to have a manager say, "That won't work." Here, the manager's skepticism is the control mechanism that impedes making a change to a process.

Controls often have "slack" in them that allows incremental changes to a proc-ess without triggering the control mechanism. Continuous process improvement techniques can be quite successful because often there's no need to change a control when changing a process.

The *structure* of an organization refers to its chart of departments, reporting relationships, and span of control.

Thus, organizations consist of people working in processes that have control mechanisms, all of which are placed into an organizational structure.

An effective entry point to find problems in an organization is through processes. By using the four lenses of analysis—i.e., frustration, quality, time, and cost—discussed in Chapter 7, we can identify problems not only with processes but also with people, control mechanisms, and structure. Process analysis produces a wonderful diagnostic on what works and what doesn't.

WHERE DO MOST ORGANIZATIONAL PROBLEMS ORIGINATE?

Process-thinking pundits claim that 85 percent of all problems can be attributed to processes. The remaining 15 percent falls into the people category. I'd like to modify that slightly: *85 percent of all organizational problems fall into process, control mechanisms, and structure, with the bulk of that in process.*

An interesting dynamic takes place in organizations where managers blame people for problems: The people being blamed will use a series of defensive routines to deflect the criticism. Often, they'll blame someone else or another department. Consequently, problems imbedded in a process don't get fixed, and it's more than likely that they'll reoccur. The blame dynamic creates a vicious cycle with little chance of really solving the problem.

Thus, when a problem arises, the most effective plan of action is to examine the process in detail using the four lenses of analysis. If the problem isn't a process issue, you should still be able to locate the root cause by using the four lenses.

The root causes of organizational problems can be categorized as:

- Problems with process, control mechanisms, and structure: 85 percent
- Problems with people: 15 percent

THE FIVE STYLES OF WORK MANAGEMENT

When my associate Jerry Talley and I looked at how organizations manage work, five distinct management styles emerged. Organizations tend to move logically from one style to the next because the preceding style sets the stage for the one following. Moving from one style to the next requires a developmental transition. For this reason it's difficult to skip a step.

Also, each step in the transition is an evolutionary advancement in how effective an organization can be. The thinking, tool sets, and methodologies of each style allow an organization to improve in quality, cost reduction, service delivery, and customer satisfaction. Each time an organization moves to the next management style, the rewards accelerate.

The transition from one style to the next is preceded by a belief change or experiences that cause management to think differently. When this change takes hold, it sets the stage for a new way to manage work.

When these management styles were benchmarked against the Malcolm Baldrige National Quality Award winners of 2000 to see if their transitions match the theory of work management, the Baldrige winners stated that the five styles we defined mirrored their own journeys. Following is a discussion of each style.

TRADITIONAL WORK MANAGEMENT

The first style of work management is called "traditional." Figure 1.1 shows a diagram of a typical organization chart. At the top is the president, to whom a variety of departments report. Within each department the authority is hierarchi-

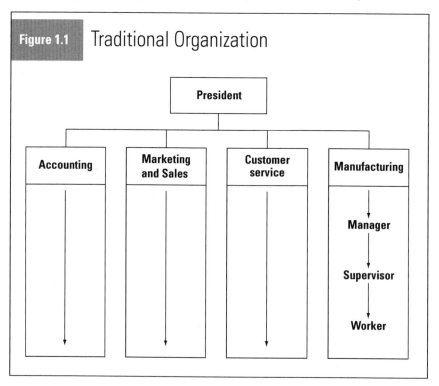

Figure 1.1 Traditional Organization

cal, with the department head at the top, then the manager, supervisor, and, finally, the worker.

In a traditional organization, the "brains" are represented by everyone in a management position, while the "arms and legs" are those at the worker level. When something goes wrong, the immediate response is to find the guilty party. Management in traditional organizations attributes most problems to people. You hear comments such as, "They weren't trained"; "They didn't follow procedures"; "It was a poor job fit"; "They weren't motivated"; and "They lacked the skills."

Another aspect of the traditional organization is lack of trust. Workers don't trust management, and management doesn't trust workers. Lack of trust exists between departments as well. Finger-pointing and blaming between departments can be quite common.

In traditional organizations, problems get fixed in a variety of ways. One of the most popular is to do something about the people because it's commonly believed that almost all problems are somehow people-related. For this reason, training is a popular approach. When a problem comes up, someone is usually quick to rush to a training solution.

Another people approach is to change responsibilities through organizational restructuring. Managers who are trusted and deemed skilled are assigned more responsibility, while managers who underperform are penalized by losing responsibilities.

Finally, review steps are added to the workflow. Managers want to catch problems before they go too far. If managers' lack confidence that the work will be done properly, then it must be reviewed.

There are several flaws in the traditional style of work management. They are:
■ Management and supervisors believe they have all the answers.
■ Although a manager or supervisor thinks he or she is saving time by dictating a solution to a problem, it creates a lack of buy-in by those affected by the solution.
■ Creating a solution for one area can create problems in others.
■ The wrong solution might be picked because no one else has input. More minds devoted to a problem often result in a better solution.

Traditional organizations usually exist where competition is either very low or nonexistent, such as in the public sector, or in monopolistic businesses such as utilities. Products get produced and services get delivered in traditional organizations. However, the internal cost in both dollars and morale can be high.

A traditional organizational structure might be appropriate for companies where activities are simple and repetitive, and the turnover is high. A fast-food franchise might be one example. (However, high turnover could also be caused by lack of staff input, a hallmark of traditional management.) Also, in an emergency, when fast decision making is required, a traditional "command and control" approach makes sense.

THE INVOLVEMENT APPROACH

To transition to the next work management style requires the following belief by senior management: *Some of the workers have good ideas.* This realization leads to the work management style called "involvement."

How are those good ideas harvested? An early attempt at getting ideas from workers was through the employee suggestion system. A worker filled out a form and submitted it. Often months went by before a decision was made about the suggestion. Also, many of the ideas were rejected. As a result, enthusiasm and participation in employee suggestion systems declined in many organizations.

During the 1970s and 1980s, a process improvement technique from Japan called Quality Circles became popular in the United States. It involved workers getting together to discuss problems and offer solutions. However, the Quality Circle approach didn't last. What happened?

The biggest problem was that the ideas workers proposed weren't acted upon. People lost interest in participating when they discovered nothing came of it. Supervisors were responsible for implementing these ideas, but in many cases, they didn't. The reason could be that these supervisors experienced a conflict in roles. They were made supervisors because they were the best workers in their group. Now they were expected to get ideas from their subordinates and implement them. For many in this position, the benefit of implementing subordinates' ideas wasn't apparent. Also, soliciting ideas requires facilitation and team problem-solving skills, which many supervisors lacked.

Today involvement is seen in teams, committees, ad hoc groups, and task forces. People come together, analyze a problem, propose a solution, and sometimes implement it. Figure 1.2 shows an organization chart that represents the involvement concept.

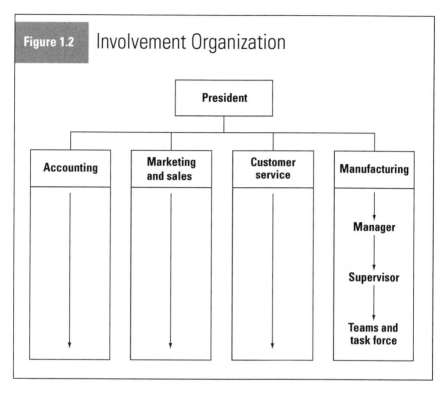

Figure 1.2 Involvement Organization

Problems With Traditional and Involvement Models

Several fundamental flaws exist in both traditional and involvement organizations. The most damaging is the belief that if a company optimizes the pieces, it optimizes the whole. How often do we find that one department uses Microsoft Windows, another UNIX, and a third Macintosh? Now try to share data. Each department has optimized its own organization, but seamlessly linking data becomes a huge problem.

Another issue is dispersing linked goals to separate departments. For example, a sales department is rewarded strictly on sales goals. If a flood of orders comes in, then manufacturing might be extremely stressed in consequence, which in turn could lead to quality problems. Ultimately, that poor quality will hurt sales. Aren't sales and quality equally valuable?

When each department has its own agenda and performance metrics, then disconnects between departments are inevitable, and these ultimately impede the whole. As you move forward in the work management structure, you'll see how this problem is solved.

In traditional and involvement organizations, the narrowly defined job is seen as a way to increase productivity. (Think of Henry Ford's production line.) But as work is cut up into smaller and smaller pieces, handoffs and their resultant quality problems arise. Imagine two relay races, one of which requires fifty baton passes, and the other requires ten: In which race would participants be more likely to drop the baton?

Finally, traditional and involvement organizations lack the knowledge of process design principles. Without these as guidance, the well-intentioned change—whether it's restructuring, reorganization, or something else—can wildly misfire, leading to decreases in quality, cycle time, and worker and customer satisfaction.

PROCESS MANAGEMENT OF WORK

The next style of work management requires a major shift in thinking. Instead of assuming that most problems are people-related, *management now believes most problems have their root cause in the process.* A process is defined as the flow of work or information leading to some output or result. A process is how work gets done.

Accordingly, this next style is called "process." Organizations gain several benefits when transitioning to process. First, blame goes way down. If most of the problems occur in the process, it doesn't make sense to look for a guilty party. People are now asked to analyze and change processes instead of covering their behinds or pointing fingers. Tension in the work place decreases and the environment becomes much more enjoyable.

Second, because most of the problems are in the process, fixing them means that quality and customer satisfaction will soar while costs and cycle time decline. Process organizations become more effective and efficient, which shows up in both sales and profits.

Many managers have a hard time making this shift in thinking. Some organizations will start down the process path, but the prevailing belief that most problems are people-related undermines the effort. Some organizations try process tools even while senior management is still blame-oriented and maintains a "command and control" mode.

TQM and Other Quality Initiatives

The process philosophy and toolsets were largely originated by two Americans, W. Edwards Deming and Joseph M. Juran. Both of these men helped introduce the concepts and tools of total quality management (TQM) to Japan after World War II. The automobile and electronics industries embraced the concepts. Organizations that adopted the TQM approach experienced significant reductions in cost and cycle time while improving quality and customer satisfaction. Inevitably, these companies began taking market share from their U.S. competitors. Today, Toyota is the second-largest automaker in the world, surpassing Ford. In addition, Toyota has taken TQM and tailored it into the Toyota Production System, which in the United States we refer to as "lean manufacturing."

The work management continuum is both developmental and evolutionary. Organizations that are further along it are likely to be more competitive and offer higher value than those that are less evolved. Japanese companies drove this point home against their U.S. counterparts. It took losing significant market share before U.S. companies embraced the concepts of TQM.

TQM was very popular during the 1980s. Millions of dollars were spent on training. Some organizations had great success with the methodology, but others didn't. Today, we don't hear much about TQM, but we do hear a lot about Six Sigma.

The Six Sigma methodology was developed by Motorola in the mid-1980s and adopted by General Electric a decade later. Recently, it's soared in popularity as many organizations adopt its toolset, methodology, and philosophy. Six Sigma overcomes many of the problems inherent within TQM and has proven to be a robust system for improving process performance and boosting quality.

Further into this book, some of the more powerful tools of process analysis —namely, process mapping and process design principles—will be discussed and explained. Additionally, some Six Sigma and lean manufacturing tools will be introduced. Six Sigma is a robust methodology for quality problems, and lean is excellent for time reduction. A combination of the two is fast becoming the process improvement methodology of choice in many U.S. organizations. In addition, the concept of process management will be outlined so that readers can help move their own organizations into a process mindset.

In Figure 1.3, the manufacturing department has identified several processes in its area. These have been improved using quality and lean tools. Generally speaking, those who manufacture things are the first to embrace process tools. That's because the process of making things is very visible: Errors, scrap, waste, and bottlenecks are all obvious. The process organization in Figure 1.3 has an aligned

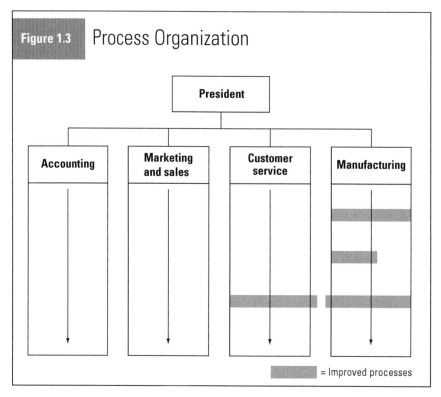

Figure 1.3   Process Organization

= Improved processes

department, customer service, that's starting to use process improvement tools as well. However, it could be that accounting has a traditional manager, and the marketing department manager uses an involvement approach. Hence, at any point in time, a transitional organization might be a blend of several management styles.

A popular improvement technique today is the *kaizen* blitz, which combines involvement (i.e., a team of workers) with data analysis and process thinking. During an intense five-day span, workers analyze data and come up with solutions to process issues.

It's not uncommon that traditional or involvement departments will throw "bricks" or attempt to impede process-oriented departments. The process mindset represents a huge departure from the usual people orientation, and some departments might come under attack as they begin the process journey.

Is Your Organization Process-Oriented?

If you think your organization is process-oriented, use this test. When a problem arises, the first course of action is to look at the process and use process improvement tools to fix the problem. Also, a significant amount of the process analysis is done by people involved in the process itself. There should be little or no blame generated. If any of the above doesn't happen in your organization, then you're not fully process-oriented.

The Dilbert cartoon below captures three work management ypes. What three did you see? If you're a regular *Dilbert* reader, you know that Dilbert's pointy-haired boss is a traditional manager who's both dysfunctional and Machiavellian. The cartoon's wide appeal is due in part to how well readers can identify with Dilbert as well as his work environment.

In this strip, Patty, a new process manager, is introduced to Dilbert and his office mates. It doesn't take long for the entire group to reject her, especially the boss. Dilbert tries to make her feel better because she lasted longer than "Timmy the facilitator" (an involvement work management trait). In this one strip, cartoonist Scott Adams has illustrated three work management styles: traditional, involvement, and process.

CROSS-FUNCTIONAL MANAGEMENT OF WORK

The transition to the next management style might happen this way: Imagine someone in manufacturing standing up from his or her desk and looking at the order-to-delivery process as it spans several departments. Although great results have been achieved within the manufacturing department by using process tools,

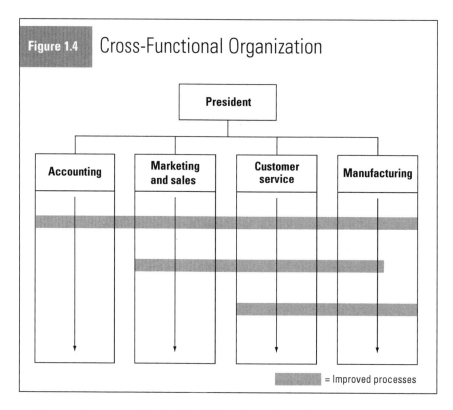

Figure 1.4   Cross-Functional Organization

problems still remain with the "handoffs" from sales. This person in manufacturing begins to wonder, "What if we redesigned the larger process from beginning to end, with a clean sheet of paper? What might that look like?" This mindset was popularized in *Reengineering the Corporation,* by Michael Hammer and James Champy (HarperBusiness, 2001).

Organizations began rethinking these larger processes and dramatically changing them, sometimes with the aid of information technology. Because cross-departmental processes were ripe for improvement, great gains were achieved. Accordingly, the next management step is called "cross-functional." Figure 1.4 illustrates the concept.

Through their reengineering efforts, many organizations were able to drastically reduce cycle time and costs while increasing quality and service. However, reengineering's success was mixed due to turf issues, resistance, and lack of senior management commitment.

An article by Thomas A. Stewart in the August 23, 1993, issue of *Fortune* testifies to the power of reengineering. Organizations that reengineered their proc-esses correctly, he says, gained in speed, productivity, and profitability, in some cases—such as GTE's—even doubling revenues or halving costs. Stewart noted that reengineering isn't appropriate for all organizations, and that the failure rate is high—between 50 percent and 70 percent.

Part of that failure can be attributed to misconceptions about the technique. Reengineering doesn't mean simply improving old procedures and firing un-productive employees. "Reengineers start from the future and work backward," he says. "In effect they ask, 'If we were a new company, how would we run this place?'" In most cases, reengineering:

■ Requires dramatic changes within an organization
■ Cuts across all departments
■ Involves considerable investment in training and information technology

"Don't do it if you don't have to," Stewart warns. "Save reengineering for big processes that really matter, like new-product development or customer service. The best corporate candidates for reengineering are companies facing big shifts in the nature of the competition."

MATRIX WORK MANAGEMENT

Although a reengineered process can deliver exceptional gains, over time some of the gains can begin to erode. People begin to revert to their old work habits. Barriers between departments rise again. Why does this happen?

In a large cross-functional process, the pieces of the process are "owned" by each department, which has an individual agenda and performance metrics. De-partments are encouraged to optimize their piece of the larger process, but in this effort the company as a whole can become suboptimized. It's not uncommon for gains to backslide because no one oversees or manages the larger cross-functional process.

The belief that leads to the next management style, which is called "matrix," is that larger cross-functional processes need someone to oversee and continually improve them. In an attempt to solve this problem, process improvement leaders created a new job, the process owner.

The title "process owner" can be somewhat misleading, however. Ownership implies control over resources. In many organizations, the process owner is responsible for the process performance but can't make decisions concerning personnel. This is a classic mismatch between responsibility and authority. In those organizations where process owners have no authority over resources, their titles should reflect their true positions. "Process consultant" or "process advisor" would be more appropriate. Figure 1.5 illustrates this concept.

IBM, Johnson & Johnson, Shell Oil, and UPS all have process owners, notes Hammer. The results from using a process owner can be impressive. For instance, a process owner at American Standard helped the company deliver toilets in one week, compared to twelve weeks at the company's Mexican facility. More organizations are recognizing the need for an oversight and management function for large cross-departmental processes.

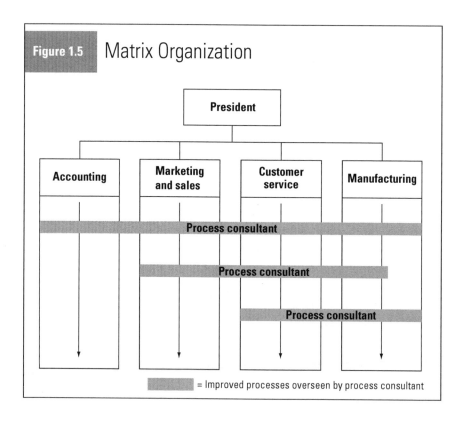

Figure 1.5   Matrix Organization

F-TYPE WORK MANAGEMENT

Eventually, senior management will recognize the problems that withholding authority from the process consultant can create. *Shouldn't the person who oversees the process also have authority to fix it and allocate resources as necessary?* It's difficult to find organizations that have placed true authority in the hands of the cross-functional process person.

A great example of an organization where the process person has true authority is a professional football team. The team has three process owners, offensive coordinator, defensive coordinator, and special teams. Each of these people "owns" the processes within his respective areas. For example, the offensive coordinator actually works with several departments, which are offensive line, wide receivers, quarterback, running back, and tight ends. Each of these departments has a "coach." It's the coach's job to develop the talent in his respective area. The coach then works with the coordinator to field the best personnel for each process or "play." The special teams coordinator often pulls talent from both defensive and offensive coordinators. The availability of these resources is based on the team strategy as well as each individual's strengths and weaknesses.

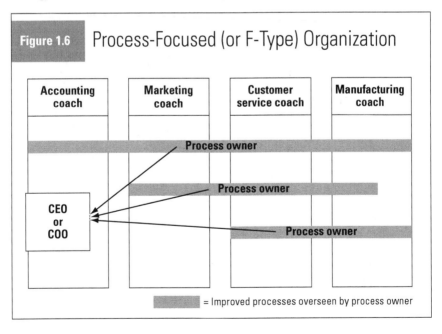

Figure 1.6 Process-Focused (or F-Type) Organization

This is the F-type management style, for football—or for finally because organizations that incorporate this style are at long last truly process-focused. Figure 1.6 illustrates the concept.

WORK MANAGEMENT SUMMARY

Work management is both developmental and evolutionary. It's developmental because each style serves as a foundation for the next. For that reason, it's hard to skip a style. It would be like expecting a crawling baby to get up and run; it's not developmentally ready. Asking a traditional organization to become a process organization is equally difficult. There are rare instances where the transition through the types can be accelerated, but it's not recommended. It's best to go at a pace that builds the foundation for the next type, wherever your organization is. If it's largely involvement, then find departments where a process mindset can be successfully inserted. When quite a few departments have embraced process thinking, then you're ready for cross-functional changes.

Work management is evolutionary. As organizations move through the five management styles, they become more efficient and effective, as the graph in Figure 1.7 demonstrates. Consequently, if your company is competing against more evolved organizations, it could become a losing battle. Conversely, if your organization is more evolved than your competitors, you should be able to gain market share from them.

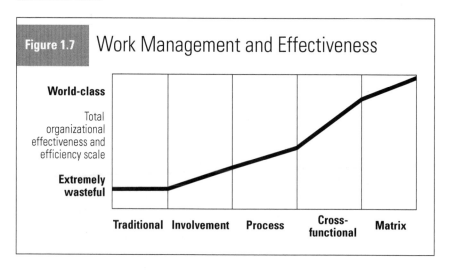

Figure 1.7   Work Management and Effectiveness

World-class

Total organizational effectiveness and efficiency scale

Extremely wasteful

Traditional   Involvement   Process   Cross-functional   Matrix

The most evolved organizations typically exist where competition is the stiffest, such as the auto industry. To survive in a global and cutthroat industry, you must be at least a process organization. The auto industry is witnessing the winnowing out of less evolved organizations and more business consolidation.

Moving from one style to the next should be your organization's goal. The rewards are greater efficiency and effectiveness—and perhaps even survival.

Caveat: If your strategy is flawed, then it won't matter how efficient you are; you'll still find yourself out of business. The most efficient buggy whip manufacturer was nevertheless doomed when the automobile arrived. However, if you're offering what the customer wants, and you're the most efficient at producing it, then your future will be secured.

USING PROCESS MAPPING IN TRADITIONAL ORGANIZATIONS

In traditional organizations, as mentioned earlier, management is the brain, and the line staff is the hands and feet. Management makes decisions, and the staff is expected to execute them. When problems arise, management's knee-jerk reaction is to find the guilty party. Once the guilty party is found, they're often penalized so the problem won't happen again. These dynamics create mistrust between management and staff. Finger pointing and blaming are endemic in traditional organizational cultures.

If you want to use the process mapping tools in this book and your organization is traditional, then you'll have to proceed with some care. Because there's usually a history of mistrust in traditional business cultures, it's not uncommon for people to wonder what the "real" purpose of process mapping might be. Inevitably, some will think, "Are they planning to eliminate my job?"

The first step is to clearly delineate the need for using the process mapping tool kit. One of your reasons might be to improve quality. Another might be to identify bottlenecks. Or perhaps you want to improve upon timeliness. Whatever your reasons, people must understand why this methodology has been chosen and what will be accomplished. Expect some to ask: "How will this affect my job?" or, "What's my role in this initiative?" Be ready with answers to these and other concerns.

Because there's a great deal of mistrust, open and frequent communication is necessary. Explain how people will be kept informed. Allow for two-way communication through small group or "town hall"-type meetings.

These suggestions apply to all organizations, but traditional and involvement organizations tend to have the highest levels of mistrust. Hence, openness and honesty is a must.

When you actually start process mapping, you could go to each individual and ask questions about his or her work. This technique fits a traditional culture, but it hampers problem solving and efforts to gain a broad perspective.

Another highly recommended option is to use more of an involvement approach. Bring some of the people who actually do the work together. Interview them about what they do (i.e., create the process map), and then open the discussion up to frustrations they experience doing the work. When people realize you're serious about hearing and then acting on their frustrations, morale and enthusiasm leaps. Buy-in for changes should be high because these workers were instrumental in improving the process. People support what they help create and, conversely, people resist, fight, and sabotage what's rammed down their throats. Later in this book, a detailed method for using the frustration lens as a diagnostic and improvement tool will be discussed.

Process tools are apt to be accepted in areas where management already wants to create more involvement and where worker frustrations are high. Look for a department where these conditions exist and begin mapping efforts there. As you involve people at the lowest levels, you'll see high enthusiasm for change, and implementation will be much smoother. Build from your successes. As other departments witness the gains, they'll be more open to using process tools in their areas.

You'll run into the greatest hazards in a traditional organization when you begin cross-departmental process mapping and improvement initiatives. Turf battles and resistance can be prevalent and cause the effort to stall or derail. It's better to scale down the effort and achieve some limited success than to have a larger effort hit a brick wall.

Chapter 2

Process Mapping

N ow that you understand how important processes are to your organization, you're ready to move on to mapping a process. To begin, you must familiarize yourself with flowchart symbols and what each represents. Once you learn the symbols, the next step is to practice mapping a process.

FLOWCHART SYMBOLS

A variety of flowchart symbols represent different activities, but the most common symbols are the seven described below. Popular software programs such as Microsoft Visio offer complete templates, where users can drag and drop the appropriate symbol into their process map. The basic symbols are fairly simple, however, and are worth memorizing.

Box

The box represents an activity. Within the box are verbs and nouns. Figure 2.1 shows examples of activity boxes that have an activity described within. The box is probably the most commonly used flowchart symbol.

Diamond

The diamond represents a review, inspection, or decision. Inside the diamond are questions. For reviews or inspections, common questions are, "Does it pass?" or "Is it OK?" Likewise for these two situations, the number of routes out of the diamond is two: It either passed, or it didn't. It was OK, or it wasn't.

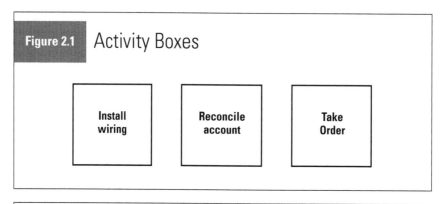

Figure 2.1 Activity Boxes

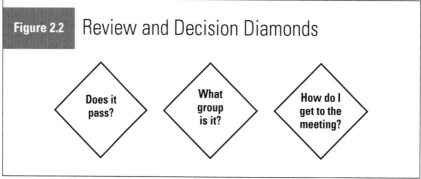

Figure 2.2 Review and Decision Diamonds

However, in the case of a decision, the number of paths the flow can take might be greater than two. If, for instance, you're asking, "How do I get to the meeting?" You might have several answers, including: Drive my car; carpool with a friend; take a taxi; take public transportation.

Figure 2.2 shows examples of diamonds.

Arrow

The arrow indicates the direction of the flow. It also can represent transport.

Figure 2.3 depicts an arrow.

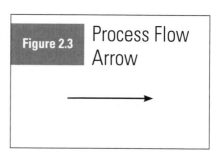

Figure 2.3 Process Flow Arrow

Triangle

Triangles represent filing or storage. They also have a verb and noun within them.

Figure 2.4 shows an example.

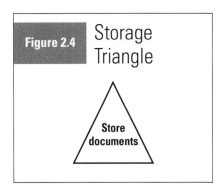

Figure 2.4 Storage Triangle

Store documents

The Big D

The "Big D" represents a delay. Batching, bottlenecks, equipment breakdowns, and waiting for information are examples of delays. Figure 2.5 illustrates this symbol.

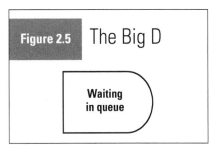

Figure 2.5 The Big D

Waiting in queue

Ovals

Ovals represent the start and end of a process map. Figure 2.6 shows an example of an oval.

Circles

Circles represent a cross-reference to another process. Figure 2.7 shows an example of a circle.

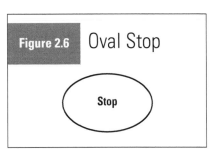

Figure 2.6 Oval Stop

Stop

MACRO FLOWCHARTS

Process mapping can be done at three levels of detail. They're called macro, functional-activity, and task-procedure. Each has its pros and cons and is used at an appropriate time and place.

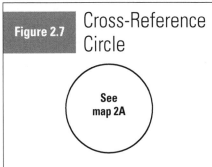

Figure 2.7 Cross-Reference Circle

See map 2A

The macro level is the least detailed of the three. Macro flowcharts usually depict two to seven steps that comprise the critical elements of a process. If a macro flowchart has more than seven steps, then it's getting too detailed. Figure 2.8 shows the macro flowchart of the order-to-delivery process for an equipment manufacturer.

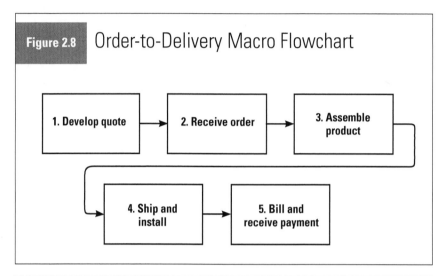

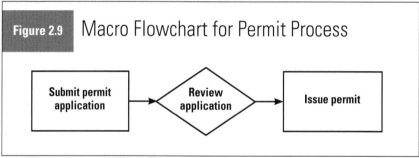

Figure 2.9 shows an example of a macro flowchart for issuing a permit at a city public works department.

The macro flowchart is used at the beginning of a process improvement project or when someone wants to illustrate the main parts of a process. This type of flowchart offers the following advantages:

■ It captures the "big picture," allowing you to see the main elements of a process.
■ It defines the boundaries or scope of a process. You can see the beginning and the end.

The disadvantage of the macro is that it's not detailed enough to spot problem areas.

Creating a Macro Flowchart

You can map the flow either from left to right or top-down. Each box or diamond should comprise either a grouping of activities or a key step in the process. Remember if you map more than seven steps, you're probably getting too detailed. If this happens, go back and see if you can combine some steps into one.

What to Watch Out For

Although it may seem apparent that creating a macro flowchart isn't difficult, that may not be the case. When working with a team, there's often discussion or debate on the process boundaries. It's good to let these discussions run their course because the conversation is valuable for the team. Consensus needs to emerge regarding the boundaries of the process.

FUNCTIONAL-ACTIVITY FLOWCHARTS

Also called a deployment flowchart, the functional-activity flowchart represents the middle level of detail, and its title explains what it does. The "functional" in the title refers to job titles of people working in the process, not department titles. "Activity" refers to the activities or work performed by each individual.

Some process maps include only the activity and not the job titles. It's important to include who performs the activity because:

- You can see where most of the work is being performed.
- You can determine who does the value-added steps and who doesn't.
- You can see where problems in handoffs occur.
- Without that information, you can't calculate activity, process, and quality costs.
- You can spot unnecessary reviews.
- You can see if it makes more sense for someone else to be doing the work.

Note: Each of the activities in a functional-activity flowchart can be broken down into individual tasks or procedures, which is the final level of flowchart detail and called "task-procedure." With functional-activity charts, you want to avoid documenting the minute procedures an individual performs because the process map would become incredibly long and much too detailed.

It's at both the functional-activity and task-procedure levels that the four lenses of analysis are used. These lenses are quality, cost, time, and frustration and will be discussed in detail in Chapter 7.

Figure 2.10 on pages 26–27 represents a functional-activity flowchart of the permit process shown in Figure 2.9. As you can see, the three steps in the macro flowchart of the process have expanded into the activities and job titles.

When starting a process map, record what happened, not what should have happened. This is called an "as-is" flowchart. An easy way to do this is to recall the last time that the process you're examining was performed. Then record exactly what happened. You're simply remembering history.

When you map an actual event, you'll find that only one thing can happen at a diamond. The product can't both pass and fail inspection; it must have done one or the other. Therefore, expect to have only one arrow come out of your diamonds.

For any process there can be multiple variations. Generally, the variations occur at the diamonds. If you map every variation that could occur there, your chart will likely end up looking like spaghetti and meatballs. These overly detailed flow-charts are incredibly difficult to follow. To make a flowchart more understandable, create separate flowcharts for the main variations in a process. While this increases your work, it's much easier to see the differences from one variation to the next. Another person should be able to look at your flowchart and read it easily.

Creating a Functional-Activity Flowchart

To begin creating a functional-activity flowchart, write the name of the process at the top of the page. What specific event are you remembering? List that as well. For example, your heading might read, "Process: Order-taking. Specific example: Acme order done last week."

Define the process boundaries. Where does this process start? Where does it end? You're looking for activities or decisions that mark both the beginning and end of the process. An incorrect response is, "The process starts in April." That doesn't describe the activity or decision that indicates the process is beginning. Expect discussion among team members concerning the start and stop points. Let the discussion run until consensus emerges.

If you're mapping from the top-down, write the job titles of the people who work in the process across the top of the page. (*Note:* Information technology and software systems deserve job titles, the rationale being that these systems perform activities.) If you're mapping horizontally, write the job titles in a column on the left-hand side of the page.

Mapping vertically or horizontally is the user's choice. The advantage of going left to right (or horizontally) is that very large processes can be displayed on the walls of a room with an uninterrupted flow. A vertical map, on the other hand, is apt to hit the floor and have to loop back up again, which can make it difficult to follow the flow of work.

If you're mapping from the top down, separate the job titles by vertical lines. For left-to-right mapping, separate the job titles by horizontal lines. These are called "swim lanes." They make it easy to follow the work of individuals. You can see where handoffs occur as well as the balance or imbalance of work among participants in the process.

With vertical maps, the process starts at the top of the page and moves down. For horizontal maps, the process starts on the left and flows to the right. Use verb-noun combinations to describe the activities and questions to describe the diamonds.

Number each box and diamond. Try to stay in sequence as the process flows. Sometimes this is difficult with parallel activities, but don't let that concern you. What's important is that every box and diamond has a unique number. You'll want these numbers as reference points when you use the four lenses of analysis later on.

Advantages of Functional-Activity Flowcharts

- You can easily spot problems and not get bogged down in details.
- Disconnects between individuals and departments are easy to spot.
- They can be used to calculate process, cycle, wait, and move times, among others.
- They can be used to generate activity costs.
- They can be used it to generate process costs.
- They can help to identify quality issues and calculate quality costs.

On the downside, these flowcharts can't be used to train someone on the detailed procedures relating to a specific activity. Figure 2.11 on pages 28–29 shows the permit process with each box and diamond numbered.

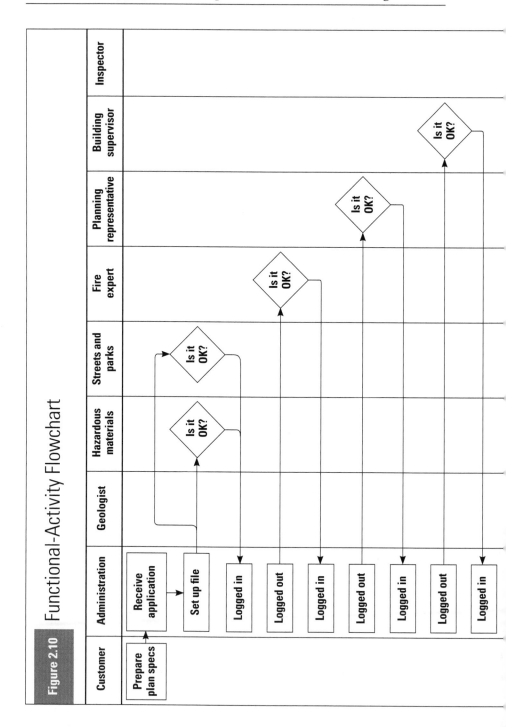

Figure 2.10   Functional-Activity Flowchart

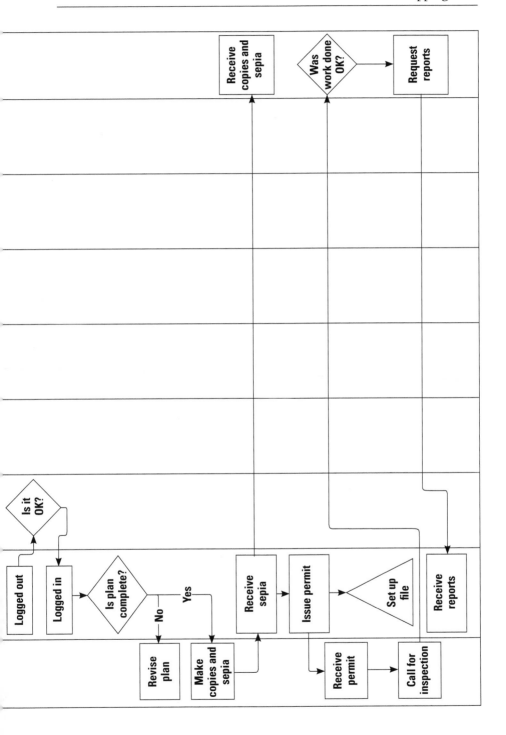

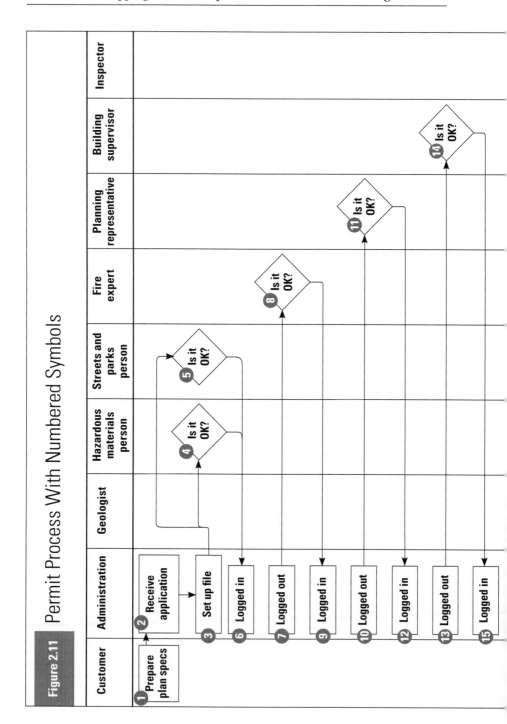

Figure 2.11   Permit Process With Numbered Symbols

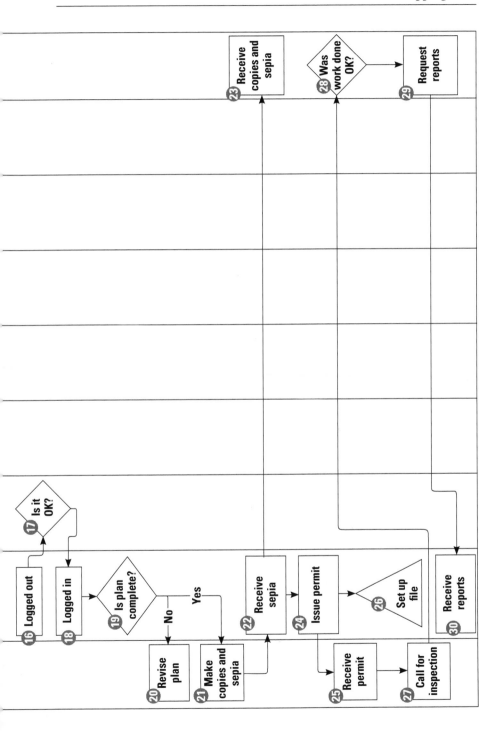

TASK-PROCEDURE FLOWCHARTS

The most detailed flowcharts are created at the task-procedure level. At this level you're looking at one box or diamond from the functional-activity flowchart. You want to include the level of detail you'd use to explain a particular task to someone during training.

The task-procedure flowchart is used in four situations. The first is when a problem keeps showing up at a certain box (i.e., activity) in the functional-activity flowchart after applying one of the four lenses of analysis. Using the task-procedure flowchart, you can dig into details to find the root cause of problems for this particular activity.

The second situation is when new activities are created through a "clean sheet" redesign. In the new process, a particular task might not be documented yet because it's brand-new. Therefore, you must create the documentation so it can be performed as expected.

In the third situation, the task-procedure flowchart is used for certification purposes, for example, validating and testing procedures.

Finally, this flowchart can be used for training purposes. Experienced operators can create them and then apply them when training is required.

Creating a Task-Procedure Flowchart

The first step in completing a task-procedure flowchart is to name the task or procedure and write it at the top of the page. Write the number one in the sequence column to indicate the first step in the activity you're charting. The next column indicates how long the first step takes; use the appropriate increments of time for the task, which could be in seconds, minutes, or hours. In the symbol column, check the appropriate symbol for the activity being performed at this step. For example, if this step is an operation, check the box. If it's an inspection, check the diamond, and so forth.

In the next column, titled "Frustration," note if there's anything frustrating at this step. If there is, the rank it: "H" for high, "M" for medium, and "L" for low. If there's no frustration, leave the column blank.

Now describe this step in detail in the description column. Be thorough enough so that someone who knows nothing of the task could accomplish it easily.

Figure 2.12 Task-Procedure Flowchart Template

Task _____

Sequence	Time	Symbol	Frustration?	Description	Why do we do this step?

□ =Operation   ◇ =Decision and/or inspection   ➤ =Transport   ⧠ =Delay   ▽ =File and/or store

Figure 2.13 Medication Administration Record (MAR) Task-Procedure Flowchart

Task Review of MAR

Sequence	Time	Symbol	Frustration?	Description	Why do we do this step?
1	1 min.		low	Find or generate MAR for new date	Each day requires a new MAR
2	30 sec.			Find previous day's MAR	Must compare these two MARs
3	2 min.		low	Check patient No., medication name, dose, schedule time, allergies	To confirm correct info
4	4 min.		high	Look for time changes	Looking for multiple factors
5	2 min.		low	Look for orders that expire in 24 hours	Flag these so MD is aware
6	5 min.		medium	Look for newly written orders	Check patient chart for recent orders
7	2 min.		low	Look for protocol orders	Standard orders that refer to protocols
8	10 min.		high	Look for missing orders	Missing orders are critical
9	1 min.			Look for section placement	Check for IV
10	5 min.			Generate MAR discrepancy form	Use this form to communicate with pharmacy

☐ = Operation ◇ = Decision and/or inspection → = Transport ☐ = Delay ▽ = File and/or store

Finally, complete the column titled, "Why do we do this step?" This column is necessary for two reasons. First, when using this flowchart for training, people will wonder why a certain step must be performed. This column anticipates that question and provides an answer. When people know the rationale for a step, they're more likely to remember to do it in the future. Second, if you have a hard time putting a rationale in the "Why do we do this step?" column, it's probably an indication that this step is unnecessary.

Task-Procedure Analysis

There are two methods of analysis for the task-procedure flowchart. One is to focus on the Frustration column and come up with ideas to address high and medium frustrations. There's a high correlation between frustration and quality. By eliminating frustration, quality improves.

The second method of analysis is to scan the "Time" column. Concentrate on the steps that consume the most time. Shrink time as much as possible, but be sure to maintain the quality for each step.

Figure 2.13 is a task-procedure flowchart of a nurse's medication administration record (MAR). Notice that step eight is both the most time-consuming and highly frustrating. This step is an obvious candidate for improvement. The frustration for the nurse at step eight was that she had to backtrack and figure out why the medicine is missing from the new MAR. There can be multiple causes for this, and tracking down each is what creates the frustration. The team working on this flowchart brainstormed a number of ideas to eliminate this problem and was able to find a quick hit that was easy to implement and didn't cost anything.

In Figure 2.14, you can see how one level of flowchart detail cascades down to the next. We start with the macro, which is then exploded into a functional-activity flowchart. In fact, we could have taken only one of the macro steps and created a functional-activity flowchart for it. In Figure 2.14, all three macro steps are expanded into the functional-activity flowchart. Finally, one box (or activity) on the functional-activity flowchart can be expanded into the task-procedure flowchart.

Each level of detail has its uses in a process improvement effort. Start with a macro flowchart, then move to a functional-activity and finally a task-procedure.

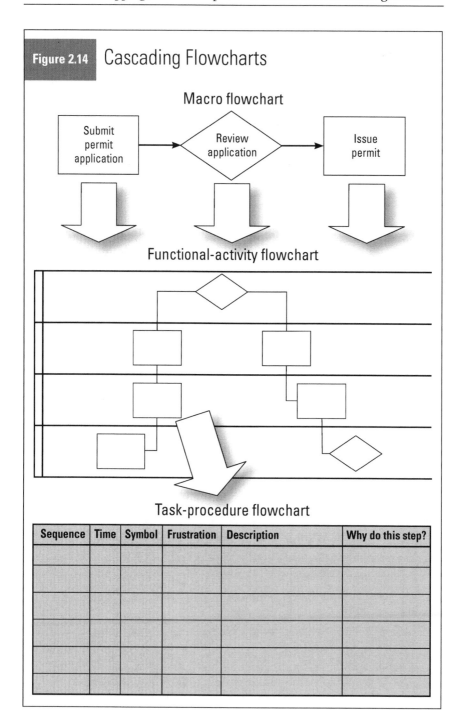

Figure 2.14   Cascading Flowcharts

Macro flowchart

Submit permit application → Review application → Issue permit

Functional-activity flowchart

Task-procedure flowchart

Sequence	Time	Symbol	Frustration	Description	Why do this step?

INSTALLING PROCESS CONTROLS

For control purposes, a fourth level of detail, the control level, occurs between the functional-activity and the task-procedure levels. It's not as detailed as a task-procedure flowchart, but it provides critical information for both internal and external audits driven by the Sarbanes-Oxley Act. At the control level of detail, information is given for each activity that comes from the functional-activity flowchart.

Control Documentation at the Activity Level

Consider the functional-activity flowchart of the customer order process as illustrated in Figure 2.15 on page 36.

An activity is broken down into seven distinct types of information. They appear on an activity detail sheet that represents everything a person must know about to successfully complete an activity. An example of an activity detail sheet is shown in Figure 2.16 on page 37, which refers to step two from the functional-activity flowchart of the customer order process depicted in Figure 2.15. The seven key components on the activity detail sheet are:

- General information
- Brief description
- Task list
- Forms, policies, procedures, and manuals
- End-work products or deliverables
- Applications
- Corporate controls

The general, description, and task list components are mandatory for all activities, but the remaining four categories are included depending on their relevance to the specific task being performed. Following is a more detailed description of the components.

- *General information:* Identifies which activity is being performed and by whom. For the customer order example in Figure 2.15, the sales representative performs the "record order" task (i.e., step two in the process map). The overall owner of the process is the customer service manager, and the business owner is the director of sales.

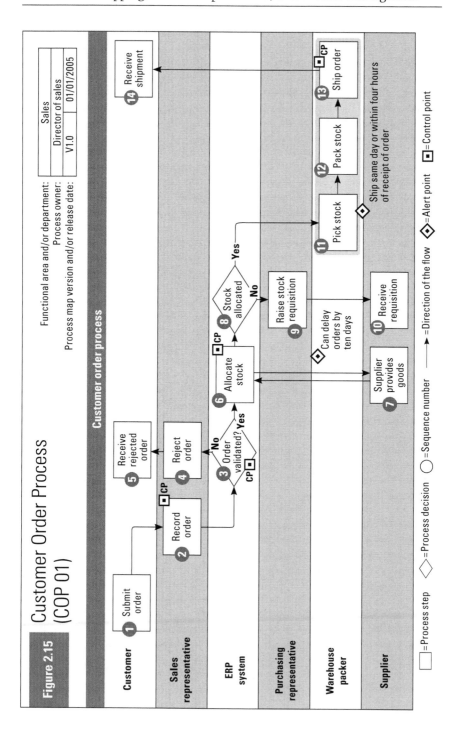

Figure 2.15   Customer Order Process (COP 01)

Functional area and/or department: Sales
Process owner: Director of sales
Process map version and/or release date: V1.0   01/01/2005

Customer order process

Customer — 1 Submit order

Sales representative — 2 Record order · CP — 5 Receive rejected order — 4 Reject order

ERP system — 3 Order validated? CP · No / Yes — 6 Allocate stock · CP — 8 Stock allocated No / Yes

Purchasing representative — 9 Raise stock requisition — 10 Receive requisition

Warehouse packer — 11 Pick stock — 12 Pack stock — 13 Ship order · CP

Supplier — 7 Supplier provides goods

Can delay orders by ten days

Ship same day or within four hours of receipt of order

14 Receive shipment

□ = Process step   ◇ = Process decision   ○ = Sequence number   → = Direction of the flow   ◆ = Alert point   ■ = Control point

Figure 2.16	Activity Detail Sheet

Customer Order	Version number: 1.0
Activity Detail Sheet	Release date: January 1, 2005

General No.
Step: 2
Step Name: Record order

Swim lane: Sales representative
Process Owner: Director of sales
Business Owner: Vice president sales

Description
The record order activity is responsible for capturing the preliminary information of a new customer order. This step will encompass everything from product/service identification to quantities and availability. Upon the successful identification of this information, the process continues to the order-validated decision.

Tasks
- Select the product and quantity being ordered.
- Determine if product is in stock, back ordered, or discontinued.
- Inform the customer of alternate options or delay in filling the order if the product is not in stock.
- Repeat the above three steps until all products and quantities have been identified.
- Price the order.

Forms/Policies & Procedures/Training Materials
- Customer Service Handbook
- Corporate ERP System Manual
- Order Request Policy

End Work Products/Deliverables
- A preliminary order with product and quantities

Applications
- Corporate ERP System
- Corporate Intranet (used for supporting product documentation and materials)

Controls
- A discontinued product without any on hand stock cannot be selected for an order

Company confidential—do not distribute	Page 1 of 14	Friday, June 15, 2005

- *Description:* A brief overview of what must be done to successfully complete the activity and move on to the next one on the process map.
- *Tasks:* Individual actions that must be performed to successfully complete an activity. As a general rule for activity detail sheets, tasks should never be detailed to the work-instruction level. This safeguards against problems with process documentation management as well as the unintended consequence of curbing manager and employee creativity for improving processes. However, the rule doesn't mean that tasks shouldn't be broken down into individual work instructions such as task-procedure flowcharts, training aids and/or materials, or reference materials.
- *Forms, policies, procedures, and manuals:* A list of materials that either directly support or reinforce work being performed for an activity within a given process. This includes such things as standardized forms (to ensure consistency), policies and procedures (to convey corporate rules), manuals and/or handbooks (for "how to" guidance), or miscellaneous information (e.g., research or information relevant to the work at hand). The information can dictate what will later be interpreted as controls and/or business rules.
- *End-work products or deliverables:* Expected outcomes that occur at the end of an activity within a given process. This information typically includes documents, data entry, processing decisions, information verification, management reporting, management approvals, and so on.
- *Applications:* A list of information technology resources required to complete a specific activity within a given process. This information typically includes ERP systems, office automation tools, e-mail, document storage, intranet, Internet, extranet, imaging, and so on.
- *Controls:* A specific action, constraint, or condition mandated by management that must be executed successfully at all times. Corporate management relies on these controls to ensure that the organization is meeting the requirements of government regulators, investors, boards of directors, customers, suppliers, and employees. Controls typically are the items that auditors focus on during spot reviews or checks, process breakdown investigations, periodic internal audits, and annual external audits.

WHAT ARE PROCESS CONTROLS?

Business rules applied or executed during the course of a process activity are called process controls. These rules ensure that an organization is operating in the manner that adheres to corporate policies and procedures.

A control can take many different forms within a process. These include conditions that require certain decisions or responses, mandatory actions or reviews, and management oversight or monitoring. Below, the controls are applied to an everyday business activity—a retail store—to demonstrate examples of each:

- *Condition:* A merchandise return without a receipt for items that cost more than $100 requires manager approval prior to completing the return.
- *Action:* A cashier must balance his or her cash drawer and report any discrepancies at the end of every shift.
- *Review:* A complete store inventory is performed once a quarter.
- *Oversight:* The store manager must review the weekly sales figures for discrepancies and/or trends.

Each of these examples represents an actual control that's used in most retail stores to ensure financial integrity and a controlled environment. If you examine the controls' wording, you'll notice that a simple yes-or-no query can be applied to and answered for each of them. The way in which a control is written is critical because that determines how it will be tested and enforced. Ambiguously worded controls increase the likelihood of employees coming up with different interpretations and methods of execution.

Control Point Matrix

The control point matrix document shown in Figure 2.17 on page 40 highlights all the main controls in a particular process. This document is linked to the functional-activity flowchart shown in Figure 2.15 on page 36.

The first column, the process reference number, refers to the process flowchart for this control point matrix (CPM). In this example, the process reference number is COP 01. The second column, the activity number, corresponds to the step number from the functional-activity flowchart. The first step with a control is step two.

Control Point

A process control point is a mandatory business rule that must be completed during the normal course of business to satisfy a managerial mandate. Manage-

Figure 2.17   Control Point Matrix

Customer order process

Sales department

Process reference No.	Activity No.	Control point	Risk(s)	Key	Type	Category	Source	Component	Caption	Assertion	Executive owner	Process owner	Evidence
COP 01	2	A discontinued product without any on-hand stock can't be selected for an order.	– Fictitious and/or duplicate sales are recorded – Delivery and/or purchase commitments are improperly recorded	Y	Prevent	Configuration	System	Control activity	Sales Accounts receivable	Existence and/or occurrence	VP sales	Director of sales	Stock, committed transactions
COP 01	3	An order can't be placed for any customer with a past due amount greater than ninety days.	– Accounts receivable amount is inaccurate – Fictitious and/or duplicate sales are recorded	N	Prevent	Configuration	System	Control activity	Sales Accounts receivable	Existence/and or occurrence	VP sales	Director of sales	Receivables past due report
COP 01	3	An order can't be placed for any customer greater than the customer's pre-approved limit without sales manager's approval.	– Unauthorized sales orders are placed and filled – Accounts receivable amount is inaccurate	N	Prevent	Authorization	Manual	Monitoring	Sales Accounts receivable	Accuracy	VP sales	Director of sales	Authorization code
COP 01	6	Stock that's already allocated can't be assigned to another order	– Unauthorized sales orders are placed and filled – Delivery and/or purchase commitments are improperly recorded	N	Prevent	Configuration	System	Control environment	Sales Accounts receivable	Accuracy	VP sales	Director of sales	Sales order module configuration rules
COP 01	13	Receivables can't be posted to the general ledger until the shipment has been released to the carrier.	– Accounts receivable are improperly valued or recorded – Fictitious and/or duplicate sales are recorded	Y	Detect	Configuration	System	Control activity	Sales Accounts receivable	Accuracy	VP sales	Director of sales	Accounts receivable ledger

ment relies on these controls to ensure that the financial reporting and control environment are intact and operating correctly. Without both these components in place, a company exposes itself to the possibility of fraud or misrepresentation concerning its current financial condition.

The third column, control point, explains the problem that could happen at this step. This is done to prevent the problem from actually occurring. For instance, at step three, a control point prohibits placing an order for any customer whose account balance exceeds a past due date of 90 days.

Process Control Risks

If the problem at the control point occurs, what effect does it have? This is explained in the process control risks column. At step two, for example, if a discontinued product is selected, the effect is to create fictitious or duplicate orders. Remember that it's just as important to know what a control is supposed to prevent than it is to identify the control itself. If you don't understand what you're trying to prevent, you'll never know if the control is working and will be unable to test it to make sure.

Process control risks should be based on the language or risks that have been identified by either an internal audit or external audit group. This ensures that the process control is understood as well as interpreted correctly by the various audit groups.

Key Process Controls

All controls are considered either "key" or "non-key" depending on their importance and placement within a given process. It's important to remember that all controls start out as non-key or operational controls. These are the ones put in place to ensure integrity and adherence to a specific process, policy, and/or procedure. Key controls are a much smaller group. They're identified by management as the ones used to detect or prevent any material misstatements in the organization's financials reports.

For example, step thirteen is a key control because the product is shipped to the customer at this point, which triggers a sale.

Types of Process Controls

Each of the two types of controls performs a specific function: one prevents, and the other detects. The prevent control is used to stop or identify a problem before it becomes an issue. A detect control identifies a problem after it's occurred. Of these two types, the prevent control is always considered to be more desirable because it won't require rework or additional effort to correct.

Categories of Process Controls

Categories are the policies and procedures that help ensure that all management directives are carried out. The process control categories are:

- *Management review:* An independent review by management performed to verify proper completion or execution
- *Reconciliation:* Independent verifications that help ensure the control activities are functioning as intended
- *Authorization:* Transactions that must be authorized and executed in accordance with management's intent
- *Configuration:* Controls that have been programmed within systems to ensure integrity and accuracy
- *System access:* Limiting access to, and controlling the use of, assets and records to safeguard them
- *Segregation of duties:* Ensures that no one person is in a position to initiate and conceal errors and/or irregularities in the normal course of his or her duties
- *Key performance indicator:* Transactional measures that are tracked to ensure corporate performance goals are met
- *Exception or edit:* Monitoring and documenting exceptions that have taken place within systems or processes

Source of Process Controls

The source of the control represents where or how a control is implemented. Typically controls fall into one of three classifications: system, manual, or both. System controls are business rules that are implemented uniformly across the organization by programming the corporate systems. Manual controls are business rules that require individual interpretation and/or intervention to complete. The "both" classification occurs when part of a control is implemented within a system but still requires manual interpretation prior to processing the control. Of these classifications, system controls are always more desirable because a consistent interpretation is enforced by programming the business rules.

Components of Process Controls

Controls consist of five interrelated components. These are derived from the manner in which management runs the business and are integrated with the management processes. The components are:

- *Control environment:* The "tone at the top"—i.e., management's attitudes, abilities, awareness, and actions regarding control within the organization. The environment provides the discipline and structure for the overall system of internal controls. Examples include management's integrity and ethical values, philosophy and operating style, and assignment of authority and responsibility within the organization.

- *Risk assessment:* Identifying and analyzing relevant risks associated with achieving objectives. When assessing risk, both external and internal factors must be considered. External risk factors lie outside the organization, usually beyond management's control. Examples include economic changes, technological developments, and natural catastrophes. Internal risk factors are within the organization, usually within management's control. Examples include new personnel, low morale, and new or upgraded information systems. Risk assessment takes into consideration what can go wrong and the likelihood of it occurring.

- *Control activities:* Policies and procedures to ensure that management directives are carried out. Control activities expect a certain action or condition to be completed or achieved. Examples are proper authorizations, manual or automated reconciliations, and segregating duties.

- *Information and communication:* Systems that provide management with reports detailing facts about operational, financial, and compliance matters. Information must be relevant and communicated to appropriate personnel in a timely manner for it to be useful, and it must flow in all directions. The information and communication system helps ensure that employees are aware of what's expected of them in accomplishing the organization's goals and objectives.

- *Monitoring:* The process that assesses the performance of the internal control process over time, ensuring that it's operating as expected. Supervisory personnel should perform the monitoring function, focusing on high-risk areas. Monitoring includes observation and testing activities. Internal control systems change over time (e.g., new personnel and/or technological advancements are added), and an adequate internal control system can become obsolete or less effective. Monitoring ensures that as change occurs, the internal control system is adjusted to fit current circumstances.

Process Controls Captions

Each line item on the corporate income statement and balance sheet is considered a caption. Each of these items must have corresponding controls to ensure the statement's overall integrity and accuracy.

Process Control Assertions

An assertion is an expressed or implied representation by management about the financial statements and their components. The list of possible assertions represents all the various manners in which a specific control could affect a particular caption within the corporate income statement and balance sheet. All of the assertions are directly tied to the Generally Accepted Accounting Principles and used by management to classify, measure, and disclose financial information affirming that the financial statements are correct. The seven assertions are listed below:

- *Completeness:* All transactions and other events that occurred during a specific time period were indeed recorded for the period in which they took place.
- *Existence and/or occurrence:* All transactions for assets, liabilities, and ownership interests exist for a specific date and represent events that actually occurred during that period.
- *Accuracy:* All transactions, balances, and classifications have been correctly processed and recorded for the correct time period.
- *Measurement and/or valuation:* All transactions are mathematically correct and appropriately recorded for in the correct time period.
- *Ownership (rights and obligations):* The rights (i.e., assets) and obligations (i.e., liabilities) are correctly recorded for the correct time period.
- *Presentation and/or disclosure:* All items in the financial statements have been properly recorded and accounted for in the correct time period.
- *Various:* Any combination of multiple assertions listed above is relevant and

appropriate.

Process Control Owners

A process control's owners are individuals responsible for properly executing and interpreting the specific control. Because business processes can span multiple departments and/or roles, it's important to identify who will be responsible for executing a control properly. In some cases the process owner might not be responsible for a control or able to change it because a different department or organization established it. An example is a control within the sales process that states, "All new sales contracts must be approved first by legal prior to execution." This process is owned by sales but must conform to a control executed and interpreted by the legal department.

Evidence for Process Controls

The last thing that must be identified is the evidence used to demonstrate that a control has been executed or interpreted correctly. It's extremely important to have the evidence to prove a control is indeed in place and working. Identifying evidence for a control usually requires research or implementing formal procedures. Examples of evidence are system logs, signatures on documents, electronic approvals, e-mails, faxes, etc. Identifying evidence is a difficult exercise for most people because often it isn't tracked or completed correctly.

Typically this step requires creating and implementing more detailed policies and procedures. Most organizations have trouble differentiating between tracking and maintaining evidence versus simply trusting that they've done their jobs correctly.

What Happens to Controls?

After controls have been identified, they're turned over to the internal audit team to review for accuracy and provide additional information required by external auditors. Once this is done, the internal audit team evaluates the controls to determine the manner and frequency in which a specific one will be tested. These tests are then conducted and tracked to identify any discrepancies and/or problems with a control. If a problem is identified, the team will work with the process owners either to correct the problem or create a new control.

Chapter 3

Key Stakeholders' Roles and Responsibilities

"People support what they help create."
–Anonymous

W hen you want something done, what's more desirable, commitment or compliance? Obviously, you'd want commitment from those who will be performing the task. That being the case, why is it that so many organizations have compliant people instead of committed ones?

Top-down, "command and control" bureaucracies usually produce only compliance. How many of us can get excited about executing someone else's decisions? Not many. Also in many organizations, managers don't appreciate employees who ask questions and want more involvement. Hence, both the organization's structure and managers' beliefs contribute to making employees compliant rather than committed.

If these conditions produce compliance, what conditions produce commitment? It comes from people who are actively involved in problem solving and decision making. By being actively involved, people assume "ownership" of their work.

You can build commitment by giving teams the authority to solve day-to-day problems. That way, you create problem solvers instead of problem finders, and these people enjoy their work much more than before.

Successfully delegating decision making hinges on the teams' skills. Basic ones, such as group problem solving and decision making, meeting facilitation, and effective communication, are the necessary building blocks of high-performance teams. With these in place, managers have the necessary confidence to progressively delegate decisions to the team.

SUCCESSFUL PROCESS IMPROVEMENT REQUIRES EMPLOYEE BUY-IN

Optimal process-improvement results occur when there's substantial employee involvement. The principle of employee involvement rests on two premises:

- Employees know the job best and if given an opportunity will contribute great ideas for improvement
- Employees involved in developing change recommendations will support, not resist, their implementation.

Employee involvement happens in a variety of ways at various stages of the improvement effort. These might include:

- Participation on a process improvement team
- Providing input for the existing process
- Responding to redesigned work processes developed by the process improvement team
- Assisting in implementing newly redesigned processes
- Creating incremental improvements on an ongoing basis

WHAT'S IN IT FOR US?

Employees typically like being part of an improvement effort because they can:

- Address frustrations
- Remove bottlenecks
- Reduce bureaucracy
- Redesign their own work
- Simplify processes
- Increase teamwork and morale
- Increase communication
- Exert more influence
- Learn new techniques

PROJECT MANAGER'S RESPONSIBILITIES

The project manager's role is critical to the success of a process improvement effort. The ideal candidate is a strong leader who can work through obstacles. The partnership relationship between the project manager and facilitator ensures successful project completion.

This is what you should expect a project manager to do:

- Ensure that the work gets done
- Define the process boundaries
- Define subprocesses and their owners, and establishes priorities
- Direct the various process implementation stages
- Establish measurements and set targets to improve process effectiveness and efficiency
- Maintain contact with the process customers to ensure their expectations are understood and met
- Keep the process team informed about organizational changes that might affect the process
- Support the process improvement team's recommendations to senior management
- Reward and recognize the process improvement team and its members for small wins

Characteristics of a process manager:

- Has a passion for improving the process, and an ability to drive it forward
- Knows about the process being redesigned
- Is authorized to commit resources
- Is authorized to act on recommendations
- Has successfully completed projects in the past
- Is relatively senior within the company
- Is well respected

PROCESS IMPROVEMENT TEAM'S RESPONSIBILITIES

The bulk of the work in a process redesign is performed by the process improvement team. For this reason, these people must have some free time so they can work on the project. If it's a reengineering project, at a minimum you should expect one day per week to be freed up for team members. If you can't get this type of commitment, then scale the effort down.

Team members are to:

- Collect and/or verify data related to the process (e.g., workload, turnaround time, quality issues)
- Flowchart the "as is" process
- Design the customer interview activity
- Design the employee interview activity
- Benchmark other organizations to learn about alternate methods
- Redesign work processes
- Communicate process improvement activities to employees
- Present recommendations to senior management
- Develop implementation plans
- Advocate, explain, and review the redesign with employees
- Monitor design implementation
- Train other organizational members

Team composition

Who should be part of a process redesign team? People who work in the process—the best and the brightest—and those who want a change. It's also important to include:

- *Information technologist.* Many processes are enabled with technology. The IT expert should know current and future IT capabilities.
- *An outsider or maverick.* This person's job is to challenge the team to think outside the box. Look for someone who doesn't work in the targeted process because he or she must see the process with unbiased eyes. This person should be well respected in the organization so that others will listen to his or her opinion and observations. A person who questions the status quo is a good candidate. Make sure he or she is comfortable in challenging the thinking of other team members because that's his or her job.
- *Human resource specialist.* Sometimes work evaporates, and new work is created. This can lead to training, pay, and other HR issues.

PROCESS IMPROVEMENT FACILITATOR'S RESPONSIBILITIES

The facilitator can be either an internal employee or an external consultant. If the facilitator is external, this person should train his or her replacement for future projects. The facilitator's role is to:

- Set the agenda and facilitate the process improvement team meetings
- Coach and train process team members
- Coach and mentor future facilitators
- Partner with the project manager on any issues that arise
- Enforce compliance to team ground rules
- Evaluate the performance metrics
- Talk regularly with the people who work in the process
- Provide feedback to people working in the process
- Meet with department heads about conflicts, priorities, and issues
- Update senior management regularly on progress, problems, etc.
- Remain neutral and refrain from voting in team decision making

Characteristics and Skill Sets of the Facilitator

- Extremely knowledgeable of process improvement tools (e.g., Six Sigma, lean, BPM, design principles)
- Skilled at leading team meetings
- Capable of handling "problem people"
- An organized and logical thinker

SENIOR MANAGEMENT'S ROLE

Senior managers can make or break a process improvement effort. Their commitment to the project is critical. They must be sure to allow an adequate amount of time and resources to get the job done. Below are skills that senior management should bring to the project.

Honor the Past

What can you say about the organization's past accomplishments? How can you acknowledge the hard work that's already been done? When you talk about a problem, people can easily jump to the conclusion that *they* are the problem. Your comments must reinforce that the problem is in the process, not them.

Establish a Compelling Reason for Change

Create a document that convinces people the organization must change. State reasons clearly and simply. Appeal to employees' logic as well as emotions. Provide information concerning external and internal forces that are causing the change. Provide factual data to back up the case.

Create a Vision of the New Organization

What will the new organization look like? How will it be better than the existing one? Describe the WIIFMs (What's in it for me?) for each organizational stakeholder (e.g., employees, customers, management).

Communicate

Create a communication strategy to keep in touch with people regularly. Create two-way communication channels through small groups and discussions sessions. Go out and meet the troops.

Revamp Control Mechanisms to Support the Change

How are your appraisal process and criteria going to change? How is decision-making going to change? How is your reward and recognition system going to change? Align your organization's systems to drive the needed changes in processes and behaviors.

Senior Managers' Responsibilities

- Decides which recommendations to accept
- Shoots or confirms sacred cows
- Resolves turf issues
- Manages realignment of strategy, systems, and structure as necessary
- Settles internal disputes created by the redesign

- Runs interference with external agencies
- Communicates with the rest of the organization on the process improvement effort
- Hires outside resources

Which Managers Should Be Involved?

- Senior executives within the area of the redesign or improvement effort
- Executives from other departments and at higher levels whose concurrence is necessary

Manager Involvement

When putting a team together, you'll choose people who are actually doing the work to be on the team. What, then, is the manager's role? He or she could become the project manager, which has been discussed earlier.

If a manager wishes to be on the team, then some ground rules must be followed. The manager must relinquish decision-making power to the team. A strong manager accustomed to steamrolling won't benefit the team. Decisions are arrived at through consensus. Consensus helps ensure buy-in and support by those who have to make the new process work successfully.

Sometimes a team isn't very aggressive in pursuing improvement options. In that case, a strong manager might be needed to spur the team forward. However, it's a good idea to see if the team will move forward without outside help before asking the manager to step in.

If the manager isn't on the team, then what role can he or she perform? The manager can provide resources, remove obstacles, coach, and serve as a liaison with other teams. A supportive outside role can prove a big asset to the team as well as to the success of the redesign or improvement project.

Supervisors' and Middle Managers' Roles

In a process improvement effort, the roles of supervisors and managers involve the following tasks:

- *Keep people informed.* When people don't know what's happening, their imaginations will run wild. Distortions and fears will alarm them. Share whatever information you can on the improvement effort.

■ *Get people involved.* Remember: People support what they help create. The opposite is also true: People resist and sabotage things that they have no part in creating. Constantly look for ways to involve staff.

■ *Listen, listen, listen.* Be available to hear what everyone has to say. Don't hole up in your office. Show people you understand their concerns.

■ *Allow for anger, depression, and yearning for the "good old days."* It's OK for people to react in an emotional way to the changes. It's natural and expected.

■ *Be a good role model.* Show your support for the improvement effort. Don't criticize senior management. Be patient, open, honest, and concerned.

■ *Look for solutions when you find concerns and/or problems.* Most process improvement efforts will have rough spots. Try to anticipate them and formulate solutions. When problems come up unexpectedly, collaboratively work to solve them.

Chapter 4

Getting Started on Process Improvement

A process improvement effort begins with finding broken processes. Imagine you're scanning your organization, looking for what's broken. How would you know if something needs fixing? The symptoms listed below all point to potential problems. Review the processes in your organization and list those that have any of these symptoms.

SYMPTOMS OF A BROKEN PROCESS

- Customers (either internal or external) are unhappy.
- Some things just take too long.
- The process wasn't done right the first time (i.e., it produced errors, rework, mistakes, or scrap).
- Management throws people at the problem, but it doesn't improve.
- Employees report a high frustration factor while working.
- Processes span several departments, and there is finger-pointing and blaming.
- Processes aren't measured or controlled.
- Inventory, buffers, and other assets sit idle.
- Data redundancy is common.
- Too many reviews and signoffs.
- Complexity, exceptions, and special cases are common.
- Established procedures are circumvented to expedite work.
- No one manages the total process.
- Management throws money at the problem, but it doesn't improve.
- Managers spend a great deal of time "firefighting."

Customers Are Unhappy

Customers can be either internal or external. You're an internal customer when you receive something from another department or staff member. This might be a report, document, service, or response to a request. As a customer, do you get the quality you desire? Does the product or service meet your expectations? If not, an internal supplier's process isn't performing properly.

Do your external customers have complaints? These should be addressed at once because your organization's survival depends, ultimately, on customer satisfaction.

Some Things Just Take Too Long

Common sense tells you if a process takes too long. You know that the actual work time involved is low, and yet it takes days, weeks, or even months to get what you want. Common time-consuming examples are financial reports, turnarounds on requests, purchases, or an information technology service.

Work Is Not Done Right the First Time

In these cases, you're looking for processes where persistent and excessive mistakes, scrap, and rework occur. Another telltale symptom is missing, incomplete, or incorrect information.

Management Throws People at the Problem, but It Doesn't Improve

This symptom manifests itself in two ways. First, a department head, manager, or supervisor keeps asking for more people. Eventually these pleas are heard, and more staffing is provided. A year or so transpires, but even with extra help the problem hasn't improved. Placing extra staff in a bottlenecked, convoluted, or fractured process doesn't solve the problem.

Second, manager turnover is high. Look for cases where department heads, managers, or supervisors are frequently replaced. For example, during a five-year period, five different people have held the same position. Chances are a busted process has resisted these managers' attempts to fix it. Senior managers keep hoping that someone will solve the problem, so they continue to replace managers instead of addressing the process.

Employees Report a High Frustration Factor While Working

Many employees become frustrated when they work in processes that are confusing, full of bottlenecks, and/or justified by the comment, "That's the way we do it around here." When people complain, look for the root cause of the problem in the process rather than focusing on the personalities involved.

You'll hear people complain, "I wish I didn't have to do (whatever process is frustrating them)." There's no law that states work must be frustrating. Frustration indicates a process has design flaws. Everyone should be encouraged to propose solutions to frustrating processes. This is one reason why the frustration lens, discussed in Chapter 7, is such a powerful tool.

Processes Span Several Departments and Causes Finger-Pointing

With this symptom, you'll hear comments such as, "If those people in (a particular department) would do it right, we wouldn't have this problem!" Handing off work or information from one department to the next often creates problems. It doesn't occur to the department upstream to view the department downstream as a customer. For example, the sales department is asked to provide missing data for a customer order. The sales department believes it's responsible for bringing in sales and that the customer service representative should address the problem of missing data.

Processes Aren't Measured or Controlled

Look for processes with consistent steps but where output time and quality vary considerably. For example, five people working in the same process, each with his or her own method, will hamper standardization and create unwanted variability.

Inventory, Buffers, and Other Assets Sit Idle

In a manufacturing organization, idle assets indicate a "push" rather than a "pull" system. Building to order and creating a continuous flow are typical solutions.

Data Redundancy Is Common

This is a common problem that occurs when multiple databases don't share information easily because each department uses its own, unique system. Rather than linking the systems, excessive information exchange, data reconciliation, and data redundancy stand in for effective solutions.

Too Many Reviews Lead to Inefficient Work

How many people must "sign off" on requests? Do some managers in your organization spend most of their time reviewing and approving? Although this might seem counterintuitive to some, quality can actually improve when some review steps are removed. For example, if work is reviewed eight times, the desire to do quality work for the first review is low. The upstream worker expects his or her mistakes will be caught during the next seven reviews. However, if there's only one review, both the worker and reviewer are motivated to get it right the first time. They know no one else will catch the problems.

Complexity, Exceptions, and Special Cases Are Common

These are processes or situations that fall outside the everyday routine of work, but when they do, they create chaos. Organizations generally have standard operating procedures for typical processes, but unusual, exceptional, or special cases can create havoc because there's no SOP for handling them.

Established Procedures Are Circumvented to Expedite Work

To what extent does your organization circumvent established procedures? When this occurs, it means your regular process is slow or cumbersome. If the circumvented process performs satisfactorily, why not make it the standard operating procedure?

No One Manages the Total Process

In this situation, consider cross-departmental processes. Each department is managing its piece of the process and is measured and rewarded on how well its piece performs. However, no one is managing or overseeing the process as a whole.

Thus, upstream fixes can cause downstream problems because the department upstream is focusing only on its piece. When an organization establishes a matrix or F-type management style, these problems disappear.

Management Throws Money at the Problem, But It Doesn't Improve

This is a variation on throwing people at the problem. How often have you been promised a better process through technology? Did the technology actually improve the process? In many cases the answer is, "No." By paving the cowpath, a convoluted process was not improved.

Managers Spend a Great Deal of Time "Firefighting"

How much of your day do you spend firefighting? If your efforts aren't making fundamental changes in processes, then the fires most likely will recur. Remember that the root causes of 85 percent of all problems are in process, control mechanisms, and structure.

PROCESS SELECTION MATRIX

From the previous list you've probably recognized a number of symptoms that need to be addressed in your own organization. The next step is to create a process selection matrix to help you decide which process to improve first. To begin, the senior management team creates a list of processes that are candidates for improvement. Next, this team generates selection criteria, which can include cost-savings potential, incidence of quality problems, time or responsiveness issues, internal staff frustration, customer complaints, whether the problem represents "low-hanging fruit," feasibility, and so forth.

Usually each management team creates its own unique solution criteria. What criteria are important to you? An example from one organization is shown in Table 4.1. The matrix is created by listing the processes in the left column and the selection criteria across the top of the page.

Next, score the problems against the selection criteria. Use a score from one to five, with five indicating the greatest opportunity for improvement. In cost-savings potential, customer complaints, and staff frustration a five would indicate great

Table 4.1	Process Improvement Selection Matrix					
Process	Cost-saving potential	Customer complaints	Low-hanging fruit	Feasibility	Staff frustration	Total score
Customer ordering	5	5	2	2	4	18
Purchasing	4	2	4	3	4	17
New product development	4	1	3	2	4	14

opportunities for improvement. A five in low-hanging fruit means that the problem represents an obvious improvement opportunity. (And if you asked employees for improvement ideas, they'd come up with several quickly.) Feasibility means the organization won't have to spend money, rewrite software code, undertake a major reorganization, or change organizational policies. This category also indicates the ease in making a change.

If your organization is new to process improvement, you'll want to emphasize low-hanging fruit and feasibility. Process change can be difficult. If you want to start an organizationwide process improvement initiative, your first process improvement efforts must succeed. By building upon a series of successes, you create a base of support for process improvement. Imagine a snowball rolling down a mountain. When it hits a tree, it stops dead. If that happens with your effort, people could say, "We tried process improvement, Six Sigma, lean, and reengineering, and they don't work here."

However, if the snowball continues rolling, picking up more snow and momentum, it's much more likely to keep going when it hits a tree. Major change efforts need early successes to build momentum and buy-in. For this reason, problems that rank high in the low-hanging fruit and feasibility categories are important initially.

In Table 4.1, purchasing scores highest in terms of low-hanging fruit and feasibility and second highest for the total score. Although customer ordering held the highest score, it might make sense to launch the process improvement initiative with purchasing due to its higher scores in low-hanging fruit and feasibility.

However, selecting the customer-ordering problem as the first redesign candidate also makes sense for a number of reasons. Processes that deliver value to the external customer typically are the most important in any organization. If external customers are unhappy, the entire organization suffers in terms of revenue and long-term viability. Unless those processes are operating effectively, the others quickly become irrelevant.

Choosing the first process to launch an improvement effort means looking at a number of criteria and discussing the importance of each. One way to assess their importance is to assign a weighting factor to each criterion. In Table 4.1, each criterion is weighted equally, but that might not be the case for your organization.

SELECTING THE RIGHT CHANGE METHODOLOGY

After the selection criteria are factored against the process list, you can rank the processes in order of importance. That done, you must decide on which improvement methodology to use. When should you use continuous improvement, Six Sigma, total quality management, lean, or reengineering? How do the techniques compare to one another? Table 4.2 helps you answer that question.

Process mapping is a key feature of all the methodologies listed in Table 4.2. Lean has its own process mapping tool set called value stream mapping, which Mike Rother and John Shook explain well in their book, *Learning to See* (Lean Enterprise Institute, 2003). Regardless of which methodology you choose, process mapping skills will be necessary.

If you're considering a significant change, then choose business process reengineering or lean. Keep in mind, however, that the success rate for reengineering is low. That's because BPR requires big changes in just about everything—people, jobs, processes, control mechanisms, and structure. This certainly isn't easy, and resistance can be extremely high. But a strong commitment from senior management and project managers, and using effective change management techniques, can boost the success rate to 75 percent. You can improve your success rate by following the process redesign methodology guidelines discussed in Chapter 5.

Lean works particularly well for problems involving time reduction. The methodology is used primarily in manufacturing, but service organizations can apply many of the tools and concepts. (For an excellent overview of lean's effectiveness in the service industry, read "The Lean Service Machine," published in the October 2003 issue of *Harvard Business Review*.) Like reengineering, lean is one of the few techniques that can create dramatic improvements in an organization, although it's used for incremental improvement as well. Lean design principles are included in Chapter 10's discussion of design principles.

Six Sigma is great for quality problems. Although it includes reengineering, it lacks design principles and is weak on benchmarking and best practices. Total quality management traditionally has focused on quality through process improvement and continuous process improvement, but it's weak in reengineering. Some basic Six Sigma and TQM quality tools are included in this book. In addition,

Table 4.2	Change Methodology Comparison Chart			
Change methodology	**Amount of change**	**Scope of the change**	**What gets changed**	**Key tools used**
Business process reengineering (BPR) Lean	Reduction of 50 percent or more in time, costs, and quality problems	Cross-functional or within one department	−People (jobs) −Process −Control Mechanisms −Structure	−Process maps −Design Principles −Benchmarking and best practices −Lean tools
Process improvement	Reduction of 20 percent or less in time, costs, and quality problems	Cross-functional or within one department	−People (jobs) −Process	Same as above, plus Six Sigma and lean tool kit
Continuous process improvement	Small reduction in time, costs, and quality problems	Often the activities or tasks of one person, or a subprocess	−Subprocess −Tasks	Six Sigma and lean toolkit
Change methodology	**Resources**	**Senior management commitment**	**Probability of success**	**Examples**
BPR Lean	Dedicated staff time, at a minimum one day per week freed up for team members	Definitely. They need to be firmly behind the effort	Less than 40 percent	Redesigning the entire budgeting process for the organization to shrink time by 50 percent
Process improvement	Less than the above	Depends on the political sensitivity of the process	70 percent or more	Redesigning the departments process for doing a budget
Continuous process improvement	Minimal, a few team meetings	No	90 percent or more	Incrementally improving the redesign of the department's budget process

several design principles that specifically address quality problems are discussed in Chapter 9.

Table 4.2 can help you devise tactics to overcome obstacles. For example, suppose you're one month into a reengineering project. Senior management is anxious for results and wants to know when some will be delivered. In this scenario, you might switch from reengineering to continuous improvement and implement some of the quick wins you find by using the frustration lens on your process map. Or you might reduce the scope of your effort from several departments to one and make changes there.

Another reengineering obstacle might be lack of team enthusiasm. Some team members might say, "Why are we doing this, when nothing ever changes around here?" In this scenario, move from reengineering to continuous process improvement and implement some quick, positive changes. When team members see actual changes, they'll convert from skeptics to supporters. You can then move up to process improvement. As each success builds buy-in, you'll eventually be able to resume the project's original scope.

If management stalls or impedes quick wins from continuous process improvement, it's time for you to leave the project. Some efforts are doomed, and it's best to know when to stop.

The ten-step redesign methodology outlined in the next chapter is for reengineering and process improvement projects. Continuous process improvement will be discussed in Chapter 10.

Chapter 5

The Ten-Step Process Redesign Methodology

"At this very instant in time, your organization is perfectly
designed for the results that it's getting."
—Anonymous

igure 5.1 illustrates the ten-step redesign methodology. Each of the
steps will be briefly described in this chapter. In subsequent chapters,
individual steps will be examined in more detail.

STEP ONE: INTRODUCTION TO PROCESS REDESIGN

The first step in the process redesign methodology is the introduction to process
improvement, and it has two parts. The first consists of a series of meetings and
activities to pick the process that will be redesigned. This material was covered in
Chapter 4.

Scoping the Project

Begin by creating a macro flowchart for the process that will be redesigned. The
purpose is to communicate to the team, project manager, and facilitator the scope
and major activities within this process. The flowchart also defines the boundaries
of the process. If you're scoping "world peace," for instance, it should show up in
the macro flowchart.

Scoping can be an issue. If your organization is new to process redesign, it's best
to take on projects that are within your control. Although issues and problems can
come from upstream and outside the organization, it's best to tackle these after you

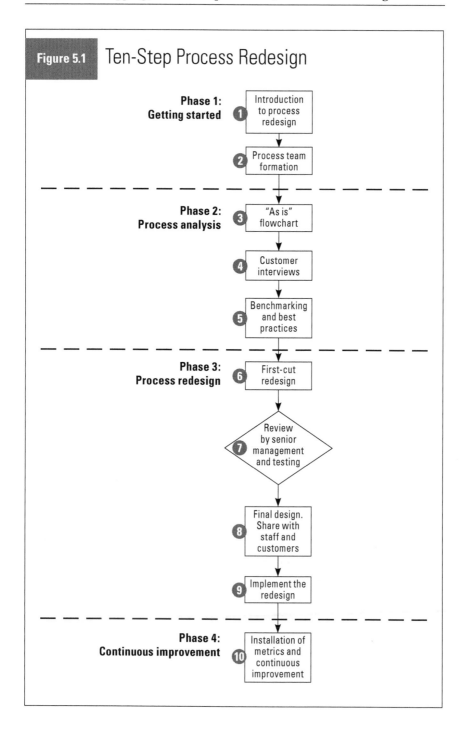

Figure 5.1   Ten-Step Process Redesign

have your own processes in order. After you've improved the processes within your control, address issues upstream. Chapter 10 discusses how to do this.

After you've scoped the process, ask the senior management team what it wants the process improvement effort to accomplish. The improvement can focus on such topics as time, quality, cost, customer satisfaction, and worker frustration. Ask the senior management team to quantify the improvement desired. Is it looking for a time reduction of 50 percent? Zero defects? The process improvement team must have specific goals for the improvement effort. The team will create a baseline as it reflects current performance, measure improvement against the baseline, and compare it to the goals established by senior management.

Meeting With Senior Management

Another meeting with the senior management is necessary to discuss three topics:
- Barriers to process improvement
- Job loss
- Crafting the kick-off speech

Chapter 10 examines a variety of barriers to process improvement, and these issues should be discussed with senior managers. Pay particular attention to how turf issues at the department-head level will be addressed, should they arise. If senior managers don't believe turf issues will be a problem for a large, cross-departmental change effort, then you should anticipate trouble down the road. Cross-departmental efforts usually create turf issues.

Another important topic is job loss. This usually occurs when a new process is created. Some existing work evaporates, some new work is created, and some work moves. Job loss is inevitable for work that evaporates. The ideal solution is to deploy the newly available staff in some other area of the organization. Ask senior managers if they have initiatives they'd like to pursue but that need staff to implement. Most likely the answer will be, "Yes." If that's the case, then a plan should be developed to retrain and place employees affected by the redesign.

In redesign projects where employees must leave the organization, a plan must be developed for outplacement, severance packages, and so forth. Both job and employment loss must be discussed when a senior manager talks with those employees who will be affected by the process redesign. People will naturally be concerned about their livelihoods, so it's best to address these topics right away.

The third topic to discuss with senior management is crafting the kickoff speech that's given to all affected staff. Chapter 6 discusses this in more detail, but a key element in this speech is honoring and showing appreciation for the hard work employees already have done. If management announces that a certain process needs fixing, it's not a far leap for staff to think *they* need fixing. Senior management must make it clear that the problem is in the process, not the people.

Another aspect of the kickoff speech is making the case for change. This is comprised of two groups of issues known as "go to" and "away from." Away from elements include the pain, danger, frustration, and costs that reside in the present and/or future situation if nothing changes. Away-from issues are highly motivating for immediate action, but motivation drops sharply when the pain or danger subsides. Go-to elements offer a desirable destination, rather like a vacation. It's a compelling vision of the new organization that inspires people to work toward achieving. As the organization gets closer to the go-to vision, motivation rises dramatically.

Meeting With Affected Employees

Once you've discussed the redesign project with senior managers, they should then meet with all affected employees. At this time the kickoff speech is given, the project goals are outlined, and the case for change is explained. The project manager, process improvement team, and facilitator are introduced. Finally, the meeting is opened for questions and answers. This meeting usually lasts two hours, and when it's over, you're ready for step two of the process redesign method.

STEP TWO: CREATING THE TEAM

After you've created the macro flowchart and senior management has established improvement goals, the next step is to assemble the process improvement team. Along with the process improvement team members is a project manager, facilitator, and information technologist.

Project Manager

A critical player in the process improvement effort, the project manager should be someone who has already led an organizational change effort. He or she should have experience handling problems that occur during process redesign. This person should also hold a relatively senior position within the company. If you're planning on a cross-functional process change, then your project manager must be comfortable with, and powerful enough to address, department heads. The project manager should be well respected in the organization and have a passionate interest in changing the targeted process. One of the two critical success factors for any process improvement effort is the project manager's ability. The other is senior management's commitment. If both of those factors are strong, then your improvement project's success rate will be high.

Process Improvement Team

After the project manager has been selected, the process improvement team must be chosen. Look for the best and brightest who work in the targeted process. Potential team members should be enthusiastic about improving the process. From this list of potential candidates, the project manager chooses the team.

The number of team members depends in part on the scope of the process under redesign. It's a good idea if there's a team member to represent each key piece of the process. Keep in mind that although it's quite possible to work successfully with teams of up to twenty-four members, teams with more than eight members will have a harder time dealing with team dynamics. Also, people who work in the process should make up the largest component. Managers and supervisors are welcome as long as they don't intimidate other team members.

Another key team member is someone who doesn't work in the process. He or she should come from another department within the organization. This person, known as the "maverick," is responsible for asking, "why?" and preventing team members from succumbing to "group think." He or she should challenge the team to think outside the box, so choose someone who's comfortable with this role. Disagreements are healthy for a team as long as members respect one another.

Facilitator

This person serves as a walking resource and should be knowledgeable about lean, Six Sigma, design principles, benchmarking, best practices, team facilitation, and coaching. He or she will set the agenda and lead the team through all the process improvement steps. If an external facilitator is used, this person should train at least one person within the organizations to assume the facilitator's role for future projects. The facilitator-in-training progressively will take on more responsibility in process improvement efforts as his or her skills and confidence increase. Conversely, the original facilitator works him- or herself out of a job.

The facilitator should be neutral regarding team decisions. For a facilitator to push a particular solution or idea is an abuse of power and can fracture the team. Although the facilitator might have some good ideas, these should be presented outside of team meetings to the project manager or other team members. If they see merit in the ideas, they can present them during team meetings. The facilitator should assume the role of coach or trainer, not fixer. The fixer or problem-solver role has traditionally been what most managers have played in U.S. organizations. However, at Toyota the manager leads through questioning. (For an informative portrayal of coach versus fixer, see Steven Spear's article, "How To Lead at Toyota," published in the May 2004 issue of *Harvard Business Review*.)

The facilitator can bring in pertinent case studies and examples for team members to review. Examples of benchmarking and best practices also fall into this category. Team discussions about case studies can uncover insights that will aid the team in building a conceptual framework for process improvement fundamentals, such as design principles.

Information Technologist

As the name implies, this person is knowledgeable about technological resources. Many process designs are enabled through appropriate hardware, software, Internet solutions, and so forth. The information technologist can greatly assist the team during the redesign phase. If you can't get this person during step two, then try to bring him or her in at step six, the clean-sheet redesign.

Meeting With the Team

During the first meeting with the team, the facilitator and project manager reinforce the message given by senior management. The points to reinforce are honoring and appreciating past efforts by team members, and that the redesign is focusing on the process, not people. Also, the project manager should restate the case for change.

During this initial meeting, the first task is to create the team ground rules. Sample ground rules are included in Chapter 6. The second task is to answer the question, "How are we going to communicate to all stakeholders who have a vested interest in this project?" This, too, is addressed in the next chapter.

STEP THREE: CREATING THE AS-IS FLOWCHART

The third step in the ten-step process redesign method is the as-is flowchart, whose purpose is to create a functional-activity flowchart of the process undergoing redesign. The four lenses of analysis discussed in Chapter 7 are employed at this step. Usually the frustration lens is used, followed by any other appropriate lens, such as time, quality, or cost. The choice of which lens to use depends on the goal of the process improvement effort. If the goal is to reduce time, then the obvious lens to use is time. If the goal is to reduce costs, then quality and cost lenses are appropriate.

The as-is flowchart precedes the customer interview in step four because questions can arise while creating the flowchart that you won't have thought of if you interviewed customers first. Consider, for example, a newspaper's ad-flow process. The as-is flowchart indicates that the sales staff controls access to the customer. For complex ads, it might make sense for a designer to talk directly with the customer, but the sales department is against this idea. Therefore, an additional question to ask customers would be, "Are there occasions when you'd want to speak directly to the ad designer?" This question might not have come up if the as-is flowchart wasn't created prior to customer interviewing.

Best-Practice Questions

The as-is flowchart can provide the team with potential benchmarking and best practice questions. The ones and twos from the frustration and idea bin can be turned into questions (see Chapter 7 for an explanation of the frustration and idea bin). For example, one team might have the idea to put their organization's contract template on the Internet. The team asked organizations, "Do you put your contract template on the Internet?" When a respondent answered, "Yes," the team's follow-up response was, "Please tell us how well that works." There's always a likelihood that someone else has thought of some of the ideas your team has. If that's the case, the team should find how well the idea worked. The team should consider what it can learn from someone else's experience implementing that idea.

The Walk-Through

After the team completes the as-is flowchart, check it by conducting a walk-through. This is where you actually follow the process to trace the steps as outlined in the flowchart. Make a point of approaching people other than those you interviewed when you created it. You can begin the exchange by commenting, "We interviewed your colleague, and this is what she said happens at this step. Do you do the same thing?" If this person answers, "no," then you have a standardization issue. If you're given a negative answer, follow up with, "What is it that *you* do?" Then ask the frustration question, "When you're at this step, is there anything that frustrates you?" Make a note of the frustrations, and ask the person if he or she has any ideas about eliminating them.

Assuming you've uncovered issues concerning standardization during your walk-through, you'll need to indicate the variations in the as-is flowchart. Obviously, one of the problems with the process could be this lack of standardization.

STEP FOUR: CUSTOMER INTERVIEW

Step four is the customer interview. At this step, your goal is to find out what the customer needs, wants, desires, and requires from the process. In addition, you'll ask any questions that were generated from the as-is flowchart in step three. Refer to the customer report card in Chapter 8 for more details on this step.

STEP FIVE: BENCHMARKING AND BEST PRACTICES

Step five focuses on benchmarking and best-practices research. To do this, divide the team into three groups. The first should find out what your direct competitors do relative to the process you're investigating. The second group should look for organizations similar to your own but that aren't direct competitors. These might be organizations that are in a different geographical region or that provide a product or service that's similar but doesn't compete with yours. The third group should look for organizations that use a similar process, regardless of industry, and that are considered world-class.

This last group is most likely to achieve a breakthrough in new ideas. People often spend their entire careers in one industry, and over time they'll begin to think pretty much the same as others in the industry. This is known as "group think." By looking outside your industry, particularly at world-class organizations, you're more likely to shake off group think and discover new ways of approaching problems.

An example of this is an opera company that wants to redesign its subscriptions process. What's a subscription like? It's like taking an order, in this case for opera tickets. Who does the best job at taking orders? Lands' End Direct Merchants is considered world-class in this area. So team members ask that organization questions about taking orders and gain three innovative ideas to use in redesigning the subscription process. These ideas weren't found by talking with other opera companies.

Benchmarking and best practices are discussed in more detail in Chapter 8.

STEP SIX: CLEAN-SHEET REDESIGN

Step six is the clean-sheet redesign. Each team member writes a story of the ideal process. We challenge the team with stretch goals. Every team member reads his or her story. Team members are encouraged to list ideas that they like from these presentations. In most cases, the team will be able to come up with a new process, based on the new ideas, that all agree on. In cases where the team can't agree on a single new design, you can determine the best design through the testing process that occurs in step seven.

For example, a team comes up with four different designs for a new process. The team role-played each of the new designs to establish which one worked best. Two of the designs failed the test, and the remaining two were combined together into one new process design. Thus, it's not necessary for the team to agree on a single design initially. Test each of the variations with simulation, practice, and role-playing, and let the results decide the winning design.

STEP SEVEN: PRESENTING THE REDESIGN TO SENIOR MANAGEMENT

At step seven you'll share the new design with senior management. It's a good idea to brief senior management after every meeting so that when the new design is presented, it won't create any surprises. In fact, the team should have a sense of senior management's approval even before the formal presentation.

A key discussion with senior management at this time is implementation options and risk management. Which of the options make most sense? Should the team test the design by role-playing, should they run a pilot test, or should the design be phased in? Senior management must feel confident that any risks in the new design are managed properly.

STEP EIGHT: SHARING THE REDESIGN WITH STAFF AND CUSTOMERS

After senior management has signed off on the new design, at step eight the design is shared with staff and customers. Observe their reactions to the new process. Are there problems the team overlooked? Will some adjustments need to be made in the design?

In addition, the team should look for people not on the team who would be interested in participating in the implementation phase. Avoid staff members who say, "This effort wouldn't be necessary if people just did their jobs." Instead, look for people who say, "This new design is exciting and should really help." Ask them if they'd be interested in helping the team implement the design. If they say, "yes," then you know you're staffing your implementation effort with supporters rather than naysayers.

The final group that will see the new design is customers. You want to gauge their reaction and get their comments. If you decide to run a pilot of the new design, you might find some customers interested in participating.

Step eight is completed after staff and customers have seen and reacted to the final design.

STEP NINE: IMPLEMENTING THE REDESIGN

Step nine involves implementing the redesign. This might start with a practice run, followed by a pilot test, and finally phased in. Implementation strategies vary from process to process. Each design has its own risk and implementation factors, so choosing implementation options will be different for each time. Step nine is finished when the new design is completely rolled out and fully implemented.

STEP TEN: INSTALLING METRICS AND CONTINUOUS IMPROVEMENT

Step ten sets up a system of continuous improvement. Measurement and feedback mechanisms are installed in the new process. A process advisor or consultant monitors the metrics for problems. Selected employees who work in the process are assembled for continuous improvement activities that are facilitated by the process advisor. Ongoing process control and improvement are then structured into the process.

ELEVEN CHARACTERISTICS FOR CREATING A SUCCESSFUL REDESIGN

- Senior management is committed and designates the process redesign as a high priority.
- Management and employees understand design principles and their implications from the outset.
- Communication and training during the redesign effort ensure proper attention is paid to employee concerns and the organizational environment.
- Substantial and continuing customer input is encouraged.
- Maximum involvement of employees is encouraged at every step of the redesign effort.
- High-quality staffing is a priority of the process improvement team.
- At least one absolute zealot of the redesign process is in a position of influence.
- Change is driven by results for the customer.
- Appropriate use is made of information technology.
- The redesign includes a strong measurement component such as baseline data, targets, and benchmarking.
- Broad change issues and alignment questions that emerge during the redesign are effectively managed.

Chapter 6

Introduction to Process Improvement and Creating the Process Team

This chapter covers the first two steps of process redesign: introduction to process improvement and creating the process team. Figure 6.1 highlights these steps within the ten-step methodology.

MAKING THE CASE FOR CHANGE

The case for change is comprised of two groups of elements called "away from" and "go to." Away-from issues usually are pain-, danger- or frustration-driven. People want to get away from these negative states. Pain, danger, and frustration are highly motivating for immediate action. For instance, if a fire suddenly erupted in your office, you'd quickly move to safety. However, when you were a safe distance away, your motivation for action would suddenly drop off. Interestingly, "firefighting," the common response to away-from issues, is a recurrent event in many organizations. There's a burst of activity, the problem goes away (if only temporarily), and everyone involved returns to business as usual. Figure 6.2 on page 79 illustrates the concept.

Away-From Reasons for Change

What is it about the current situation or process that's painful, dangerous, unpleasant, or frustrating? You could answer this question from the employees' perspective, the organization's, and the customer's.

From the employee's perspective, the pain might be in the work itself. Or it might be from the pressure placed on them to meet challenging goals. It could be

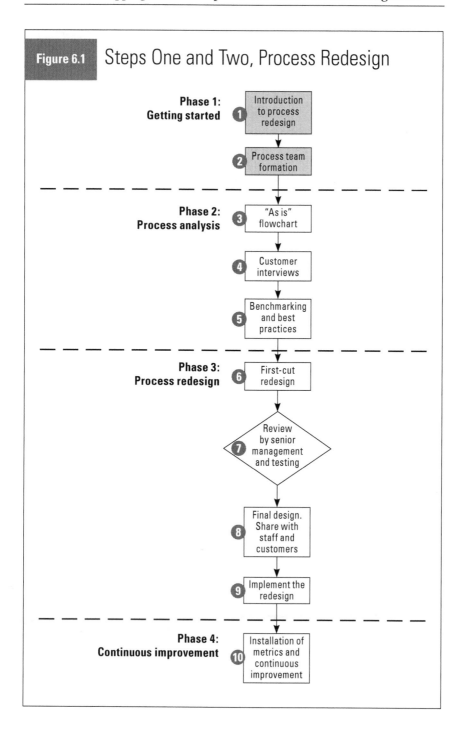

Figure 6.1   Steps One and Two, Process Redesign

Phase 1:
Getting started
1. Introduction to process redesign
2. Process team formation

Phase 2:
Process analysis
3. "As is" flowchart
4. Customer interviews
5. Benchmarking and best practices

Phase 3:
Process redesign
6. First-cut redesign
7. Review by senior management and testing
8. Final design. Share with staff and customers
9. Implement the redesign

Phase 4:
Continuous improvement
10. Installation of metrics and continuous improvement

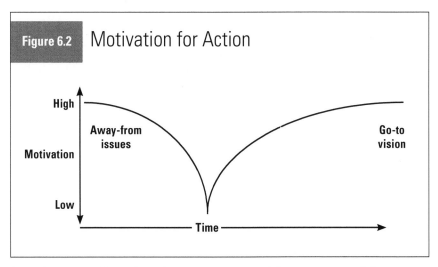

Figure 6.2   Motivation for Action

from the potential loss of employment or income if the organization fails. Pain can be cast as a present or future condition. If the organization doesn't change, some negative event could happen in the future that would hurt employees. People should see how the current situation or process hurts them now, or could do so in the future.

From an organizational perspective, the pain can be cast as cost, quality, timeliness, or some other organizational metric. How are these areas eroding? What effect does the negative situation have on the organization? What will happen if nothing is done about it?

If customers are feeling discomfort or dissatisfaction, the organization is at risk. Customers vote with their dollars. If you lose enough votes, ultimately the organization goes out of business.

Go-To Reasons for Change

Although away-from issues focus on problems, go-to scenarios promote a desirable destination. Collectively, they present a picture of how the organization could be and are cast as situations worth achieving. With go-to scenarios, motivation increases the closer an organization gets to them. Think of going on vacation: As the departure date draws closer, we become more excited.

Frame go-to scenarios as specific improvements for employees, the organization, and customers. Answer the question, "What's in it for me?" from the employees' perspective.

Figure 6.2 shows how motivation and time relate to away-from issues and go-to scenarios.

How often should you make the case for change? Enough times for 60 percent to 80 percent of your staff to understand why the change is being made. The message must be delivered multiple times and in multiple formats. Senior management's job is to make a compelling case for change and communicate it so that most employees not only understand the need but also buy into it as well.

Present a Persuasive Kickoff Speech

Many change efforts begin with a kickoff speech that offers little explanation, background, or justification. People often come away from these nonevents confused, angry, and cynical. These speeches usually leave out important information. What should you include in a kickoff speech? There are specific topics concerning the past, the present, and the future that should be addressed.

When talking about the past, be sure to:

- Honor the past
- Highlight past successes
- Highlight people's contributions
- Highlight attitudes that helped in past crises
- Show appreciation for the hard work people have done

When talking about the present, be sure to define:

- The current situation
- Problems and issues (i.e., away-from reason for change)
- Who's involved
- Why problems occurred
- What will happen if nothing is done

When talking about the future, discuss:

- The target goal (i.e., go-to reasons for change)
- What past traits, characteristics, and talents will help with the future challenge
- What new traits, characteristics, and talents will be needed
- Improvements in:
  - ☐ Quality
  - ☐ Service

- ☐ Cost
- ☐ Timeliness
- ☐ Features

- ■ New products and/or services

Identify the change methodology that will drive the process:
- ■ Six Sigma
- ■ Business process reengineering
- ■ Merger
- ■ Lean
- ■ Reorganization
- ■ Describe what will be measured and how the company will know that it's succeeding
- ■ Create a link between these measures, performance appraisal, and bonuses

Address the potential for job change. Tell employees what changes they can expect to see in terms of:
- ■ Job descriptions
- ■ Work location
- ■ Increased decision making
- ■ Pay levels
- ■ Workload
- ■ The potential for job loss

Emphasize that everyone has a part to play and explain:
- ■ What senior management will do to support the effort
- ■ How senior management will change to support the effort
- ■ What each person must do to make the effort succeed
- ■ How the change effort will affect individuals

Before you finish the speech, be sure to:
- ■ Acknowledge that mistakes will occur, and emphasize that they'll be treated as learning opportunities.
- ■ Get employee buy-in by involving them.
- ■ Promise to keep employees informed and follow through on that promise.

CREATING THE PROCESS TEAM

For teams to work effectively together, team ground rules should be established. Here are some that are commonly used.

- *Decisions are made by consensus.* In consensus, everyone agrees. Voting presents a problem, in that there are always losers. These people might not support the winners. If disagreement occurs, you must discuss it until consensus is reached. Consensus means everyone will go along with it, but not everyone has to like it.
- *As a team, you'll spend 100 percent of your time on process issues.* If there's a people issue, it will be discussed away from the group with the project manager or facilitator. This doesn't mean that there won't be people issues. There will be, and they can effect process performance and team dynamics. However, if people issues arise, they must be discussed outside the team meetings.
- *Treat everyone with respect.*
- *Everyone on the team is equal.* Although there may be managers in the room, their vote counts no more that anyone else.
- *There are no dumb questions.*
- *Do what you say you're going to do.* Process improvement requires work and commitment. The project manager and team members count on all employees to do what they commit to.
- *If you think you can't meet your task deadline, notify the project manager as soon as the problem becomes apparent.* Don't wait until the team meeting to state that your task isn't done. Don't spring any surprises on either the project manager or the team. The project manager might be able to suggest some ideas to help you get the assignment done on time. Or he or she might want to adjust the timeline because your day-to-day job is interfering with team tasks.
- *Share the workload.* A successful team doesn't let some people do all the work and let others have a free ride.
- *When you walk into the team meeting, remove your department hat and put on your team hat.* Although you must keep your perspective on the work performed in your area, team goals supersede turf issues, departmental agendas, and politics.
- *Don't talk over someone else.*
- *Don't interrupt.*

Asking a Team Member to Leave

Periodically, projects involve team members who are consistently disruptive, unreliable, or irritating. For these people, the three strikes rule applies. After the first infraction, the team member is coached outside the team meeting regarding the problem behavior. The desired behavior and team rules are emphasized. After the second infraction, repeat the process, and let the person know this is the last warning. At the next infraction, the person is removed from the team. Invariably, on the third strike, the person won't argue about wanting to stay on the team.

Process improvement work is similar to a pack of sled dogs pulling a heavy load. You can't afford to have one dog pulling in a different direction or dragging its tail in the snow. All the dogs must pull in the same direction, toward the same goal, and follow the same rules.

Creating the Communication Plan

The team should ask itself, "Who must be kept informed of this process improvement effort?" Draw up a list of all the critical stakeholders and record all the available means to keep them informed. Then create a matrix comprised of the who and the how. Figure 6.3 shows an example.

In keeping with the change management principle of no surprises to senior management, this group is kept informed after every team meeting. Dramatic change ideas often are discussed in team meetings, and you want to run these by

Figure 6.3	Who and How Matrix

	Method of communication			
Stakeholder group	Phone call or face-to-face meeting after every team meeting	Monthly staff meeting	Newsletter	Condensed minutes on the intranet
Senior management	Yes, by project manager	Yes, by project manager	Yes, by meeting secretary	Yes, by meeting secretary
Other employees in the process but not on the team		Yes, by project manager	Yes, by meeting secretary	Yes, by meeting secretary
Downstream department		Yes, by project manager	Yes, by meeting secretary	Yes, by meeting secretary

senior managers before you present your recommendation to them at step seven. In addition, change resistance, turf issues, and corporate policies often surface, and the senior staff must be kept apprised of them. You don't want to present your recommendation after three months' work only to encounter shock and resistance from senior management.

Usually organizations have regularly scheduled staff meetings where team members can update others on the process improvement effort. In addition, team members are encouraged to communicate informally with non-team members about the progress the team is making. Process improvement efforts don't involve state secrets, so there's no need to hoard information. However, on the rare occasions that sensitive topics are covered, agreements are made between team members to keep the discussion private.

The team facilitator occasionally will ask team members what they're hearing about the effort. This is to gauge the level of support or resistance in the organization to mitigate rumors or fears before they get out of hand. It's a good idea to check in with the team periodically about organizational issues, both inside and outside the meeting room.

Chapter 7

The Four Lenses
of Analysis

I n Chapter 2 you learned to make a functional-activity flowchart. This chart of an "as is" process is the first task in step three of the redesign methodology. Remember, the as-is flowchart summarizes what is actually happening, not what you want to happen. Therefore, it's important to build a flowchart from an actual event. Also, it's important to number each box, diamond, and triangle in the chart. These numbers will serve as reference points when you use the four lenses of analysis discussed in this chapter.

Figure 7.1 highlights the steps covered in this chapter.

THE FRUSTRATION LENS

The frustration lens diagnoses the process from the perspective of those who work in it. The purpose is to learn what frustrations people experience when doing their work. You can ask people about these as you create the as-is-flowchart, or you can complete the chart first and ask later. Use the first method if the process is relatively short and there aren't many frustrations. Use the second for complex processes, particularly if there are a lot of frustrations.

With a large process, keep in mind that if you start talking about frustrations as you map it, you will take an extremely long time to finish the flowchart. Looking at a finished chart allows the team to concentrate on areas that cause the most frustration, rather than bogging down in a flurry of small irritations.

Before you begin asking people what frustrates them, set up a ground rule. Tell them, "While we're in this room working together, we'll focus 100 percent of the time on the process, not the people involved in it. If someone has a people issue, he or she should take it up with the project manager or facilitator, outside of the meeting."

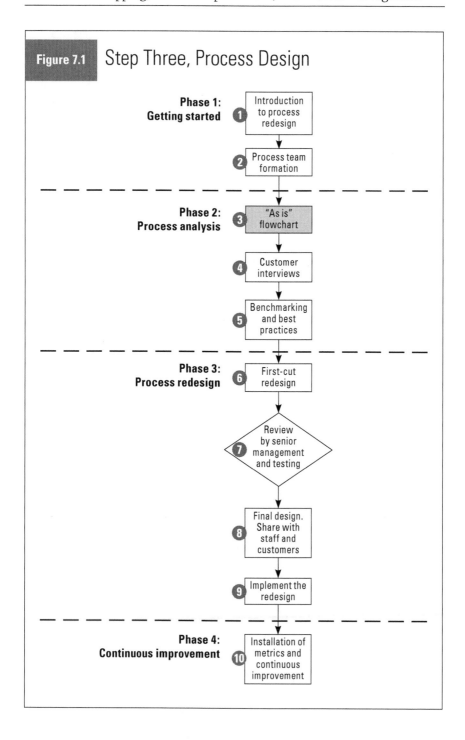

Figure 7.1   Step Three, Process Design

The frustration lens offers the following advantages:

- *Frustrations and quality issues are related.* Sometimes if you ask a person about quality problems, he or she might not answer for fear of retribution. (In traditional and involvement-style organizations, blame and lack of trust are often rampant during process improvement initiatives.) But if you ask what frustrates them, the quality issues surface in the course of the conversation. By focusing on frustrations, you can uncover quality problems without people clamming up.

  When someone mentions a frustration that's a quality issue, ask him or her to quantify the frequency of the problem. For instance, "What frustrates me is that the change order has errors," is a quality problem. Your next question should be, "Out of ten change orders, how many have errors?" Put the response to that on the flowchart or list it on the quality problems sheet described in the quality lens section later in this chapter.

- *Problem areas become easily visible.* People want the flow of work to be smooth and of high quality. So their frustrations often point to bottlenecks, disconnects in communication, missing information, and confusion.

- *People get to "vent" about the parts of the process that frustrate them.* Venting is cathartic. When team members see you're serious about hearing their problems, it creates enthusiasm and excitement. Buy-in for process improvement soars.

- *People begin to offer improvement ideas after frustrations and problems are identified.* People who do the work often have the best ideas about how to improve it. Structure the frustration lens so that workers also provide ideas to solve their frustrations. Ideas that will have a significant effect and are inexpensive and easy to implement (i.e., the low-hanging fruit) can be addressed immediately. People get excited when they see their ideas becoming realities. Because these ideas came from team members—as opposed to a top-down management dictate—this also creates a huge boost in morale, enthusiasm, and buy-in to process improvement.

- *Problems point to process design principles that aren't being used.* Process design principles are derived from best practices of world-class organizations and are extremely useful for providing direction and guidance on a redesign. (They're described in detail in Chapter 10.) Sometimes a person will express a frustration that links directly to a design principle. For example, a person might say, "What frustrates me is the incomplete information on the form." That links to design principle No. 17, bringing downstream information needs upstream. When a design principle surfaces during the frustration discussion, state the principle and then have the team consider how to incorporate it into the redesign.

■ *Process mapping creates a shared understanding and awareness of problems, issues, and solutions.* Sometimes finger-pointing and blaming occurs between departments. When these departments are brought together on a process improvement team, over time as frustrations are expressed and solutions offered, the negative atmosphere between the departments will begin to improve. The departments start shifting from an "us and them" attitude to a more cooperative vision. Although process improvement wasn't designed as a team-building activity, it is.

THE FRUSTRATION AND IDEA BIN

Figure 7.2 shows a sales-order process. At step two the account representative receives the sales order from the sales department. If this process was examined through the frustration lens, you'd ask the rep, "Is there anything frustrating at this step?" The rep might respond, "The sales orders have missing, incomplete, and wrong information." On a flip chart, write the number two, which corresponds to the step you're examining. Next to that write, "The sales orders have missing,

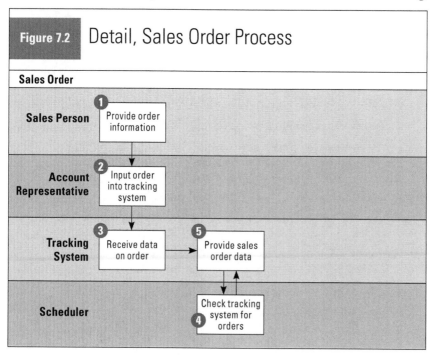

Figure 7.2   Detail, Sales Order Process

incomplete, and wrong information."

Note: Be sure to use the exact words of the person experiencing the frustration. Paraphrasing without the person's permission is insulting and implies that you can express the person's frustration better than he or she can. If you must paraphrase, state what you want to write, and then ask the person, "Is it OK to state it like this?"

Next, make sure every team member has a Post-it notepad. If anyone has ideas that will eliminate the frustration, write each idea on a note. If a person has four ideas, then you'll get four notes from him or her. Place all the notes on the flip chart so they accumulate under the frustration you just listed. It should look something like the representation in Figure 7.3.

Why Use Post-it Notes?

You could simply ask team members to brainstorm ideas to eliminate the frustration the account representative has experienced. The problem with that is twofold. First, people tend to discuss ideas when they're being generated, and discussion stifles brainstorming. Although eventually you'll want to discuss these ideas, you don't want to do so during the creative phase. Second, not everyone is an extrovert, and some people feel uncomfortable shouting out their ideas. When they can think about an idea and write it down, they're more apt to contribute. By using the Post-it note technique, the group will come up with more ideas than

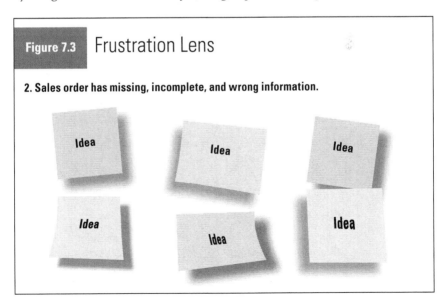

Figure 7.3 Frustration Lens

2. Sales order has missing, incomplete, and wrong information.

it would simply by brainstorming. The chance of someone offering a great idea increases as well.

Sorting Through the Idea Bin

Now that you have a series of ideas, how do you decide which ones are best? Use a two-by-two table to frame the discussion. On the table's vertical axis, ask two questions: First, does the idea eliminate that person's frustration? If it "zaps" the frustration, then the idea falls in the upper region of the vertical axis. Second, will the customer like this idea? To be considered, an idea must both eliminate the frustration and please the customer. If not, you're defeating the purpose of the process that's being fixed, which is to create customer satisfaction. However, if you think the customer would like the idea, then you're clearly in the high area of the vertical axis.

The next question, "Is the idea both inexpensive and easy to implement?" must pass both criteria to fall in the left column. Thus, ideas that have high impact, high value to the customer, and are inexpensive and easy to implement fall into quadrant one or "slam dunk." These ideas can be acted upon immediately. The only reservation about acting on them right away is that some might be unwound in a clean-sheet redesign (i.e., reengineering) of the process. You might ask, "Does the idea have merit, no matter what the new design might look like?" If the answer is yes, then go ahead and implement the idea.

By acting on ideas immediately, the team can experience an instant, positive effect of the process improvement effort. In addition, it sends a message to the rest of the organization that you're serious about improving processes.

Ideas that have high impact and value to the customer but are either expensive or difficult fall into quadrant two, which has a series of question marks in it. These stand for two questions: How difficult will it be to implement the idea? How expensive? The answers to those questions will determine whether to implement it.

Figure 7.4 shows the two-by-two matrix for sorting ideas.

Ideas that have low impact and value to customer but are inexpensive and easy to implement fall into quadrant three. Lastly, ideas with low impact and value to the customer and that are either difficult or expensive fall into quadrant four. Instead of rejecting ideas in these quadrants, ask the team, "How can these be changed so they might end up into quadrants one or two?" This will trigger another round of creativity, which might take a so-so idea and make it shine.

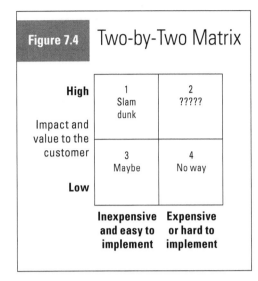

Figure 7.4 Two-by-Two Matrix

	Inexpensive and easy to implement	Expensive or hard to implement
High	1 Slam dunk	2 ?????
Low	3 Maybe	4 No way

Impact and value to the customer

THE TIME LENS

Time is a critical dimension of customer satisfaction and cost reduction. Getting products and services to customers in a speedy fashion is a value-adding activity. By beating your competitors to market, you gain sales and market share.

As a cost-reduction strategy, time reduction can be very effective. Inspection, moving, setup, rework, and waiting all add costs. The amount of time in these areas can be staggering. Table 7.1 illustrates the percentages of time in various process categories.

"Processing time" means the time spent actually doing work in a particular process. It's through processing time that a product is made or a service delivered. As you can see in Table 7.1, processing time—where actual work is performed—is remarkably low in the total process cycle time, just 2 to 20 percent. In addition, only a small portion of that amount is value-added time. Hence the percentage of value-added time in a process can be just a tiny fraction of the total process cycle time.

Wait time is measured from the perspective of the item in the process, not the

Table 7.1 Percentages of Total Process Cycle Time

Time category	Typical percentage of total cycle time in a process
Processing	2 percent to 20 percent
Waiting	30 percent to 70 percent
Rework	20 percent to 50 percent
Moving	10 percent to 30 percent
Inspecting	5 percent to 15 percent
Setup	2 percent to 20 percent

person doing the work. For example, if you're working on something and you stop to answer a phone call, the work you stopped doing must wait while you're working on something else (in this case, answering the phone). As you can see, wait time encompasses the largest percentage of time in a process.

Rework comprises the next largest category of time. Six Sigma experts often call this area the "hidden factory." These are all the extra activities performed because the work wasn't done right the first time. Table 7.1 shows that 20 to 50 percent of total process cycle time can be consumed by rework.

Both formal and informal rework steps make up the hidden factory. Formal rework is done after a formal inspection step, for example, following a quality-control check at the end of an assembly line. If an error or mistake is discovered, the item is put into the rework queue. The informal step occurs when someone upstream checks his or her work before passing it along. If this person catches an error, he or she reworks the problem.

Moving time is fairly straightforward and occurs whenever the work is moved from one place to another. Shortening the distance that the work must travel is a common technique to cut down on moving time.

The final category is setup time (in manufacturing this is called "changeover"). Setup is any activity that's done prior to performing the actual work required for the process step. In manufacturing, for example, this could be configuring equipment with dies, bits, calibration, and so forth so that it can perform the task. In service, setup could include scrolling through computer screens to find the one needed for the process. Another example is locating files or information before starting the task.

When all the categories of time are added together for one step, you get the total time for that step. Adding all the total times together will give you the cycle time for the process. Cycle time is the total amount of time from when a process starts to when it ends.

Every time category in Table 7.1 that follows processing time is non-value adding. The customer doesn't want to pay for waiting, rework, moving, inspecting, and setup. With the time lens, you'll want to focus on all the non-value added steps and try to eliminate or reduce them. After you've done that, look at the processing steps and try to shrink them as much as possible.

Process Cycle Time Analysis

Figure 7.5 shows a document that helps track all the different categories of time in a process. (You'll find a template for this sheet in Appendix C).

Figure 7.5 Process Cycle Time Sheet

In the columns below, list the components of time for each process step.

Step No.	Processing time	Setup time	Wait time	Move time	Inspecting time	Rework time	Total time

You'll need to use the functional-activity flowchart when filling out the time sheet. Each step in the flowchart, which you numbered earlier, corresponds to the step numbers listed in the process cycle time analysis sheet. Using a stopwatch, record the times for each step on the time sheet. To get a representative sample, do a time analysis of different operators at different times during the day. (This is a variation on the old time-and-motion studies done decades ago.)

Figure 7.6 shows seven steps in a process recorded on the process cycle time analysis sheet. Step four consumes the most time at 130 minutes, including a whopping 120 minutes of wait time. This step is a formal review by the department manager, and the work often stalls here for quite a long time. The manager sees he's created a bottleneck and has decided to delegate review to another person if he's busy.

Step five is the next longest step at 108 minutes and thirty seconds. The two major contributors to total time for this step are wait and rework time. Using the quality lens technique described below, find the root cause of the rework to eliminate this issue. The wait time is due to a heavy workload by this person. The team using this time analysis sheet is considering cross-training another person so that more than one person can do step 5.

Travelers

Another way to gather time data is with a document called a traveler. It's attached to the work and "travels" with it through each step. With the traveler you can calculate process, wait, and cycle times. Figure 7.7 is an example of a traveler sheet.

The sequence number in the first column refers to the numbered steps on the functional-activity flowchart of the process. The first person to log in would be the person identified on the functional-activity flowchart by his or her job title. With a time stamp or clock, the person records when the work is first touched. Under the "activity performed" column, this information should match the activity that's already been described in the functional-activity flowchart. Under the "processing time" column, the person estimates the amount of time he or she worked at this step, not counting interruptions. When the individual is done, he or she indicates the time the work was finished under the "logged out" column. Under the "sent to" column, the individual records who should receive the work next. When that person gets the work, he or she repeats logging and tracking time.

Figure 7.6	Process Cycle Time Analysis

Process Reconciling time sheets

In the columns below, delineate the components of time for each process step.

Step No.	Processing time	Setup time	Wait time	Move time	Inspecting time	Rework time	Total time
1	15 min.	30 sec.			1 min.	15 sec.	16 min., 45 sec.
2	5 min.	5 sec.					5 min., 5 sec.
3	17 min.		15 min.		5 min.	5 min.	42 min.
4			120 min.		10 min.		130 min.
5	3 min.		60 min.	30 sec.		45 min.	108 min., 30 sec.
6	6 min.				30 sec.	10 sec.	6 min., 40 sec.
7	5 min.	20 sec.					5 min., 20 sec.

Figure 7.7	Traveler Sheet					
Sequence No.:	Logged in by:	Time logged in:	Activity performed:	Processing time:	Time logged out:	Sent to:

The time when the work is logged in to when it's logged out comprises the total cycle time for each step. Subtracting processing time from total cycle time will give you wait time. The wait time between steps is calculated by subtracting logged-out time from logged-in time. This wait time is added to the person receiving the work.

Remember that cycle time equals processing time plus waiting time. In equation form, it's:

Cycle time = Processing time + Wait time

Figure 7.8 represents a data sheet constructed from the traveler that shows process time and cycle time for each step. The percentage column is calculated by dividing processing time by cycle time at each step. A high percentage means there's very little wait time for a particular step. For example, steps one, three, and five have 100 percent in the percentage column; hence, there's no wait time in those steps. However, step six has a meager 6 percent. That means work (i.e., processing) is happening only 6 percent of cycle time at this step, and wait time takes up 94 percent of cycle time.

One way to use the traveler is to construct a table like the one shown Figure 7.8. A first-pass method of analysis is to peruse the percentage column and scan for low percentages of processing time to total cycle time. Because step six is listed as only 6 percent, it's an obvious candidate for reducing wait time.

Figure 7.8	Data Sheet for Process and Cycle Time			
Activity	Processing time (in hours)	Cycle time (in hours)	Percentage	Percent of total
1	0.5	0.5	100	0.03
2	2.0	3.0	67	0.20
3	0.3	0.3	100	0.02
4	2.0	3.0	67	0.20
5	0.4	0.4	100	0.02
6	20.0	336.0	6	18.60
7	72.0	168.0	43	9.30
8	336.0	1,108.0	30	61.20
9	72.0	168.0	43	9.30
10	8.0	24.0	30	1.30
Total	513.2	1,811.2	28	100
Percent	28.3 percent	100 percent		

The final column, percentage of total, indicates the percentage of total process cycle time is consumed in each step. You can calculate this by taking the cycle time for each step and dividing it by the total cycle time for the process. For instance, at step eight, cycle time is 1,108 hours. Total cycle time for the process is 1,811.2 hours. If you divide 1,108 by 1,811.2, you'll get a percentage of 61.2. Thus, step eight consumes 61.2 percent of total process cycle time.

Obviously, if time reduction is your goal, you should look at steps that consume the most time. Because step eight consumes the most time in this process, it should be the first one analyzed. It doesn't make sense to start with step one because it consumes only .03 percent of the total process cycle time.

Design Principles for Reducing Process Time

Of the thirty-eight process design principles (explained in more detail in Chapter 10), the ones listed below are particularly helpful for time-reduction projects.

1. Design workflow around value-adding activities.
4. If the inputs coming into the process naturally cluster, create a separate process for each cluster.
5. Ensure a continuous flow of the "main sequence."
6. Reduce waiting, moving, and rework time.
7. Reduce setup and changeover times.
8. Reduce batch sizes.
9. Substitute parallel for sequential processes.
11. Reduce checks and reviews.
13. Build quality in to reduce inspection and rework.
15. Organize by process.
20. Involve as few people as possible in performing a process.
22. Ensure 100-percent quality at the beginning of the process.
23. Increase flow and speed to identify bottlenecks.
24. Eliminate bottlenecks.
30. Standardize processes.
31. Use co-located or networked teams for complex processes.

TIME-REDUCTION CASE STUDY

A large insurance company needed to address a time issue concerning its application process. A decision either to accept or reject an applicant's request for insurance coverage took nine to thirteen days. Brokers complained of the slow turnaround time. Competitors approved applications in five days, and potential customers were attracted to these companies.

A redesign team created a traveler form and attached it to hundreds of applications. Each person who was involved in processing the application recorded on the traveler when he or she received the application and finished working on it. By doing this, the cycle time for each step was recorded and wait time between steps captured. After calculating processing and wait time, the team found it took only nine minutes to process the application, yet nine to thirteen days to complete the entire process.

The As-Is Flowchart

The as-is flowchart of the application process is illustrated in Figure 7.9. The problems with the existing process included the following:

■ Work was performed in batch sizes of thirty to fifty applications each for the first few steps. This created wait time while a batch was being worked on.

■ Applications crisscrossed the processing facility, moving fifty feet or more.

■ Some applications had missing information. These were mixed in with the complete applications. Each processor would work on a batch containing both complete and incomplete applications. While the processor contacted the broker and tracked down the missing information, completed applications would wait until this step was competed.

■ Simpler applications that could be approved in processing instead were sent on to underwriting, which delayed the decision to approve.

■ Some process steps were performed quickly, but others took a long time. Due to the bottlenecks at the installation and membership steps, applications sat in a file drawer for up to five days.

The most critical customer requirements in the application process were a speedy review of the application followed by a timely decision. Thus, the new process had to be designed to achieve this objective. The design principles used in the redesign were chosen to address each of the problems listed by the team. Below are the design principles that were selected.

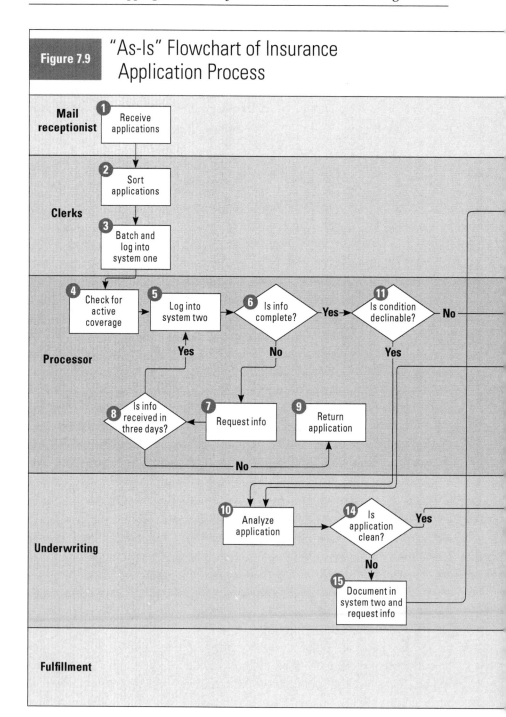

Figure 7.9 — "As-Is" Flowchart of Insurance Application Process

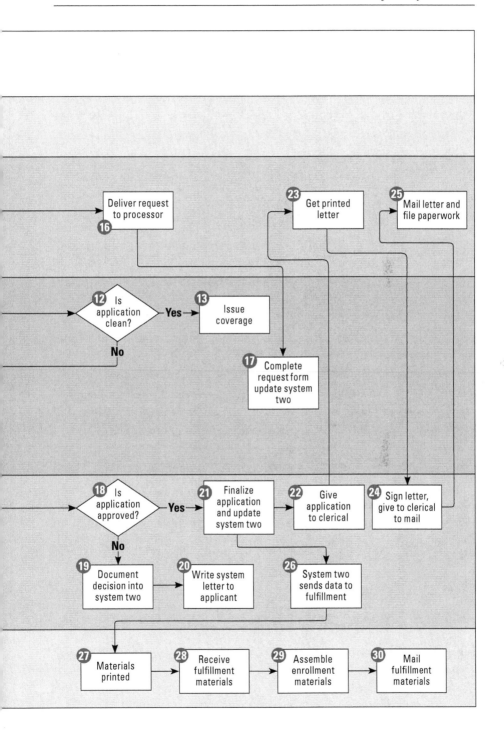

1. Design Workflow Around Value-Adding Activities

The value-adding activities were the review of and decision concerning the application. The new design had to speed the applications through the process to the point where a decision could be made. In addition, steps that didn't create value (e.g., inputting the information into a tracking software program) needed to be eliminated, taken off-line, or reduced. Because the new process would enable a speedy decision, tracking software was unnecessary, and that step was eliminated.

2. Perform Work Where It Makes the Most Sense

Because there were applications that were easy to approve (in a subprocess called "auto approve"), this step was brought upstream to the processors instead of sending such applications to underwriting.

4. Create a Separate Process for Each Cluster of Inputs

The natural clusters were incomplete application, complete application, auto approve, and complex application. When the sorting function was done, the applications were placed in their appropriate cluster, and each cluster had its own process. The incomplete applications were sent to a "pending" team, which was responsible for getting the missing information from the broker or applicant. No longer did a processor work on both complete and incomplete applications.

12. Push Decision Making Down to the Lowest Reasonable Level

Completed applications went to a processor. Here a decision was made to auto-approve some applications. If an application couldn't be auto-approved, it was sent on to underwriting.

36. Use Multi-Skilled Employees

Because this sorting (or triage) function was so important, the team recommended training several people for the job. Otherwise, if the triage person was sick or out, the process would grind to a halt. Several people were trained so there would be backups as needed.

5. Ensure a Continuous Flow of the "Main Sequence"

The main sequence is always the value-adding activities for the customer. For this process it was the speedy review of complete applications. To create a continuous flow, the redesign team used these design principles:

8. Reduce Batch Sizes

Instead of doing batches of thirty to fifty applications, they were reduced to batches of five, which reduced wait time.

6. Reduce Waiting, Moving, and Rework Time

Moving time was reduced by placing people involved in the application process right next to each other.

27. Install Metrics and Feedback to Find and Correct Problems

Incomplete applications required the most staff because tracking down information was very time-consuming. To help speed this process, a measurement and feedback system was created. The pend team logged data about the types and frequency of missing information by broker. The information was sent to the brokers, who could correct their mistake and submit more complete applications in the future.

22. Ensure 100-Percent Quality at the Beginning

Through the measurement and feedback effort, the pend team looked for opportunities to provide feedback to the broker community so that applications would be 100-percent correct when sent in.

32. Assign a Process Consultant for Cross-Functional Processes

A new position was created: the process consultant. In fact, the redesign's project manager became the process consultant. This person was the logical candidate because she knew the process end to end and had no vested interest in any one functional area. The process consultant's job was to ensure continuous improvement and coordination of this cross-functional process.

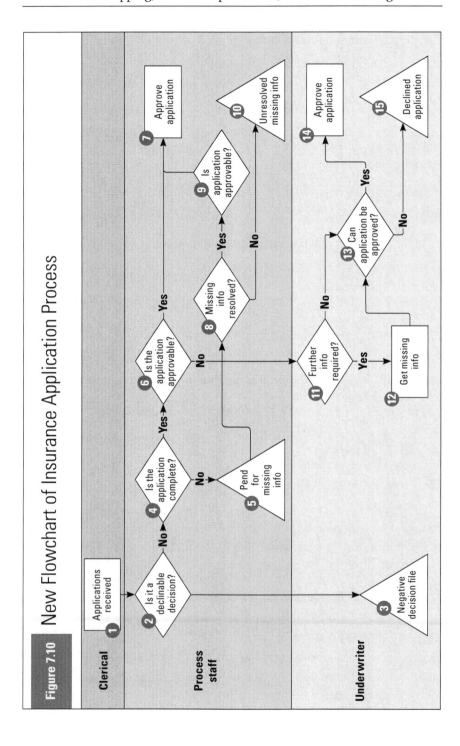

Figure 7.10   New Flowchart of Insurance Application Process

RESULTS OF THE REDESIGN

The end result of the redesign was that the insurance company could approve 14 percent of the applications in one day (i.e., auto-approve at the processor), another 20 percent were approved in two days at a triage underwriter, and the remaining complex applications were approved in five days after a more comprehensive review in underwriting.

The new process is illustrated in Figure 7.10.

Documenting the physical layout of people, materials, and equipment allows you to see the movement within a process. Because movement is a non-value adding activity, you want to shrink it as much as possible. Figure 7.11 shows the layout at the insurance company for processing applications. The physical movement from processing to quality control and from processing to underwriting was excessive.

In the layout redesign depicted in Figure 7.12, movement was shrunk dramatically by placing the people in the process next to each other. In the old design, people were grouped together according to task. All the processors worked together, all the quality control people were together, and so on. In the new design, instead of organizing by function, the organization was based on efficient flow.

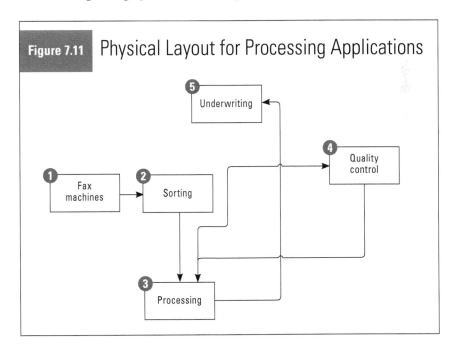

Figure 7.11 Physical Layout for Processing Applications

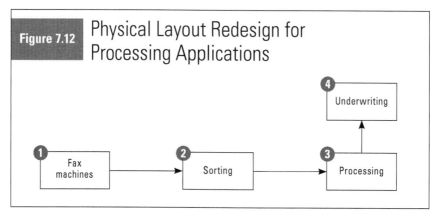

Figure 7.12 Physical Layout Redesign for Processing Applications

When batch sizes were reduced, applications needed to be processed in a steady flow. Shrinking batch size and co-location complemented each other.

Another way to visualize layout is to use the "ball of yarn" technique. Tie the end of the yarn at the beginning of the process, then walk each of the steps, unraveling the yarn as you travel. Without a visual mechanism to register the actual distance that work travels, management can often be oblivious to the effect of movement on a process.

Also, videotaping the flow of work can be quite revealing. Although flowcharts are very useful, a videotape contains much more information. Actually seeing the work performed as it passes from one area to the next helps observers realize the process is more than just an intellectual concept.

THE COST LENS

The cost lens is used for three purposes. First, when you know how much a process costs, you can calculate the return on investment generated from its redesign. Cost out both the existing and new processes. The savings between the old and the new is then offset by the investment to reach the new process (the cost of new technology, for example). Return on investment calculations such as internal rate of return, net present value, and payback can demonstrate the utility of spending money to build a new process.

Second, the cost lens allows you to see which particular steps in a process consume the most money. If cost reduction is your goal, then use a Pareto diagram of the steps, ranked from highest to lowest cost. Your cost-reduction efforts can then focus on the highest cost steps.

Third, the cost lens allows you to use activity-based costing. Using a traveler from the time lens, you can see the actual time consumed at each step. From this information you can trace costs by product, customer, or market. These are actual costs, not allocated using percentages or ratios. Traditional managerial accounting over-costs and under-costs particular products or services due to allocations. Consequently, data from your managerial accounting system can be highly inaccurate. For instance, products or services that have high volume, large lot size, low customer support, low complexity, and low technological investment generally are over-costed. The true profitability on these items is actually higher than what your managerial accounting system indicates. Conversely, products or services that have low volume, small lot size, high customer support, high complexity, and high technological investment often are under-costed. These products and services usually cost your company much more than indicated by your managerial accounting system.

Two activity-based costing sheets follow. Figure 7.13 is for service, and Figure 7.14 is for manufacturing.

The first step in filling out the activity-based costing sheet is to write the name of the process at the top of the page. The information that goes into the sheet comes from your functional-activity flowchart and the traveler. The first column is the sequence number, which corresponds to the same number on your functional-activity flowchart. Thus, at the first sequence number look at the job title for that step from your functional-activity flowchart.

The processing time information comes from the traveler. Use the increments of time that make the most sense. Increments of an hour are the most common.

The cost factor is the average hourly wage for that job title, which includes salary plus benefits. Cost factor information can be obtained from your human resources department. The labor component cost is calculated by multiplying the processing time for that step by the cost factor.

The overhead of processing time column lists how much overhead was consumed by processing time. The first step is to calculate your cost per square foot per hour of overhead. This can be accomplished by looking at all the overhead expenses in your facility for a year. These expenses include utilities, rent, depreciation, insurance, and so forth. Divide the total yearly overhead cost by the amount

Figure 7.13   Activity-Based Costing Sheet for Service

Process _____

Sequence No.	Job title	Processing time	Cost factor	Labor component cost	Overhead of processing time	Wait time	Overhead of wait time	Activity cost	Description
						Total			

Calculation is done by multiplying the processing time (in increments of an hour) by the cost factor, which equals the labor component cost. Add the overhead component of processing time. Calculate wait time. From this time, factor the overhead component of wait time. Sum up labor component cost, process time overhead cost, and wait time overhead cost. This equals the activity cost.

Figure 7.14 Activity-Based Costing Sheet for Manufacturing

Process _____

Sequence No.	Job title	Processing time	Cost factor	Labor component cost	Material cost	Overhead of processing time	Wait time	Overhead of wait time	Activity cost	Description
			Total							

Calculation is done by multiplying the processing time (in increments of an hour) by the cost factor, which equals the labor component cost. Add the overhead component of processing time. From this time, factor the overhead component of wait time. Calculate wait time. Calculate the overhead component of wait time. Sum up labor component cost, process time overhead cost, material cost, and wait time overhead cost. This equals the activity cost.

of square footage in your facility. This will give you the cost per square foot in a year. Next, divide that number by the number of hours the facility is available in a year. The final number is cost per square foot per hour. See Table 7.2 for an example of calculating cost per square foot per hour for an 18,000 square foot building.

Look at the square footage that was occupied by the person in step one. Multiply the square footage and the processing time by the cost per square foot per hour. This figure is the overhead consumed for processing time at that step.

This same technique can be used for wait time, which is also reported in increments of an hour. While products, reports, etc. are waiting, they consume overhead. Some people want to know how much overhead is consumed by wait time. To find out, take the square footage occupied by the waiting product, inventory, etc. and multiple that by the wait time, then multiply that amount by the cost per square foot per hour. The final number is the amount of overhead consumed as the product waited. Service organizations, which have little inventory, often skip this step.

The activity cost for a step is the sum of labor component cost, overhead com-

Table 7.2   Calculating Cost Per Square Foot Per Hour

Rent	$432,000
Taxes	$37,040
Insurance	$4,919
Landscaping	$5,910
Management	$22,557
Garbage	$11,031
Water	$2,310
Parking lot maintenance	$5,074
Parking lot lights	$313
Repair and maintenance	$3,588
Electric and gas utilities	$35,100
Phone	$45,000
Janitorial	$17,280
Total overhead	$622,122

(Annual overhead expenses for an 18,000 square-foot building)

To calculate cost per square foot, divide $622,122 by 18,000 square feet, which equals $34.56. To calculate cost per square foot per hour, divide $34.56 by the number of hours available in a year, which is 2,080. Thus, $34.56/ 2080 is $0.017 cost per square foot per hour.

ponent of processing time, and the overhead component of wait time. The final column is a description of the activity performed, which is pulled from the functional-activity flowchart. Add all the costs for each of the steps, and the total will be the cost for that process.

The only difference between the activity-based costing sheet for service and the activity-based costing sheet for manufacturing is the addition of material costs in the manufacturing process. The rest of the calculations are the same.

To calculate true profitability by product, customer, or market, you must first create a macro flowchart of the sale-to-payment process in your organization. Next, create a functional-activity flowchart for each of the macro steps. For whatever product, service, or customer you want to examine for true profitability, run a traveler through your entire sales-to-payment process. From the traveler, extract the processing and wait times for each step. Use the activity-based costing sheet for each functional-activity flowchart to calculate true costs. Add all the costs associated with each functional-activity flowchart to find the total consumed cost for that order. Subtract the total cost from the sale for that order, and the remainder is your true profit or loss. Figure 7.15 illustrates the process for calculating true profitability.

Consider the example of the customer order process for welding equipment by the Simpson Co. that was done on February 23, 2005. The activity-based costing sheet is a combination of the customer order process (Figure 7.16) and the activity-based costing sheet for that process (Figure 7.17). In this example, the activity cost for the Simpson order is $3,050.06. The company charged Simpson $3,500 for the order, which means the true profitability on the order was $449.94.

Although the company made money on the Simpson order, the true profitability of other orders indicated it was actually losing money on small orders. This particular company had 600 customers, and roughly 400 of them placed small orders. The remaining 200 were very profitable customers. In a dramatic shift in strategy, the company decided to discontinue serving customers for small orders. Although they had to shrink the workforce significantly, by concentrating on its most profitable customers, the company boosted profitability sevenfold.

THE QUALITY LENS

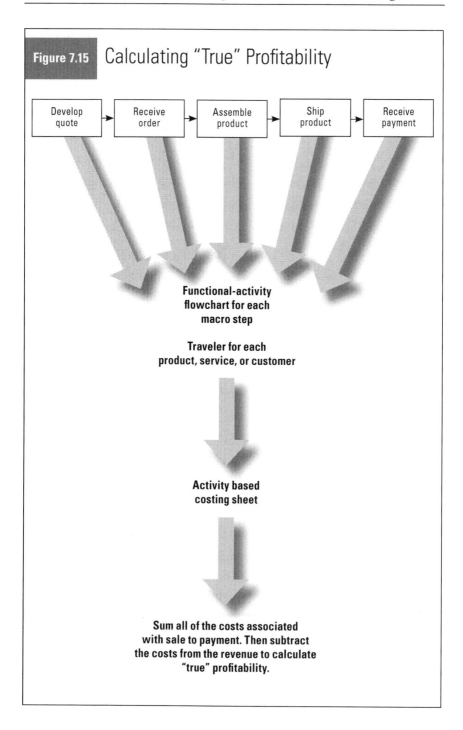

Figure 7.15   Calculating "True" Profitability

Develop quote → Receive order → Assemble product → Ship product → Receive payment

Functional-activity flowchart for each macro step

Traveler for each product, service, or customer

Activity based costing sheet

Sum all of the costs associated with sale to payment. Then subtract the costs from the revenue to calculate "true" profitability.

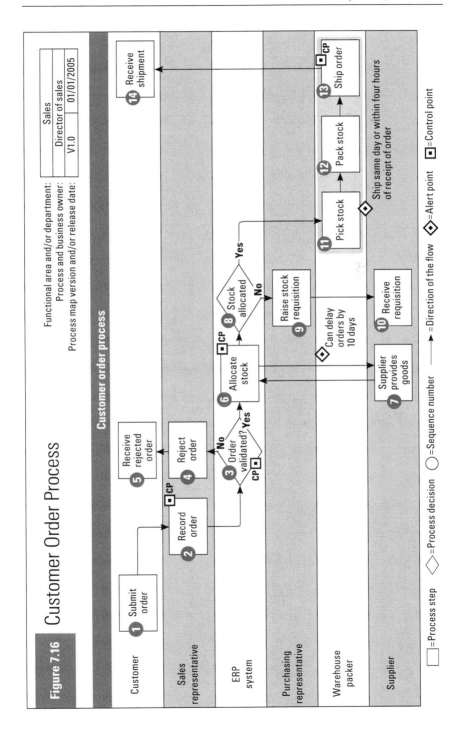

Figure 7.16   Customer Order Process

Figure 7.17 Activity-Based Costing Sheet, Customer Order Process

Process Customer order process, welding equipment, Simpson order, 2/23/05

Sequence No.	Job title	Processing time	Cost factor	Labor component cost	Material cost	Overhead of processing time	Wait time	Overhead of wait time	Activity cost	Description
2	Sales rep	0.5	150	75.00		1			76.00	Submit order
3	ERP	0.003	350			1.05			1.05	Record order
6	ERP	0.014	350			4.90			4.90	Allocate stock
8	ERP	0.003	350			1.05			1.05	Stock allocated?
11	Warehouse packer	0.5	75	37.50	2,500.00	1			2,538.50	Pick stock
12	Warehouse packer	2.5	75	150.00	45.00	4			199.00	Pack stock
13	Warehouse packer	1	75	75.00	150.00 shipping	2	8	2.56	229.56	Ship order
									Total	3,056.06	

When customers evaluate products or services, quality criteria are generally ranked as the most important. Research consistently indicates that organizations producing higher-quality products or services than their competitors gain market share and outpace rivals in sales growth.

When activities aren't done right the first time, the cost to the organization can be staggering. The cost of quality in organizations that don't have a rigorous quality initiative can be as high as 20 percent of sales.

From both customer satisfaction and cost criteria, quality is critical. Using the quality lens, you can identify quality problems, rank them, and then find the root cause to eliminate the problem.

The ideal solution is to build processes that produce quality without having to rely on review or inspections. A technique for ensuring quality known as error-proofing will be described later in this chapter.

The tools available for quality improvement are numerous and range from simple techniques to sophisticated statistical analysis. The tools present here are easy to use and don't require statistical training. The 80-20 rule—that 20 percent of the tools can solve 80 percent of quality problems—definitely has merit.

The first step in using the quality lens is to document quality issues. Figure 7.18 is a form for documenting quality problems.

Another technique for documenting quality issues is to locate them within the process. You can lay the quality lens on a functional-activity flowchart to identify and cost out the effect of each issue. Figure 7.19 shows what this might look like.

The process shown in Figure 7.19 is used in conjunction with a functional-activity flowchart of a particular process. The sequence number corresponds to the sequence number from your flowchart.

Because some steps won't have quality problems, the numbering in this template doesn't have to be sequential. Conversely, some sequence numbers might be repeated because multiple quality issues can occur at any one step. Thus, the sequence numbering in our example is two, five, seven, seven, and nine. There were no quality issues at steps one, three, four, six, and eight. In addition, there were two quality issues at step seven.

The next column, rework time, indicates how long it takes for the quality problem to be reworked. Record the time in increments of an hour. In this example, the first problem at step seven—i.e., drilled hole not aligned—requires three hours of rework. These three hours include the time to manufacture a new piece because the original was waste and couldn't be used. The next column, cost factor, repre-

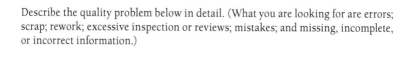

Figure 7.18   Documenting Quality Problems

Describe the quality problem below in detail. (What you are looking for are errors; scrap; rework; excessive inspection or reviews; mistakes; and missing, incomplete, or incorrect information.)

What is the affect of this problem? How does it affect you? How does it affect others? How does it affect customers? How does it affect the organization?

What must you do to fix the problem?

What does it cost to fix the problem (i.e., time you and others spend to fix it, cost of waste and scrap, cost of lost sales, etc.)?

How often does this problem occur per day, week, month, or quarter?

Figure 7.19   Calculating Quality Costs in a Process

Process   Brace subassembly

Sequence No.	Rework time	**(×)** Cost factor	**(=)** Labor cost	**(+)** Scrap waste	**(+)** Overhead costs	**(=)** Cost per incident	**(×)** No. of incidents per week	**(=)** Total cost	Quality problem
2				0.50		0.50	6	3.00	Broken flange
5	1.5	46	69		2.49	71.49	2	142.98	Bent support
7	3.0	46	138	15.10	51	204.10	3	612.30	Drilled hole not aligned
7	0.5	46	23		0.85	23.85	4	95.40	Burr on brace
9	0.5	46	23		0.85	23.85	2	47.70	Bolt missing

sents the combined salary and benefits per hour of the person doing the rework. This information is gathered from human resources. In this case, the person's combined salary and benefits per hour are $46. By multiplying the rework time by the cost factor, you can calculate the labor cost of doing rework. In the example at step seven, the labor component cost is $138 (i.e., three hours times $46).

If there's any scrap or waste associated with this quality problem, record that cost in the scrap and waste column. In the example, step seven has scrap. The metal component with the misplaced drilled hole is now useless and has become waste. Step seven has a scrap cost of $15.10.

Overhead cost is the amount of overhead consumed by the rework. Calculate this by taking the square footage of the rework area and multiplying that by the time spent doing the rework, and then multiplying that figure by the cost per square foot per hour of your facility. The cost per square foot per hour is $0.017. This was calculated by taking annual overhead costs and dividing that number by square footage and the total hours of available usage in a year. (See Table 7.2 for the calculation.)

Because step seven has rework, the overhead component is calculated by multiplying the cost per square foot per hour by the square footage occupied by the people doing rework and the amount of time spent in rework. Hence, $0.017 multiplied by 1,000 square feet times three hours equals $51 of overhead consumed by rework. (For a more thorough explanation, see the discussion on calculating cost per square foot per hour in the cost lens section in this chapter.)

By adding the labor cost, scrap or waste cost, and overhead cost together, you get the cost of one incident. So, at step seven, with the drilled hole not aligned, the total cost of one incident is $204.10

The next column lists how often an incident happens in a week. Multiply the number of incidents in a week by the cost per incident to achieve total cost. In the final column, record a brief title or description of the quality problem.

After you've calculated total costs for each incident, rank the quality problems from highest to lowest cost. Start with your highest-cost problems first and seek the root cause(s) to eliminate these problems permanently. Referring again to step seven, the problem of a drilled hole not aligned happens three times per week for a total cost of $612.30. This quality problem is the most expensive of the five and should be eliminated first.

FAILURE MODE AND EFFECTS ANALYSIS

Another technique to prioritize and solve quality problems is by failure mode and effects analysis. FMEA consists of a set of guidelines, a process, and a form to identify and prioritize potential problems (i.e., failures). By basing their activities on FMEA, a manager, improvement team, or process advisor can focus prevention, monitoring, and response efforts where they're most likely to pay off. See Figure 7.20 for an example of an FMEA sheet.

How FMEA Works

1. Identify the process.
2. List all potential problems that could occur at each step in the process (These are known as "failure modes"). Ask, "What could go wrong?" and "What has gone wrong in the past?" The problems can come from operators who work in the process, equipment documentation, past experience with the process, etc. Avoid trivial problems.
3. Rate the problem for severity, probability of occurrence, and detectability. Using a one-to-ten scale, score each potential problem with each factor. More serious problems get a higher rating; harder-to-detect problems get a higher score. These might be judgments or based on historical or test data.
4. Multiply the severity, occurrence, and detectability scores together to calculate the risk priority number, or RPN. Now rank the problems from highest to lowest RPN and prioritize actions for the highest RPN numbers.

Developing Actions to Reduce Risk

By focusing first on potential problems having the highest RPN, you can devise actions to reduce one or all the factors: seriousness, occurrence, and detectability. Generally, the seriousness category is hard to affect. However, occurrence and detectability are ripe places for improvement actions.

In Figure 7.20, a supplier that manufactures sunroofs for automobiles has performed an FMEA analysis on two steps in its assembly process. Under the first column, item part and/or function, step ten—building a glass assembly at a seal station—is listed. The next column, potential failure mode, indicates what negative thing can happen at this step. In the case of the glass assembly, the glass frame

Figure 7.20	FMEA Sheet

Failure Mode and Effects Analysis

System: Sun Roof					Design responsibility: L. Coleman		
Subsystem component model: Glass assembly SR71							
FMEA No.: 2					Page: 1		

Item part and/ or function	Potential failure mode	Potential effect(s) of failure	Severity	Class	Potential cause(s) and/or mechanisms of failure	Occurrence	
Enter a system function using verb and/or noun format	Failure mode equals loss of function or negative of function	Consequences on other systems, parts, or people			From block diagram, determine if and/or how each element can cause system failure		
Step 10. Build glass assembly at seal station	Glass frame pulls away from the glass	Seal falls off and potential water leak	6		Glass frame sweep is incorrect	8	
Step 17. Press and apply trace label	Trace label is missing	Unidentified part in storage rack	5		Assembly error	2	

Severity of effect:	Occurrence rating:	Detection:
1. None	1. Almost never	1. Almost certain
2. Very slight	2. Remote	2. Very high
3. Slight	3. Very slight	3. High
4. Minor	4. Slight	4. Moderately high
5. Moderate	5. Low	5. Medium
6. Significant	6. Medium	6. Low
7. Major	7. Moderately high	7. Slight
8. Extreme	8. High	8. Very slight
9. Serious	9. Very high	9. Remote
10. Hazardous	10. Almost certain	10. Almost impossible

FMEA No.: 2		
		Key date:
Prepared by: Swartz, R.		**FMEA date:** 1/7/2005

Current design controls	Detection	RPN	Recommended actions	Responsibility and target completion date	Actions taken	Severity	Occurrence	Detection	RPN
Method, test, or technique used to detect cause of failure		0	Design actions to reduce severity, occurrence, and detection ratings	System design department and date	Actions and actual completion date				0
Supplier testing of each lot plus in-house visual inspection	4	192	100-percent inspection, clamp frame to glass as needed	Operator 12/3/04	Added to work instructions and operators trained	6	2	1	12
In-process inspection	4	40	No action currently required	V. Louis 12/3/04					0

RPN = Risk priority number

pulls away from the glass. If this happens, the consequences are listed in the third column. In this case, the seal falls off and there's a potential water leak.

The fourth column indicates how severe the failure is. It's rated a six, or significant. The next column, class, is a special category for the customer to flag any problems with a severity rating of nine or ten.

The sixth column, potential cause of failure, indicates that the glass frame pulls away when the glass frame sweep is incorrect. The seventh column, occurrence, records how often this failure occurs. In the case, it receives an eight, or "high." The occurrence can also be calculated statistically. The eighth column, current design controls, indicates what's being done to control this problem. In this case, the supplier is testing each lot as well as conducting an in-house visual inspection. Obviously, this control isn't working very well.

The tenth column, RPN or risk priority number, is calculated by multiplying severity, occurrence, and detection. Thus, six times eight times four equals 192. In the automotive industry, RPNs of sixty or higher must be addressed.

The eleventh column, recommended actions, addresses what will be done to affect occurrence and detectability. In this example, the recommended action is to perform 100-percent inspection and clamp the frame as needed. Although this might prove an adequate short-term solution, it doesn't get to the root cause of the problem. The root cause probably lies in the frame itself, and this problem should ultimately be tracked back to the source. The twelfth column, responsibility and target completion date, indicates who will do this action and when. In this case, the operator is responsible, and the completion date is December 3, 2004.

The thirteenth column, actions taken, indicates what was done to fulfill the recommended actions, and in this case the new action was added to work instructions, and the operators were trained.

The last three columns are for recalculating the new RPN number based on the result of the recommended actions. In this example, the severity remained the same at six, but occurrence and detectability dropped to two and one, respectively. The new RPN number of twelve meets the requirement of being less than sixty.

FISHBONE DIAGRAMS

When there are multiple causes for a problem an effective tool to use is the fishbone diagram (also known as a cause-and-effect diagram). This graphically displays the potential causes of a problem. It's also used when there's a lack of clarity about the different relationships between potential causes. The fishbone provides a structure and framework when a team is looking for possible causes of a problem.

This technique helps people think about potential causes of a problem. After completing a fishbone diagram, a team can begin to see relationships between potential causes. It's also used to track which potential causes have been investigated. In addition, it helps team members communicate possible causes of a problem to the rest of the organization.

The problem gets listed on the spine of the fishbone. Next, identify possible causes of a problem. Sort these into reasonable clusters. Give each cluster a name and place it as one of the ribs on the fishbone. Develop other main ribs around each cluster of potential causes. Finally, select possible causes that will be later verified with data.

Consider the example in Figure 7.21. A CPA is frustrated that clients consistently don't bring in all the information needed to do a tax return. This problem leads to extensions, the possibility of fines, and an uneven workload as the April 15 tax deadline looms.

The problem, "What's causing the missing information?" is placed on the spine of the fishbone. The potential causes of the problem are placed on the ribs in their appropriate clusters.

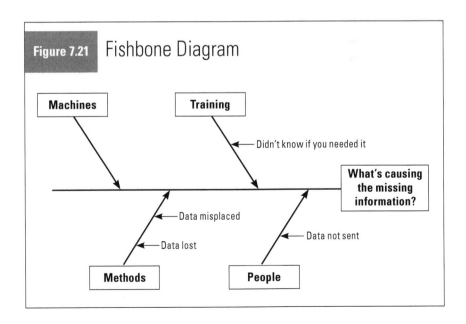

Figure 7.21 Fishbone Diagram

CHECK SHEETS

What the previous example lacks is data. You don't know the frequency of each cause. Which of the causes happens most often? To answer that question, data must be gathered. One technique for doing this is by means of a check sheet.

Check sheets are forms for gathering data that relate to uncovering both the frequency of problems and their root causes. Use check sheets to record types of defects, causes of defects, capture readings, or measure items along a continuum or scale.

Check sheets are created to capture data by incident and over time. Someone should be responsible for collecting the data. A check sheet comes with a prewritten list of common incidents. Operators simply make a tally mark next to the item on the list. Then they meet to discuss and agree on what items to list, and revise the list as things change.

The important points to remember about a check sheet are:

■ Keep it simple.
■ Label it well.
■ Include a space for data, time, and the collector's name.
■ Include key factors to stratify the data.

The CPA has potential causes to the missing information problem, but has no data. He creates a check sheet to gather the frequency of causes. During his initial meeting with the client, if there's missing information, it gets recorded in the appropriate category on the check sheet.

Consider the check sheet example in Table 7.3.

Table 7.3 Missing Information Check Sheet

	Client A	Client B	Client C	Client D	Client E	Totals
Data lost	2	1	3	1	2	9
Data misplaced	0	1	2	1	3	7
Didn't know it was needed	0	1	1	2	1	5
Data not sent	0	0	1	1	1	3
Totals	2	3	7	5	7	24

PARETO DIAGRAMS

Now that the data have been gathered in a check sheet, they must be arrayed from highest to lowest in terms of frequency. The tool for that is a Pareto diagram, which is shown in Figure 7.22.

A Pareto diagram helps a team understand the pattern of occurrence for a problem. The team can then judge the relative effect that various parts play on a problem situation. Then the team can work on the biggest contributors to any specific problem.

A Pareto diagram is used when the problem can be broken down into categories. It's helpful to locate the vital few categories to focus the team's effort.

A Pareto diagram is constructed by gathering the necessary information about the problem. List the problem categories, sorted by frequency in descending order, on the horizontal line. List the frequencies on the vertical line. Then draw the cumulative percentage line showing the portion of the total that each problem category represents.

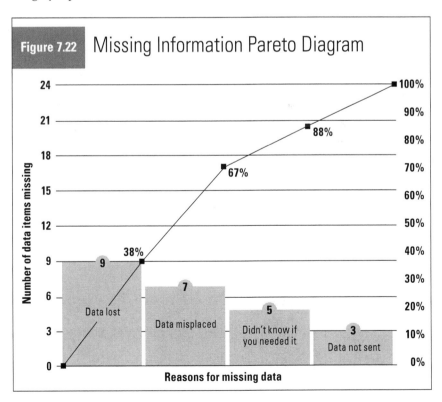

Figure 7.22 Missing Information Pareto Diagram

Data from the check sheet are placed in a Pareto chart. Obviously, you'd want to solve the "data lost" category first because it has the highest frequency of occurrence. It might require another fishbone diagram with the problem, "What causes the lost data?" on the spine, and then the probable causes on the ribs. This might lead to another data-gathering exercise, perhaps using a check sheet again.

A key element in quality analysis is seeking the root cause of a problem. The exercise is like peeling an onion. Each layer reveals new information, until you reach the core or root cause.

ERROR-PROOFING

When you've found a root cause of a problem, you want to ensure it doesn't happen again. An effective technique to address this concern is called "error-proofing," the English equivalent of the original Japanese term for the process, *poka yoke*. Error-proofing takes a disciplined approach to design procedures so that it's difficult to create an error in the first place.

How to Error-Proof

- Identify possible errors that might occur despite preventive actions. Review each step in an existing process while asking the question, "What possible human error or equipment malfunction could take place at this step?"
- Determine a way to detect that an error or malfunction is taking place or about to occur. An electric circuit in your car, for example, can tell if you've fastened your seat belt. E-commerce software is programmed to tell if data are missing from a field. In an assembly plant, trays holding parts help workers see if an item is missing.
- Identify and select the type of action to be taken when an error is detected.

Common Error-Proofing Techniques

Coming up with methods to detect, self-correct, block, shut down, or warn of a problem require real imagination and creativity. Some common error-proofing measures include:

- Color and shape-coding materials and documents

- Distinctively shaping key items such as legal documents
- Using symbols and icons to identify easily confused items
- Creating computerized checklists, clear forms, best-in-class, up-to-date procedures, and simple workflows to prevent errors from becoming defects in the hands of customers.

GETTING TO THE ROOT CAUSE VIA FIVE WHYS

After you've identified a problem, you must find the root cause of it. A simple and effective way to do this is to ask, "Why?" repeatedly. Too often, a problem's symptom is addressed rather than its root cause. When you settle too soon on a solution, the problem is likely to occur again. That's why you must delve for each underlying problem until you arrive at the true root cause.

For example, you might find that an employee named Joe is frustrated in his work. Ask:

- Why? He's feeling overwhelmed.
- Why? He's behind in his orders.
- Why? He's not been trained on the new equipment.
- Why? The supervisor wasn't aware that Joe needed training.
- Why? Joe hadn't been checked out on the new equipment.

Solution: Make sure all new employees get checked out on new equipment.

According to Jeffery Liker, author of *The Toyota Way* (McGraw-Hill, 2003), both Pareto diagrams and Five Whys are the most frequently used quality tools at Toyota. With the reputation for quality that the company has, it's hard to argue with results.

Chapter 8

Customer Report Card, Benchmarking, and Best Practices

S teps four and five in the process redesign methodology a.e covered in this chapter and highlighted in Figure 8.1.

STEP 4: CUSTOMER REPORT CARD

The purpose of every process is to create value for the customer(s). It's critical to know how well the process works in terms of creating and delivering value. To find out what customers want, you must ask. Team members should talk directly with customers rather than conduct a survey because:

- Surveys don't provide enough information.
- Surveys don't allow for follow-up questions.
- Team members should hear directly from customers to get a true understanding of what they feel and want.
- Interviews provide an opportunity for unexpected insights.

Customer Criteria

To create a customer report card, ask your external customers what they need, want, and require from the process. Pick a representative sample of customers that will give a thorough and balanced view of customer satisfaction. Stratification criteria might include size of business, perceived happiness (i.e., high to low), geographic location, or any other natural way to group your customer population.

Next, from the list of needs, wants, and desires, ask customers to rank their criteria in order. Once they've done that, ask them to grade how well the process

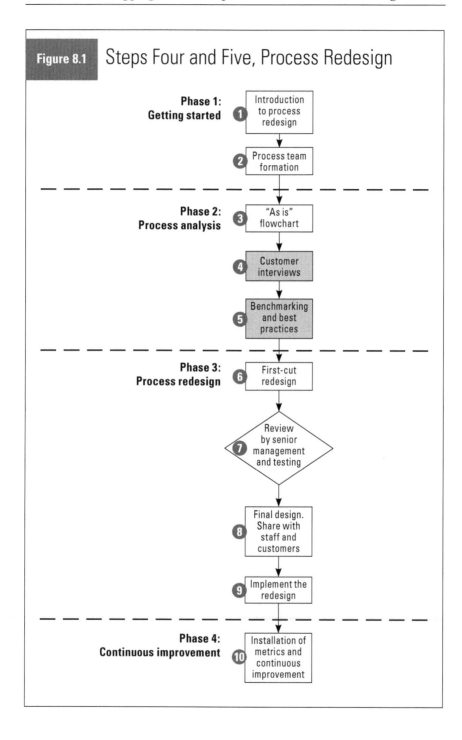

Figure 8.1   Steps Four and Five, Process Redesign

Phase 1:
Getting started
1. Introduction to process redesign
2. Process team formation

Phase 2:
Process analysis
3. "As is" flowchart
4. Customer interviews
5. Benchmarking and best practices

Phase 3:
Process redesign
6. First-cut redesign
7. Review by senior management and testing
8. Final design. Share with staff and customers
9. Implement the redesign

Phase 4:
Continuous improvement
10. Installation of metrics and continuous improvement

performs in meeting each of the criteria. Use letter grades ranging from A (excellent) to F (failing). When you stratify your customer groups, look for differences in customer satisfaction criteria and rankings. Does one group have different criteria? Are some factors more important for one customer group versus another?

An interesting pretest is to ask management to guess customers' criteria and ranking. Often the list management creates differs significantly from the actual customer list. If that's the case, it means management is making decisions based on guesses, which probably have negative consequences. For example, managers in an organization that trains chefs were asked what they thought students wanted. Number seven on the management list was an alumni association. However, that item wasn't anywhere on the students' list. To the managers' surprise, students ranked clean kitchens in the number-four slot of their list. So funds for the alumni association were diverted into maintenance and housekeeping. As a result, the organization created more value and satisfaction for the chefs-in-training. The managers wouldn't have found this out if they hadn't created the customer report card.

Ranking the Criteria

After creating the ranked list of criteria, ask the customer to define what an A grade is for each item. Encourage them to supply specific, measurable requirements. You should end up with a document that looks something like Table 8.1.

Based on the information obtained from the customer report card, you can focus your improvement efforts on high-ranking items with less than A performances. This will ensure that changes will be made to areas with the highest impact. What changes must be made in the processes to move them toward an A grade?

You can expand the customer report card to include competitors. How does your organization stack up against competitors on key customer criteria? Table 8.2 illustrates the concept.

Table 8.1 Customer Report Card		
Ranked criteria	**Process performance**	**What an "A" looks like**
1.		
2.		
3.		
4.		

For example, suppose your company provides tax services to individuals and organizations. You've lost some business to local competitors, and you want to regain market share. Consequently, you interview current and lost customers and obtain the information presented in Table 8.3.

Now compare this information to your competitors as shown in Table 8.4.

The two items that have the biggest potential for increasing market share are offering tax-saving strategies and a speedy turnaround of the reports. The strategies could be folded into the initial client visit, where time is actually added into the process. In addition, printed material on common tax-reducing actions could be mailed or given to customers.

To increase the speed at which reports are done, you'd want to find out where time gets wasted, elements of rework and errors, unnecessary movement, setup time, etc. Using a functional-activity process map and the time lens, you'd focus on all the non-value added time to eliminate or reduce those and speed up the process. Currently, quality is the overriding focus at your organization. The revised

Table 8.2   Competitor Template

Ranked criteria	Our company	Competitor 1	Competitor 2	Competitor 3
1.				
2.				
3.				
4.				

Table 8.3   Process Performance Report Card

Ranked criteria	Process performance	What an "A" looks like
1. Accuracy or tax documents	A	No audits; everything meets tax law
2. Offering tax-saving strategies	B-	Giving complete and comprehensive strategies and action plans to reduce current and future taxes
3. Speed of doing reports	C	Turn the tax document in one week or less
4. Cost of service	B	Lowest price

Table 8.4	Competitor Report Card			
Ranked criteria	**Our company**	**Competitor 1**	**Competitor 2**	**Competitor 3**
1. Accuracy of tax document	A	B	A	B
2. Offering tax-saving strategies	B-	C	B+	C-
3. Speed in doing the reports	C	B-	B-	B+
4. Cost of the service	B+	B+	B	A

goal should be to achieve a turnaround in a week or less, an A scenario as defined by the customer but one that also maintains the current level of quality.

In addition to asking customers what they need, want, expect, and desire from a process, you could come up with additional questions from your as-is process analysis. Questions often crop up when you start examining the process that wouldn't have occurred to you prior to performing a process analysis. It's for this reason you should postpone customer interviewing until you've have completed an as-is flowchart.

STEP 5: BENCHMARKING AND BEST PRACTICES

Benchmarking involves making comparisons between your organization and others that are similar. The process is typically done between competitors or comparable organizations within one industry.

A benchmarking and best-practices study should be performed in three sections: with your direct competitors, with organizations in your industry but that aren't competitors, and with world-class organizations regardless of industry. Divide your team into thirds, and assign one of the sections to each group.

The following information sources for direct competitors and organizations in your industry will be helpful for gathering benchmarking information.

Researching Industry Competitors

Industry trade associations. Trade associations are an excellent source of information. These groups perform benchmarking studies regularly, and by subscribing to the association, you can receive the results. Also, outside parties can purchase studies for a nominal fee.

Accounting firms that specialize in your industry. It's not uncommon for accounting firms to specialize by industry. See if there's one that specializes in your industry. What industry information does the firm provide? What contacts does it have for benchmarking data?

Robert Morris annual statement studies. Robert Morris Associates gathers financial data from bank lending officers. These data are arrayed by SIC code and sales volume and then broken into quartiles. This is an excellent source of income statement and financial ratio comparisons.

Valueline. This investment service provides analyses of public companies and industries.

Standard and Poor's industry studies. This investment research company is similar to Valueline and offers comparable services.

Consultants specializing in benchmarking in your industry. Some consultants are benchmarking experts. Hire those who know your industry.

Distributors. Because distributors handle competitors' products, ask them for information.

Former employees. Former employees of competitors can be good sources of information.

Information from competitors themselves. If they're public companies, order annual reports, 10Ks, press packages, and any financial reports. For private companies, get a Dun & Bradstreet report. Other standard pieces of information include company catalogs, sales promotion sheets, advertisements, newsletters, and Web sites.

Published documents. Industry surveys by market research and stockbrokerage firms might be available. Industry magazines and associations frequently feature companies and their strategies. A subscription to the hometown or regional newspaper and a visit to the library can yield in-depth articles about firms that wouldn't show up in the trade press. A database search can also turn up articles.

Indirect information sources from competitors. These include speeches by their executives at association meetings, Rotary clubs, and other nonindustry organizations. Articles in professional magazines by engineers, marketing managers, and other middle-level management can be quite revealing. Always gather as much information as possible at trade shows.

Government sources. Zoning, universal commercial code, environmental, and tax-assessment offices all have extensive information on local plants, sometimes including blueprints and lists of machinery. Federal patent filings can help you discern these companies' technological direction. Aerial photographs of plants might be available from highway administrations or public works departments.

If you must report any information to government agencies, so must your competitors. Through the Freedom of Information Act, you can request information from governmental offices.

Customers. Superb sources, they can be asked to rate competitors against your company on key costs, prices, buying factors, reputation, positioning, and other strategic points. Depending on what you're after, it's sometimes better not to reveal your company so as not to bias them. (A consultant can be of great help here.)

Suppliers. They're an excellent source of information on raw-material trends, volumes, and costs as well as emerging technologies, a company's financial strength (from any receivables problems suppliers have), company reputations, and other items.

Competitors. Calling executives and managers of your competitors can often be an excellent way to get information. But this is best left to consultants.

Reverse-engineering products. Xerox and many other companies disassemble a rival's product and then reverse-engineer it. General Motors has a 90,000 square-foot shop devoted to tearing down and analyzing competitors' automobiles.

Benchmarking Questions

You can create benchmarking questions based on the ones and twos from your frustration and idea bin (as described in Chapter 7), from team brainstorming and from the as-is flowchart. Usually the list is quite long. By multi-voting, team members attach points to questions, the points are added up, and the list is reordered from highest point total to least. The interviewer can use this list to focus on the most important questions, which is particularly helpful during short interviews. Here's an example of what you might say:

"Hello, my name is _____. I'm part of a team at _____. We're doing an analysis of the _____ process, and we understand your organization is doing some interesting things in that area. Are you the person I should speak with regarding this topic? If not, whom should I talk to? Is this a good time to talk? If not, when is a better time? I have a list of questions that should take _____ minutes to answer. If you're interested, we'll share our findings with participating organizations. Would you like a summary of our findings?

"Are you ready to answer some questions? The first is _____. The next question is _____. Is it OK to call you back if we need to clarify some things? Thank you for you time."

It's a good idea to take turns practicing the script and responding to it so interviewers are comfortable. For many team members interviewing other people for benchmarking or best practices is a new experience. Practice allows them to talk without being nervous.

Occasionally you'll find naysayers in your organization who resist new ideas. If you know of anyone with a negative attitude, have him or her listen to, or participate in, a benchmarking interview from an innovative company. This way the naysayer gets information directly from an organization where the "new" way is working. In addition, the naysayer can ask questions and address his or her concerns. This technique has been quite successful in helping to change attitudes and beliefs.

Best Practices

With best practices, you're looking for the best process. Ask, "Who has a process like ours, regardless of industry, which is considered world-class?" Take the following best-practice interview as an example. An opera company was interested in improving its subscription process. What process, it wondered, is similar to taking a subscription for opera tickets? It's basically an order-taking process, the company realized. What organization is considered the best order taker? Lands' End Direct Merchants has that reputation. Accordingly, the opera company contacted Lands' End to learn some of its process techniques. From interviews with this organization, three techniques were discovered that were incorporated into the subscription process redesign.

Finding best practices takes some creativity. Regarding the process you're analyzing, ask, "What process is similar to this?" You can also ask, "What industries are similar to our own?" You want to break out of the "group think" where people in the same industry tend to think alike and use the same techniques or processes. It's through best practices that you're apt to find a radically improved process or technique that's not been used in your industry.

Another advantage to best practice research is that organizations with "best" reputations are usually quite proud of their accomplishments. Because you don't compete with them, they usually provide information freely.

Try exploring organizations that do best practice and benchmarking research such as Best Practices LLC, APQC, BPIR.com, Benchnet.com, and The Benchmarking Network. In addition, the Malcolm Baldrige National Quality Award winners speak freely about their processes with the public and are excellent sources of best-practice ideas.

Chapter 9

Process Redesign
Case Study

An actual project makes it easier to understand how process design principles are chosen and applied. This case highlights a number of design principles that led to a successful business process redesign (BPR). As you read it, note how many of the problems mentioned also occur in your organization. Following the case study, Chapter 10 describes the thirty-eight design principles in detail.

PREPARING FOR BPR

In 1994, the city of San Jose, California, embarked on a series of reengineering projects. To ensure successful results, the city's employees were trained in basic quality management techniques and learned about the importance of customer service. Focus groups also were conducted to understand the city's various customers and stakeholders. From these and other sessions, staff gained a greater appreciation for customer service and developed an awareness for the *need* to change. Although these improvement efforts were positive, a desire existed for more fundamental change. Business process reengineering was considered the best approach for obtaining dramatic improvement.

TARGETING THE "PUBLIC" IN PUBLIC WORKS

The city conducted a business climate study to learn how well it met public expectations. One area that demonstrated a clear need for improvement was the Department of Public Works' development review process. Ralph Qualls, the department's director, was willing to give reengineering a try, although he didn't believe the promised improvements would be realized. Thirty years of public works experience told him change typically comes very slowly, if at all: "It's always a chore to get anything done quickly because there are so many bases to tag, so many layers to work through, and so many requirements that you have to satisfy before you can get anything done," he said. "Part of that is just the nature of doing business in the public sector."

Still, Qualls wanted to be supportive, so the first reengineering phase was launched. More than twenty public works processes were identified by senior department staff and included such areas as:

■ Environmental review
■ Counter service delivery
■ Traffic signal design
■ Fee collection and records management
■ Private street design
■ Floodplain management
■ Electrical design review
■ Transportation plan modeling
■ Grading permit issuance

The staff decided to target the process for issuing grading permits as its first reengineering project. It was selected because it was ripe for change: doable, a self-contained process (i.e., not constrained by other work processes), would show dramatic improvement, and would send a positive signal about reengineering's potential. Additionally, the grading staff already knew that the process needed major reconstruction.

Public works staff contracted with two outside consultants to work with a core group. The consultants led the redesign team through an eight-step methodology:

1. Flow chart the "as is" process
2. Interview customers
3. Interview staff
4. Share customer and staff interview data with core and technical teams
5. Make a first-cut at redesign
6. Share the redesign results with customers and an advisory group
7. Revise the redesign
8. Implement the new process

The staff also set a "challenge" goal of reducing cycle time for each process by 50 percent. Five interactive groups were established whose input and assistance would be critical to the reengineering effort: customers, advisory groups, core teams, support groups, and technical teams.

REENGINEERING GRADING PERMITS

Grading permits are given by the city to private individuals and contractors for certain grading work that, because of soil conditions or hazards, needs some oversight. For example, grading for a swimming pool or driveway would require a permit. Using the redesign methodology, the team created a new grading permit process.

First, the as-is process was flowcharted. This step revealed that it took the department twenty-one working days to issue a grading permit. It also showed the problems with the existing process. As many as fifteen different specialists handled different parts of the application; two different divisions were involved, creating turf problems; customers were continually handed off to new staff; bottlenecks occurred at several points; and highly skilled personnel devoted large amounts of time to administrative tasks rather than the professional jobs they were hired to do.

Team members interviewed grading permit customers over the phone and asked each of them five questions:

■ What do you want from this process?
■ What do you like about the current process?
■ What don't you like about it?
■ Who does it better?
■ What letter grade do you give to the grading permit process?

Employees also were interviewed and asked the same set of questions. Both sets of responses were shared with the core and technical teams. Interview results demonstrated that customers and staff wanted a process that was quick, fair, and thorough; involved only one stop; had clear standards and guidelines; and gave clear direction from the outset. Interestingly, customers rated the process higher than the staff, giving it a B, while staff rated it only a C.

Actual redesign work began. The staff developed a form of "triage" (or quick assessment) that sorted different types of applications into separate categories for review. In the past, the department used a one-size-fits-all approach that forced applicants with simple needs to go through the same time-consuming process as people with complex situations. Staff identified a process for three types of applications:

- Exempt: applicants not needing a permit because of an exemption
- Express: applicants doing small grading projects
- Regular: applicants doing larger projects, usually requiring input from experts, e.g., a hazardous material person or geologist

The core team also recommended that the department create a project manager position. To expedite one-stop service, the city needed a generalist who could handle all aspects of exemption and express permits. These relatively simple processes could be handled by someone with broad skills and wide decision-making authority who enjoyed exercising responsibility and acting with autonomy.

The initial redesign was drafted and shared with customers. An advisory group made relatively few revisions because the new design met the customer and staff needs identified in step four. One permit processor who had difficulty letting go of the current processes resisted the change. It took substantial support from the division head before this person was willing to give it a chance.

Implementation was accomplished quite easily. To enable the lean new process, a customer-service room was created to provide the project manager and permit applicant a place to sit down and complete the process without interruptions. Permit forms were also redesigned to make them more user-friendly.

MAKING THE GRADE

The new process far surpassed the initial goal of a 50-percent reduction in cycle time. The original cycle time for reviewing a grading permit was twenty-one days, irrespective of the type of grading project. The redesign reduced processing times to fifteen minutes for exempt permits, one to two hours (a 99.6-percent reduction) for express permits, and five days (a 76-percent reduction) for regular permits.

Now new permit reviews are handled by one of five project managers (more will be trained over time). Project managers determine whether a permit is needed and can issue on-the-spot exemptions. They also decide which applications are express and which regular. Only project managers handle express applications.

For regular process applications, the project manager and his team review them within five days.

As well as the enormous reduction in cycle time, the user-friendly forms reduced errors further and decreased staff time and customer waiting time. Consequently, staff members report they're far more satisfied with their work. One project manager notes his job is much easier with his increased authority and a reduction in bureaucratic delays. Furthermore, the new process has freed up considerable staff time for more demanding work. This adds to capacity and places employees' skills where they can add value.

It's worth noting that the process of redesigning the grading-permit process was extremely short and relatively simple. Unlike most reengineering projects, which typically take three to six months for the design phase and several months to a year or two for designing, and implementing, the new grading permit redesign took only six weeks.

Once the design team mapped out the "as is" process and realized how much waste and redundancy was involved, it came up with the triage and project manager concepts in just a few hours. The team's proposed new design was approved in one day. However, it will take months and a great deal of training to bring the new design to its full potential. The department is investing heavily in team building and other technical training to increase the number of project managers while ensuring that communication with technical experts during the regular process goes smoothly.

Unplanned benefits were also a perk of this process redesign. The extra time created by the department's streamlined processes will enable the city to offer new services. Initially, when the reengineering efforts started, top management didn't consider this possibility. The Department of Public Works not only will have more efficient and higher-quality services, but it will also be able to offer profitable new services with current resources. This is the power of BPR.

CRITICAL SUCCESS FACTORS

Eight factors contributed to the successful redesign of San Jose's grading-permit department:

- *Reviewing BPR goals*—Staff awareness was created for customer needs and the current gap between these needs. The city's performance was assessed against these criteria.

■ *Elimination of layoffs*—San Jose's Department of Public Works was downsizing at the same time, which presented a challenge to a successful redesign. However, senior management made it clear that the actual BPR project wouldn't cost anyone a job. Some staff members would have different jobs, but nobody would be laid off.

■ *Effective flowcharting*—Mapping out the current process proved very powerful. Once the flowchart was on the wall, the problem was clear. Too many steps were built into the grading permit process. Given such visual proof, nobody argued that there shouldn't be a change.

■ *Project champions*—The project had two champions: the director of the permit development department and a middle manager in the same division, who led the core team. Both kept the project moving quickly.

■ *Active participation*—Key people in the affected divisions were actively involved in the redesign effort. Their participation made them believers in the redesign and kept them on board throughout.

■ *Speed*—Staff and customers saw immediate results with the redesign, which proved both a surprise and a tremendous motivation to continue reengineering.

■ *Successful reengineering teams*—Employees were persuaded to give up their free time and serve on the redesign teams.

■ *Investment*—Initial financial investment, primarily for consultant services and new technology, was essential. To save the city money in the future, money needed to be spent up front.

The as-is grading permit process is illustrated in Figure 9.1.

USING THE FRUSTRATION LENS ON THE AS-IS FLOWCHART TO REVEAL DESIGN PRINCIPLES

The redesign team was composed primarily of staff members who worked in the process. This included the administrative person, inspector, geologist, planning person, and so forth. People who carry out a process often have the best ideas for fixing it. In addition, because these people would be using the new process, it was important that they be enthusiastic supporters. Thus, those who work in a process undergoing redesign should be actively involved in analyzing, designing, and implementing improvements (design principle No. 33).

DESIGNING AROUND VALUE-ADDING ACTIVITIES

The purpose of every process is to satisfy customers of the process. Customers of the grading permit process wanted their permit applications reviewed quickly. When asked what "excellence" meant in terms of a speedy turnaround for a permit, they said, "Two weeks." From the customer's perspective, the value-adding activities were the quick review and issuing of the permit. The team had to design a process that efficiently and effectively met those requirements (design principle No. 1). Logging permits in and out of the system wasn't something customers cared about; thus, it was a nonvalue-adding activity.

QUALITY UP FRONT AND TRIAGING

At the second step of the permit process, when the administrative person was asked what frustrated her, she said, "The applications have missing, incorrect, and incomplete information." Whenever a quality issue crops up in response to the frustration question, the next step is to quantify the problem's frequency. The logical follow-up question in this case was, "Out of 100 permits, how many have missing, incomplete, or incorrect information?" The administrative person replied, "All of them."

When the first several steps in a process have quality issues, you can be sure this will create havoc downstream. The design principle for that problem is to ensure 100-percent quality at the beginning of the process (design principle No. 5). This was accomplished by putting a review at the start of the process. Only complete applications were allowed to move past this review.

The team members identified three natural clusters of permit types. One cluster was applications for inconsequential projects (for example, patching a sidewalk), which were didn't need a permit. The next cluster was small grading projects, such as building a swimming pool or driveway, which didn't need to be reviewed by a geologist, hazardous materials expert, civil engineer, and so forth. The final cluster was large grading projects such as a subdivision or high-rise that required all of the experts to review. The relevant design principle is if inputs coming into the process naturally cluster, then design a specific process for each cluster (design principle No. 4).

For clusters, such as a high-rise or subdivision, where each is unique, you must deal with complexity issues. For these categories, think team, and co-locate it if

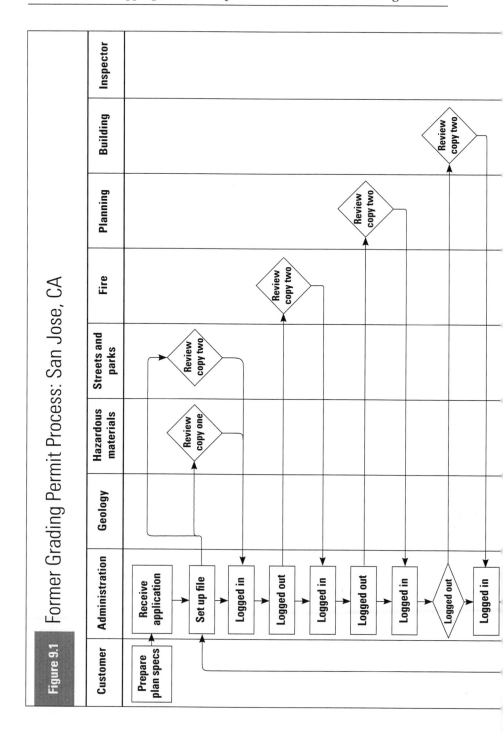

Figure 9.1   Former Grading Permit Process: San Jose, CA

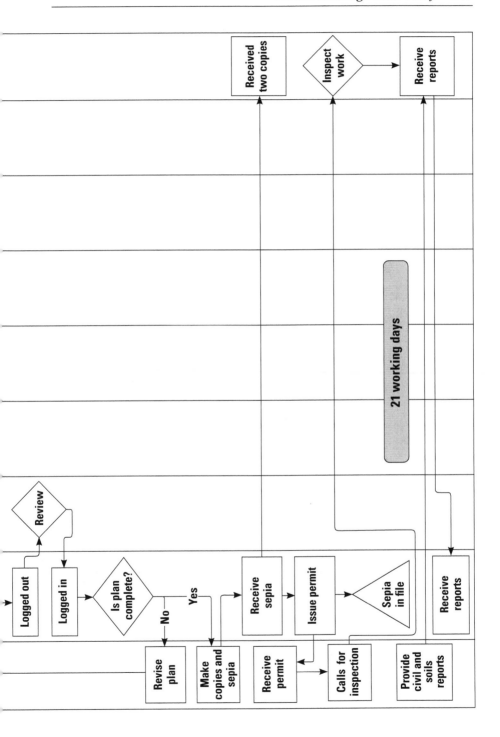

possible (design principle No. 31). Five teams were created, each led by a project manager. Team members had their offices next to one another, When a complex application was received, all team members would examine it simultaneously at a conference table. No more logging in and out.

SINGLE POINT OF CONTACT AND EMPOWERMENT

One of the frustrations customers of the process expressed was being transferred from person to person. No one could give them clear guidance on when the permit review would be completed. What the customer wanted was a single point of contact (design principle No. 3). In the redesign, the project manager became the single point of contact.

In the old system, the director of public works signed off on the permits. Did it make sense for this person to sign off on something about which he knew very little? The team thought not. Decision making (i.e., sign off) should be pushed down to the lowest levels that make sense (design principles eleven and twelve). Hence, the project manager was given sign-off authority.

Returning to design principle No. 5, to ensure 100-percent quality at the beginning of the process, the team decided that someone should review the permits as soon as they were received. If permits were complete, they could be passed along. Deciding who should do the review initially proved difficult because the administrative person wasn't knowledgeable enough. Also, each of the other experts could do an adequate review in his or her area of expertise but not outside it. The team decided a generalist engineer would be the best candidate for the job. There are occasions where it makes sense to create generalists, and this was one of them (design principle No. 37).

Cross-Training

Senior management wanted every team that dealt with the complex permits to be self-sufficient. That required a good deal of cross-training. The department employed only one geologist, and this person needed to clone herself to accommodate each of the four teams. Where it makes sense, cross-train and create multiskilled employees (design principle No. 36).

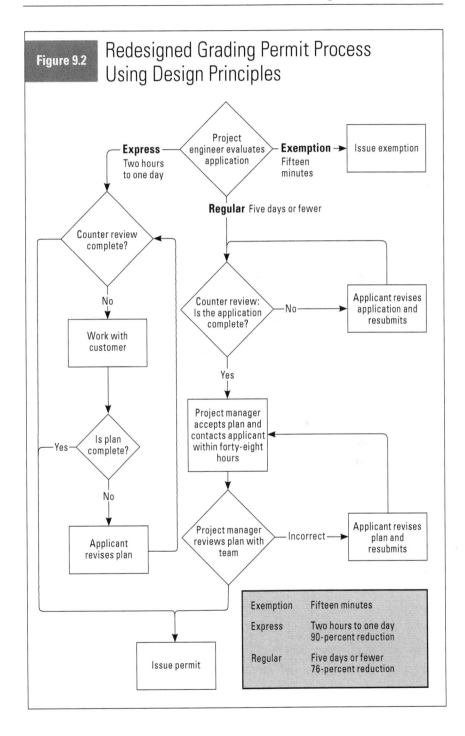

Figure 9.2 Redesigned Grading Permit Process Using Design Principles

SUCCESSFUL COMPLETION

When all of the design principles were put together, the new grading permit process looked like the one depicted in Figure 9.2.

Customers were looking for a two-week turnaround time for the permit process. With permits now making it through the process in three to five days, customers were astounded. In fact, they were delighted. Letters arrived to the city praising the new responsiveness. How do you create customer delight? By surpassing customer expectations. As you can see, the design principles' power is impressive.

Chapter 10

Design Principles for Process Redesign

D esign principles are distilled best practices gleaned from world-class organizations. The thirty-eight principles described here represent the major concepts involved in most process redesign projects.

When you look at a process through each of the four lenses described in Chapter 7, you'll find problems. Which of the design principles address those problems? How would you incorporate the relevant principles in a redesigned process?

Not every design principle applies to every process. Think of a menu at a Chinese restaurant and select only those principles that make sense to you for the situation you're analyzing. Never abandon common sense when you apply them. As a general guideline, the following categories of principles should prove helpful:

■ Principles 1–16: use for work structure
■ Principles 17–19: use for information flow
■ Principles 20–30: use for design guides
■ Principles 31–37: use for organizing people
■ Principle 38: use for general guidance

1. DESIGN THE PROCESS AROUND VALUE-ADDING ACTIVITIES

This principle requires you to be clear about what the customer of the process requires. When you transform information or material into what the customer wants, you're creating value-adding activities. Study the as-is process flowchart and determine exactly where these activities are performed. Now pull them out of the as-is process and ask, "How can we do these steps [i.e., the pure, value-adding activities] in the most efficient and effective way possible?"

As you answer the question, try not to discuss who will do any particular activity or where it will be performed. Combining the activity's "what" and "who" at this stage will distract the team from developing a creative, unique process solution. Your efforts to create an elegant process can get bogged down in a debate about who should do what. After you've created a great process flow, you can begin debating about who should do the work.

To create a new process, the "pieces," such as job descriptions, work location, and who should do the work, must be extremely flexible. Team members should be aware that the existing configuration of jobs, work location, and organizational structure are all up for reassessment. There should be no constraint on their thinking; everything should be regarded as a "clean sheet." This freedom from existing patterns allows people to think outside the box and create a dramatically improved process.

Some redesign methods look for the nonvalue-adding activities and then eliminate or reduce them. The problem with this approach is that it can create acrimonious relationships with people who do such work. When you tell them their work adds no value to the process, they'll defend their positions, often becoming angry and defensive. You can circumvent this situation if you look for value-adding activities instead and optimize them. You can't argue with the customer about what's value-adding, but by focusing and optimizing on those activities, the nonvalue-adding activities simply fall away, and you can avoid a confrontation that will invariably create resistance to the redesign project.

2. WORK IS PERFORMED WHERE IT MAKES THE MOST SENSE

Once you've designed a great flow, it's time to figure out who should do what. Let your common sense guide you. When you apply design principle No. 1, some existing work will evaporate, new work will be created, and work might move from one department to another.

During the permit-process redesign, the team couldn't decide who should do the initial review. It required the expertise of an engineer with a broad background rather than a specialist. That position didn't exist in the original process structure. To implement the new process, the permit department had to develop a job description for a generalist engineer and then hire someone for this new position. Don't be constrained by current job titles and locations. Create the ideal position(s) to make the process flow with the greatest efficiency and effectiveness.

3. PROVIDE A SINGLE POINT OF CONTACT FOR CUSTOMERS AND SUPPLIERS

A common symptom of having no single point of contact is transferring customer calls from person to person. Another symptom is when staff doesn't know whom to talk to or where to go for information.

A single point of contact can be a person such as a project manager, process consultant or customer service representative. In addition, a single point of contact could be a data repository like an intranet.

4. IF THE INPUTS COMING INTO THE PROCESS NATURALLY CLUSTER, CREATE A SEPARATE PROCESS FOR EACH CLUSTER

Often a single process attempts to handle every variation. It's an example of the one-size-fits-all approach. However, process inputs and outputs can often vary by complexity, type, size, and so forth. For some variations, the process might work smoothly, but for others it might be cumbersome and slow.

For instance, when you shop at a grocery store and have eight items to purchase, you pick the express checkout lane. The store has two checkout processes, one for many items and one for few. The regular checkout line has a bagger, but one isn't needed for the express line.

If your inputs naturally cluster, then a decision diamond should be made at the front end of your process. The question in the diamond is, "What cluster is it?" The input cluster is then routed to the appropriate process.

5. ENSURE A CONTINUOUS FLOW OF THE "MAIN SEQUENCE"

In a manufacturing process, steps that directly add value to the customer, such as delivering supplies, building the product, and shipping it, represent the main sequence. In lean terminology the main sequence is the "value stream." In a service process, the steps that make and deliver the service are the main sequence or value stream. The customer pays for the output of the value stream. It's the means by which your organization gets revenue.

Lean thinking recommends that nothing should impede or slow down the value stream. Design principles six through ten deal with this issue.

6. REDUCE WAITING, MOVING, AND REWORK TIME

By using the process cycle time analysis sheet, you'll find those areas with the greatest amount of waiting, moving, and rework. Use a Pareto diagram and attack the greatest time-wasters first.

7. REDUCE SETUP AND CHANGEOVER TIMES

Setup includes anything you must do before performing the task required for a given step. Setup for manufacturing means configuring equipment so processing can be done. Do this by performing all setup activities off-line, having machine parts and fixtures that automatically fit, pre-work completed ahead of time, etc.

In service organizations setup might require looking for a file or scrolling through a computer screen before a person can actually do the work. Have all the information a person needs for an activity readily available so little time is wasted in setup.

8. REDUCE BATCH SIZES

Batching causes wait time for items at the end of the batch. Batching causes inventory to build as it moves through your process. As you cut batch sizes, you start creating a smoother flow through the process. Ultimately, a batch size of one is the ideal.

9. SUBSTITUTE PARALLEL PROCESSES FOR SEQUENTIAL PROCESSES

A good example of this principle is found in new product development, where concurrent engineering is used rather than sequential. Where steps in a process can be done independently of one another, without having to be in sequence, consider parallel processing.

10. PERFORM PROCESS STEPS IN THEIR NATURAL ORDER

Sometimes the sequence of steps in a process needs reordering. Be sure to question the logic of one step preceding another.

11. REDUCE CHECKS AND REVIEWS

In traditional and involvement organizations, management usually has little trust in workers to get the work done properly, so there's constant checking and reviewing. When an organization moves into a process management of work style, trust should start shifting to the process rather than focusing solely on people. If a process operates at a six sigma quality level (i.e., 3.4 defects per million), the need for review should be minimal or nonexistent. Thus, as a process becomes more robust (i.e., defect-free), the need for review is inversely proportional.

Multiple reviews also encourage poor quality at the initial step. For example, if someone knows his or her work will be reviewed multiple times, the incentive to do quality work for that first pass is low. However, if both the worker and reviewer know there will be only one review, first-pass quality suddenly improves. This might seem counterintuitive, but removing unnecessary reviews actually boosts quality.

12. PUSH DECISION-MAKING DOWN TO THE LOWEST REASONABLE LEVEL

Are managers and executives signing off on things they really don't know much about? If that's the case, push decision-making down to where the work is actually being done. Eliminating unnecessary signoffs can dramatically decrease cycle time.

13. BUILD QUALITY IN TO REDUCE INSPECTION AND REWORK

Identify each step that causes downstream rework and delay, and then brainstorm how to make the step perfect, or at least close to perfection, every time. Use error-proofing techniques to eliminate mistakes in process steps.

14. SIMPLIFY STEPS

What could be done to improve the process so that it can be tremendously easier? What steps, operations, or procedures, could be greatly simplified?

15. ORGANIZE BY PROCESS

Instead of breaking a large, cross-departmental process into departmental pieces, group all employees involved in the process under one manager who has full responsibility to get the work done quickly.

16. CONSIDER HYBRID CENTRALIZED/DECENTRALIZED OPERATIONS

In some organizations it makes sense to maintain sales close to the customer but have a centralized accounting department. This would be an example of hybrid centralized/decentralized operations.

17. BRING DOWNSTREAM INFORMATION NEEDS UPSTREAM

When using the frustration lens, ask people at each step what frustrates them. Imagine you're several steps into a process, and a person responds to the frustration question with, "What frustrates me is that when it gets to me, there's missing, incomplete, and incorrect information." When you hear a reply like that, this design principle should be considered.

There are two ways of implementing this principle. If what's coming through the process is routine and not complex ("We pretty much do the same thing day after day"), then the upstream person should be trained or given a template or check sheet so he or she can capture what the downstream person needs.

However, that solution won't work when what's coming through the process is complex and changes frequently. For complex inputs, the downstream person must be brought upstream during a redesign to get information directly from the source.

18. CAPTURE INFORMATION ONCE AT THE SOURCE AND SHARE IT WIDELY

If a process requires entering the same data more than once, then this design principle is appropriate. Root out data redundancy, re-keying, and reconciliation. Enterprise resource planning (ERP) software is designed to accomplish this principle. However, be sure you know your processes first before installing an ERP system.

19. SHARE ALL RELEVANT INFORMATION

Respect everyone's information needs. Hoarding information leads to mistakes and rework.

20. INVOLVE AS FEW PEOPLE AS POSSIBLE IN PERFORMING A PROCESS

The children's game "Telephone" illustrates the importance of this design principle. In the game, ten kids line up, and the first whispers in the ear of the next child. Each child passes the message along from ear to ear. The last child announces what the message was, and everyone laughs because the relayed version differs substantially from the original.

In a relay race, the baton pass is the most important thing. How often does a slower team beat a faster one because there was a problem with the baton pass? (During the 2004 Olympics, the U.S. men's and women's relay teams suffered from poor baton passes and didn't win the gold medals.)

We can think of the handoff of work or information as the baton pass or message in "Telephone." Every handoff is an opportunity for error. By eliminating baton passes, you eliminate that opportunity.

You can accomplish this by expanding the job scope upstream and downstream so that a person "runs" with the work longer. This requires retraining and often a change in compensation to reward knowledge or pay for new skills.

There are a couple advantages to cross-training. First, work often doesn't arrive at an organization in a nice even flow. Instead there are spikes and bottlenecks in the workload. With more cross-trained workers, bottlenecks can be broken as more workers tackle them.

Second, if a person does more of the work, he or she will take increased pride in the outcome. This person can see his or her major contribution to the whole. This pride increases the desire to produce a quality product or service.

21. REDESIGN THE PROCESS FIRST, THEN AUTOMATE IT

One of the worst things an organization can do is take the as-is flowchart and lay information technology on top of it. This is bad for two reasons. First, information technology can be extremely expensive. There might be much less expensive but equally effective solutions, such as redesigning processes or training. Second, despite the investment, the problem might not be solved. It's crucial to first employ process design principles, benchmarking, best practices, and lean thinking before automating an as-is process. Otherwise, you might end up with a modestly faster but much more expensive and still ineffective process. How often have people been promised improvements through an IT solution only later to find little or no improvements? Make sure you understand your organization's processes. Don't assume that IT will be the solution.

The process improvement team will begin to envision a new process after benchmarking, best practices, and using design principles. Then have a conversation with IT on current and future IT capabilities. In this way, you can marry innovative process ideas with enabling IT tools.

22. ENSURE 100-PERCENT QUALITY AT THE BEGINNING

Quality problems encountered in the first several steps of a process will have exponentially negative effects downstream. The time spent by the downstream people fixing the problems can be excessive. There are certain places in a process where an investment in time and money are warranted, and the beginning is one of them. Time and money spent upfront to ensure quality more than pays for itself in preventing reviews and rework later on.

23. INCREASE FLOW AND SPEED TO IDENTIFY BOTTLENECKS

Japanese manufacturers do this to identify bottlenecks and then eliminate them.

Oil refiners do this to their processes to increase production (they call it "de-bottlenecking"). In role-playing, practice, and simulation you can stress the process to the breaking point. It's better to break it during a test than during actual production.

24. ELIMINATE BOTTLENECKS

As part of lean thinking, each step in a process should operate at "Takt" (or metered) time. You can calculate this by taking the total time available per day in seconds and dividing that by the demand rate per day. Those steps that are much slower than Takt time must be broken into smaller increments or redesigned to achieve Takt time.

25. DESIGN FOR MANUFACTURABILITY AND SERVICEABILITY

This design principle is a variation on bringing downstream information upstream. It's not uncommon for a product design to be difficult to manufacture or service. To eliminate this problem, bring a manufacturing expert or service technician upstream into the design meetings so that the design can be easily manufactured and then serviced.

26. USE DESIGN FOR SIX SIGMA (DFSS)

DFSS is a systematic methodology for achieving world-class quality in product development and manufacturing.

27. INSTALL METRICS AND FEEDBACK TO FIND AND CORRECT PROBLEMS

If you can't measure it, you can't control it. If you can't control it, then you can't improve it.

28. FIND OPPORTUNITIES FOR CONTINUOUS IMPROVEMENT

As quality issues arise, tackle them ASAP. Don't stop after one reduction in cycle time, even if it's a breakthrough. Continue to measure it, learn about it, and improve the process.

29. USE SIMULATION, PRACTICE, OR ROLE-PLAYING TO TEST NEW PROCESS DESIGNS

Opportunities to test new process designs occur infrequently in most organizations. Usually this is because the organization lacks the means to quickly test new designs. Computer simulation technology allows users to try iterations of new processes and see how they work. See Chapter 15 for a more detailed description of computer simulation in process design.

Role-playing and practice are ways to test a design without investing in new technology. Assign roles to people and then run sample products, information, service requests, etc. through the new process. The purpose is to find out what works and what doesn't. Eventually you'll to want to break the new process to find its weak spots. Increase pressure on the process through higher volumes, more complexity, and so forth. It's better to break the process during simulation or practice than when it's put to real use.

30. STANDARDIZE PROCESSES

Sometimes a significant variation in output is caused by five people doing the same process five different ways. This creates three concerns. First, with this kind of variation, it's extremely difficult if not impossible to improve the process. Second, when a problem occurs, how can you tell whether it's a process or training problem? Third, how can there be process control when there's no standardization? It's much easier to find the root cause of a problem when people standardize their work.

31. USE CO-LOCATED OR NETWORKED TEAMS FOR COMPLEX ISSUES

Complex problems require people to pore over information and data in real time. If problems occur regularly, consider co-locating team members. If co-location doesn't make sense, then network the team so information can flow easily.

32. ASSIGN A PROCESS CONSULTANT FOR CROSS-FUNCTIONAL PROCESSES

Most organizations manage large processes by pieces, with each department responsible for its piece. However, when you optimize the pieces, you often suboptimize the whole. Who's managing and monitoring the whole? One person must have oversight over large, cross-functional processes. This will move your organization into a matrix work management style.

33. INVOLVE PROCESS WORKERS IN ANALYZING, DESIGNING, AND IMPLEMENTING IMPROVEMENTS

In traditional and some involvement organizations, supervisors and managers are solely responsible for day-to-day problem solving. This is a mistake. People who work in a process often have the best ideas for fixing it. They see the process every day and have ideas about time reduction and quality improvement. Usually they're an untapped resource and should be part of the process improvement effort.

It should be part of all employees' jobs to look for ways to improve the processes they work in. As workers find and solve process problems, it becomes a natural extension of their work. Also, because they'll be creating the changes in the process, they'll be more apt to implement the change correctly if they were instrumental in analyzing and improving it.

Remember, people support what they help create. And conversely, they fight, resist, and sabotage things that are imposed on them.

34. FORM WORK CELLS FOR SPECIAL CASES OR EXCEPTIONS

Work cells perform very well with small lot sizes and complex products. This design principle is very similar to using teams for complexity.

35. USE MULTIFUNCTIONAL TEAMS

Assign teams full responsibility for cross-functional process improvement efforts.

36. USE MULTI-SKILLED EMPLOYEES

This principle eliminates the waiting and coordination time between steps by people with different skill sets. Multi-skilled employees create flexibility in your organization. As work fluctuates, bottlenecks naturally occur. Multi-skilled employees can concentrate their efforts on the bottleneck and break it.

37. CREATE GENERALISTS INSTEAD OF MULTIPLE SPECIALISTS

Generalists do well as quality control checks, dealing with routine matters, acting as a single point of contact, and serving as project or process leaders.

38. EMPLOY MASS CUSTOMIZATION

Use a configurator to automatically turn a custom customer request into a bill of materials. Consider how Dell is able to mass-produce thousands of computers customized to each individual and ship out each order in less than a week.

Chapter 11

Creating a
Clean-Sheet Redesign

T his chapter covers the last four steps in the process redesign methodology, which focus on the redesign itself and continuous improvement. Figure 11.1 highlights the relevant portion of the process.

STEP SIX: FIRST-CUT REDESIGN

The goal of step six is to create a new process that's significantly better than the old one. A challenge goal is to create customer delight. Interestingly, delight can be quantified. To do this, find out how your customers define process excellence and then exceed their expectations with your redesign. The San Jose permit-process redesign described in Chapter 9 did this. Developers thought a turnaround time of two weeks was excellent, but the redesign created a turnaround of three to five days. Consequently, developers were delighted, and letters poured in praising the speedy process.

Challenge the team to reduce process steps, cost, or time by 50 percent or more. By establishing a stretch goal, everything about the as-is process must be examined. To meet the goal, the process must be radically different. For that reason, put aside the as-is process when the team begins to create the new design. You don't want them influenced by the status quo.

In addition, job configuration must be extremely flexible. You probably won't create a significantly improved process simply by taking the current "puzzle pieces" of job descriptions and rearranging them. Team members must have the freedom to design new job descriptions, roles, and responsibilities to meet the needs of a new process.

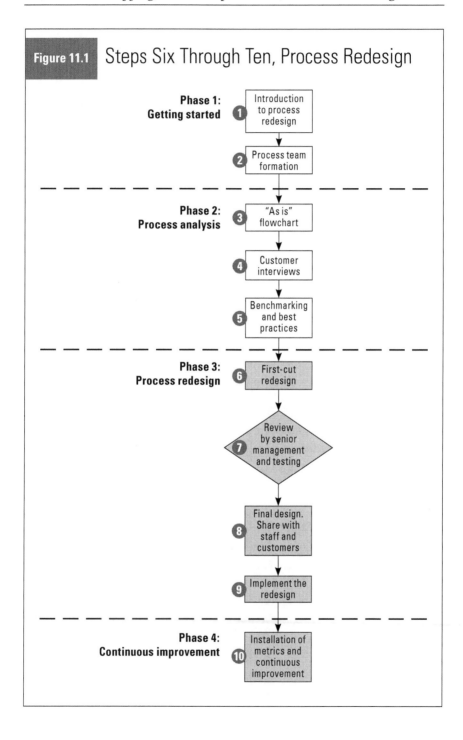

Figure 11.1 Steps Six Through Ten, Process Redesign

Organizational structure and control mechanisms should also be changeable. Both the organizational structure and control mechanisms should support and enable any new process design. Process design should drive structure and controls, not the other way around.

Generating Redesign Ideas

The two goals of a clean-sheet redesign are to:
- Delight the customers of the process
- Reduce process steps, time, or cost by 50 percent or more

To get started, team members will write a story about the new process. They have a couple of options regarding their story. Option one is to make believe they have a magic wand and could do anything. Encourage their imaginations to go wherever they wish. Don't worry about current reality.

Option two is based on the following premise. Your organization has received a windfall of cash. Your president tells you that a new facility will be built in five years where this process will be located. Your task is to create a process that will be the "best of the best" five years from now. You have the money needed to accomplish that task. You must figure out how to create the best of the best.

Team members who pursue option one can use the following technique to make their stories feasible. After someone reads his or her magic wand story, other team members must add reality back in so that the story ultimately becomes doable. Identify the improbable scenarios of the story and ask, "What aspects of this scenario can be altered so it could be done today or in the near future?" In this fashion, you can turn fantastic stories in practical ones.

Brain Writing

This technique is similar to brainstorming except that the ideas are written down instead of suggested out loud. Each team member writes a story about how he or she would change the process so that it delights customers and saves time. The story perspectives can be from a customer, someone working in the new process, or someone observing the new process.

To achieve the goals of customer delight and 50-percent reduction in time, cost, or steps, team members will have to include as many process design principles as make sense in their stories. In addition, innovative ideas from benchmarking and best practices should be incorporated.

When everyone has finished his or her story, it must be read to everyone else. As team members listen to the stories, they should jot down the ideas that appeal to them. After all the stories have been read, the facilitator will create two lists: ideas that most of the team likes, and ideas that require more discussion.

Discuss ideas until the team reaches a consensus about which ideas to use in the redesign. Nine out of ten times a team can reach consensus on one design. However, if you can't reach consensus and everyone's ideas and position have been heard, you're going to have several design variations at this stage. The variations will be tested at a later stage, where simulation, role-playing, or practice will determine the best design.

Create an Activity Flowchart

Begin creating an activity flowchart. This will show only boxes, diamonds, arrows, and triangles. There are no swim lanes. If you attempt to create a new flow and also discuss who will do the work, the exercise will invariably bog down in argument. At this point you want agreement on the flow of work or information. Avoid discussing who will do what task until the new flow is established.

If the team reaches consensus about one activity flow, then create a functional-activity flowchart with swim lanes based on design principle No. 2—i.e., work is performed where it makes the most sense. However, if you might experience debate about who should do what, you'll have multiple flows. The greatest amount of variation occurs when there are multiple activity maps coupled with differing opinions about who does what. But whether you have one design or many, you've now completed step six.

STEP 7: REVIEW BY SENIOR MANAGEMENT

In step seven of the process redesign methodology, you share the new design(s) with senior management for their review, questions, suggestions, and a discussion of implementation options.

Your goal in step seven is to refine the design ideas into one workable design. You might have competing designs from process improvement team members as you begin step seven. In addition, design ideas might come from senior management. Simulation, practice, or role-playing will determine which process design works most effectively and efficiently. For example, in one situation, four new designs were proposed. Through role-playing, two designs were scrapped, and the remaining two were combined into one design.

When the team has sufficiently tested all variations of the new process and has chosen the best process, it's time to consider implementation options. At this point, you've completed step seven.

STEP 8: SHARING THE FINAL DESIGN

Step eight is honing the final design and sharing it with staff for input, comments, and questions. Finally, share the new design with customers for their comments. From all the inputs from stakeholders, some "tweaks" might be necessary. These minor changes are now incorporated into the final design.

STEP 9: IMPLEMENTATION OPTIONS

How are risk and uncertainty concerning a new process design managed? Below are five options ranging from no-risk suggestions to ones that imply higher risks.

Role-Playing, Practice, and Simulation

The least risky option is to role-play, practice, or simulate the new design. To use a military metaphor, you wouldn't be using live ammunition in this option. A professional football team employs this option (and calls it practice) Monday through Saturday. There's no risk in role-playing, practice, or simulation.

Role-playing, during which you send fake inputs through the process to test it, involves assigning relevant process roles to people (not necessarily team members). For example, someone might take the role of customer; another might play an order taker, and so on. The fake inputs could be orders, contracts, or requests. Try to make them as realistic as possible. Once the parts have been assigned, each person must play his or her role when the new process is performed.

In a practice run, the new process has been designed, real inputs are used, and the people who will actually be working in the process participate. It's different from role-playing in that a role player might not actually perform that step when the process is up and running.

Simulation involves the use of computer software and hardware. The new process flow and key performance metrics are tested under various scenarios to find bottlenecks and other problems. Chapter 15 discusses this option in detail.

Role-playing, practice, and simulation have multiple advantages. First, there's no risk. The new process can be debugged without any negative consequences. In fact, it's advantageous to try and break the new design during these test runs. Increase the volume going through the process. Add complexity to the inputs. This way the weak spots, bottlenecks, quality, and coordination issues surface. The problems can be addressed and solved safely without harming customer relationships or creating negative consequences associated with actual process operation.

Second, role-playing, practice, and simulation can demonstrate to people the soundness of the new design. Once you have the role-playing, practice, or simulation operating properly, ask senior management and those resisting the new process to observe it. Encourage questions and comments from them. When naysayers see the new process working and have their questions and concerns addressed, they often turn into supporters of the new design.

The Pilot

The next implementation option is a pilot. During a pilot, the new design is run for real but the scope of the process is constrained. For instance, you might try the pilot for one customer group, one geographic area, or one product line. The pilot can be constrained by time as well; run the pilot for six months and then evaluate its effectiveness. A pilot is slightly more risky than a role-playing, practice, or simulation because it involves real products, customers, and services. Thus a problem can have definite negative consequences.

The advantages to a pilot are several. First, risk is constrained. Pilots are closely monitored so if a problem does occur, it can be fixed immediately. Second, the people working in the pilot can become trainers as you roll the process out to the rest of the organization. Third, the pilot is another opportunity for skeptics to visit the pilot process and learn from those working in it. There's nothing like seeing a new process working for people to change their minds.

Run the New Process Parallel With the Old

The third implementation option is to run the new process in parallel with the old design. This option is often used for software implementations. If there's a problem with the new software, you still have the old process to fall back on. When the new process has been debugged, you can then shut off the old system.

Phase in New Design

The fourth option is to phase in the new design over time. (How do you eat an elephant? One bite at a time.) Look for logical groupings of activities that could be done together in a phase. Also, what's the logical sequence of staging those groupings?

When one phase is successfully completed, then move on to the next one. A phased approach allows an organization to control risk by tackling the project in distinct and manageable pieces. In addition, when each phase is completed, there's a sense of accomplishment that helps maintain momentum for the next phase as well as for larger projects.

Complete Changeover

The last implementation option is a complete changeover. When you're sure the risk is minimal, then you should start using the new process.

It's likely the redesign team will try several of the options when implementing a clean-sheet redesign. Initially, team members might choose role-playing. After that process has been debugged, they might try a pilot. When the pilot has run successfully for some time, they're ready for a complete changeover.

No matter what design your team creates, at a minimum, you should be able to test it risk-free through role-playing, practice, or simulation. Negotiate an agreement with senior management that a test of the design will occur as a part of your redesign effort. That way you have an opportunity to demonstrate a radically different way to do work in an environment that might otherwise be resistant to change.

Step nine is the actual implementation of the final design. The process improvement team will be extremely involved in this. In addition, other staff members who demonstrated buy-in to the new design and who have gotten involved via role-playing, practice, or piloting the new design will also be instrumental in the implementation phase.

The strategy for implementation is based on risk management. The team and senior management have planned the implementation strategy that makes the most sense. Once the process has been adequately tested and fully implemented, you're ready for step ten.

STEP 10: INSTALLING METRICS AND CONTINUOUS IMPROVEMENT

In step ten, measurements and feedback are installed in the new process. A process advisor is identified and assigned. The process advisor uses measurements, feedback, "walking the process," and customer data to identify problems and conduct corrective action and incremental process improvement efforts.

You've now completed a successful process improvement project. If you've paid attention to the goals of a clean-sheet redesign, you'll have dramatically increased customer satisfaction, reduced costs and process time, and improved quality. You'll probably be wondering how you can use the new process as a template for improving your organization. Chapter 12 looks at some common barriers to process redesign, and Chapter 13 describes the mindset, tools, technology, structure, and roles that will make your organization truly process-focused.

Barriers to Process Redesign

C hanging a process and the relevant jobs, structure, and controls presents unique challenges, so a process redesign project will almost always encounter obstacles, barriers, and pitfalls. Research conducted on reengineering projects has uncovered the barriers listed in Table 12.1.

Although the study focused on public-sector organizations, the barriers described in it occur in private and not-for-profit-organizations as well. If you're going to launch process improvement, there's a strong likelihood you'll also experience one or more of these obstacles. Here's how you can address each of the barriers.

NO SURPRISES TO SENIOR MANAGEMENT

Before starting any process improvement effort, senior management should understand that barriers are typical. Each must be discussed. A key question for senior management is, "If any of these barriers are encountered, how do you want to deal with them?" Listen carefully to the responses, because these comments are early indicators of commitment. If senior managers recognize how difficult each of the barriers can be and say, in effect, "Yes, there might be some challenges ahead, but we'll do whatever is necessary to get this project completed," then your probability of success is much higher.

TURF BATTLES BY FUNCTIONAL MANAGERS

Turf battles are the main issue in cross-departmental process improvement efforts. Obviously, this isn't an issue if the effort is limited to one department. Turf disputes can manifest themselves in three ways:

Table 12.1	Barriers to Process Redesign	

Common Barriers	Reported by:
Turf battles by functional managers	50.8 percent
Employee resistance to change	45.3 percent
No one in charge or with authority to push reengineering	42.2 percent
Lack of incentives from department or oversight department	41.3 percent
Difficulty of doing "out of the box" thinking	40.6 percent
Resources tied up in legacy systems	40.6 percent
Uncommitted top management	37.5 percent
Skepticism about another reform effort in our organization	37.5 percent

(From a 1994 National Academy of Public Administration study of thirty-six state and thirty-one federal agencies involved in reengineering projects)

- Department heads don't free up necessary staff to participate on a team.
- Some of the staff have been appointed to the team. However, after a while, the department head pulls some of the staff off the project to work on other things.
- When work is eliminated, new work created, and/or personnel move from one department to another, managers will resist losing people and/or taking on new work.

The responsibility for dealing with turf issues rests with the most senior person in the organization. Neither the project manager nor the facilitator has authority over department heads.

RESISTANCE TO CHANGE

Overcoming resistance to change can be accomplished in four ways. First, people support what they help create, and they resist, fight, and sabotage what's forced upon them. Thus, involving stakeholders in any process improvement is recommended. The ten-step process redesign method offers three involvement opportunities for people who aren't on the team. These occur during step three, the walk-through of the as-is flowchart; step seven, when the team asks for reactions to the redesign, and, finally, at step nine, during the actual implementation.

Remember, it's often wise to go slowly to go fast. The time invested in creating involvement might seem excessive initially, but it ultimately will save time during implementation. Also remember that coming up with a new design isn't difficult; implementing that design is by far the most difficult step.

Second, people have a right to their opinions. If you don't honor this right, you can expect rage on some level. You might not see it, but it will be there. Listen to each person's opinion and don't fight the resistors. Instead, write their concerns on a flip chart, and let them know that the team is aware of these issues. By making it OK to resist, often another, hidden reason for resisting will surface. This might be the true concern, which the resistor, for a variety of reasons, didn't state initially.

Another rationale for respecting everyone's opinion is that the "resistor" might in fact be right. If the team is headed toward problems, a person's concerns or warnings might forestall a disaster.

Third, any time you state that a process is broken or needs fixing, it's not a far leap for some people to think *they're* broken or need fixing. Frequently you'll find people who've worked in a process for years. Over time they begin to identify with how the work is done. They "become the process." Thus, when you imply that something is wrong with it, they take it personally and think there's something wrong with them. You must make it perfectly clear that the process is the problem, not them.

At the beginning of a change effort, several things should be done. People's past accomplishments must be honored and appreciated. This lets them know there's nothing wrong with their work. Next, the reason for the change must be stated. This will help staff see the need to move the process to the next level of performance. Finally, describe the change method and how they will be involved.

Resistance often is rooted in a belief or assumption. Recall a time when you used to believe something that you don't now. What happened to cause your belief to change? Was it new information and/or experiences that caused the change? Probably it was one or the other, or a combination of the two. If you listen to resistors, you'll often hear them say, "That won't work." Or, "If people just did their jobs, we wouldn't have this problem." If you want to influence these people, you must find out what their underlying belief is.

Once the belief is on the surface, you can test whether you've understood it by restating it to the resistor. If he or she agrees that you've stated it properly, the next question is, "What would it take for you to think differently about this?" In essence, you're asking the resistor, "What information or experience do you need to think differently about this?" If he or she provides you with an answer, then it's your job to provide the evidence. Some resistors will say, "I don't know." In those situations, you'll have to guess.

Imagine the resistor's belief as frozen in a block of ice. Each new bit of information or experience that doesn't support the belief acts like an ice pick chipping away at the block. Some blocks need only a few whacks before they fall apart; others will need repeated whacks from different sources before they'll crack. It would be nice to know in advance how many whacks are necessary to get someone's belief to change, but often the person is unaware of the underlying cause of his or her resistance, much less how to overcome it.

NO ONE IN AUTHORITY TO PUSH THE CHANGE

To make large changes in a process, someone high up in the organization must really want the change. Before any process change effort is undertaken, find a champion or sponsor for the effort. Small changes in a process usually can be made without senior-level support, but remember: No surprises to senior management.

LACK OF INCENTIVES

This barrier usually is framed by the question, "Why do we have to make this change now?" You must offer compelling reasons in response. Some of these could be: "We're losing money"; "The customers are demanding it"; or "Competitors are taking customers." For more ideas, see Chapter 4, which discusses symptoms of a broken process, and Chapter 6, which examines ways to make the case for change.

DIFFICULTY IN DOING 'OUT OF THE BOX' THINKING AND RESOURCES TIED UP IN LEGACY SYSTEMS

These two are addressed together. Why does a person have difficulty thinking "outside the box?" The likely reason is that he or she has created the legacy system. People support what they help create. Again, honor people's past accomplishments, show appreciation for past efforts, and then state a compelling case for change.

UNCOMMITTED TOP MANAGEMENT
AND SKEPTICISM ABOUT REFORM

These two issues are also linked. Why is there skepticism about another reform effort? The likely reason is that top management has pulled the plug on other change efforts, and hence staff is skeptical about this one.

Top management commitment is a requirement for major change. However, small changes in the process can be done without this commitment. If, initially, top management seems committed but then begins to waver, scale down your effort and go for smaller, easier process changes.

A test of top managers' commitment is whether they're willing to make the changes that are inexpensive and easy to implement from the frustration and idea bin described in Chapter 7. If they won't allow those to be implemented, it's time to abandon the effort. If they are willing to implement these, that will go a long way toward convincing the skeptics on the team. Nothing changes skeptics' attitudes like results.

SUPPLIER EVALUATION

You must examine three general areas before proceeding with process improvement. These are:

- Inputs coming into the process from the supplier
- The process used to transform the inputs
- Output to the customer

Up to this point, you've focused on the last two. However, once you've "gotten your house in order," it's time to look upstream at your supplier inputs. Inputs, transformation, and outputs are represented by the flowchart depicted in Figure 12.1.

Do the inputs from the supplier meet your requirements? Often the answer is, "Not entirely." The first step to change this is to be explicit about your requirements. When you examine a process, determine who the suppliers are. Next, pick one supplier and ask, "What do we need, want, expect, and require from this supplier?"

If you were evaluating copy services from an outside vendor, for example, typical requirements might be clean copies, fast turnaround, a fair price, helpful staff, and convenient location.

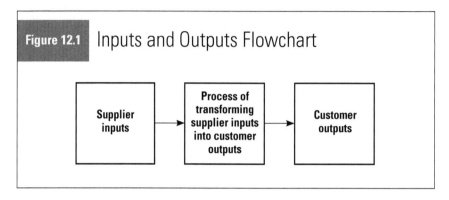

Figure 12.1 Inputs and Outputs Flowchart

Rank your requirements beginning with the most important one. Using the copy services example shown in Table 12.2, the ranked requirements might look like this:

1. Clean copies
2. Fast turnaround
3. Fair price
4. Convenient location
5. Helpful staff

Next, using letter grades, evaluate your supplier's process in terms of meeting each of these requirements. Your evaluation will look like the one shown in Table 12.2.

(*Note:* At the beginning of a process improvement effort, assume that people are doing the best jobs they can. This includes your supplier's staff as well as your own. Also assume that if there's underperformance, then something in the process is causing it. Don't assign letter grades to people or say what *they* are doing wrong. Focus on the process.)

You've now established a supplier process performance scorecard. The next step is to define what excellence looks like. What does an "A" grade require? What you want are specific, measurable criteria. For example, when you ask what an A requirement is for your top-ranked criteria—i.e., clean copies—the answer is that every copied page must look exactly like the original. Below are descriptions of excellence for each criterion.

■ Clean copies: Every copied page looks exactly like the original.
■ Fast turnaround: The order is ready in two hours.
■ Fair price: This is the lowest price available.

Table 12.2	Supplier Process Evaluation

Requirement	How well the supplier's process is working on meeting this requirement	What an "A" looks like
1. Clean copies	A-	Every copied page looks exactly like the original.
2. Fast turnaround	B	Copy job completed in two hours
3. Fair price	B	Lowest cost versus competitors
4. Don't have to drive far	B+	My driving time is under five minutes.
5. Helpful staff	B	Staff can cheerfully and easily answer all my questions.

- Convenient location: Driving time is ten minutes.
- Helpful staff: Any copying question is answered correctly the first time.

If you have a supplier, either internal or external, whose process performance is poor, what can you do to improve it?

- *Step one:* Create a supplier process performance report card as shown in the example above. List all your requirements, needs, and expectations. Rank them according to importance. Assign a letter grade according to how well each of the requirements is being met. Then define excellence for each item.

- *Step two:* Consider the items that were not given an A. These will probably require rework on your part to make the supplier input acceptable. Track all the activities you perform for a criteria that doesn't warrant an A. Cost all the activities you do to fix it. These usually include labor, materials, customer returns, etc. You want to determine a dollar figure to assign to the non-As. Costing problems out usually creates a sense of urgency and attention for decision makers.

- *Step three:* Meet with your supplier to discuss the data from steps one and two. Some suppliers might be surprised with the criteria you've listed. Some might be surprised by how well or poorly their processes are performing. Some might be surprised by the negative impact to your organization. Step three's goal is to convince the supplier to commit to improving process performance so that it warrants an A. If you have them, include examples of other suppliers who are able to achieve an A performance on your key criteria. Step three's output is a contract or agreement focusing on your key criteria and performance levels.

■ *Step four:* Create a measurement and feedback mechanism regarding your criteria and performance data. Each time your supplier provides you with a service or a product, generate a supplier process performance report card. How did the supplier's process perform on each criteria?

■ *Step five:* Share step four data with the supplier. Where there are non-A's, ask, "How can we work together to close the gap?" This partnering approach is a characteristic of involvement organizations. Don't use the data to punish the supplier, which is an approach that traditional organizations typically use.

These five steps are the keys to creating a closer relationship with suppliers so that their inputs, represented by the B in Figure 12.3, meet your requirements.

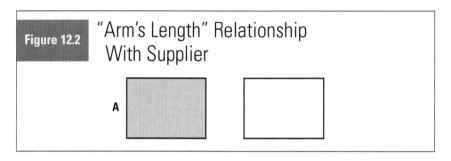

Figure 12.2 "Arm's Length" Relationship With Supplier

A

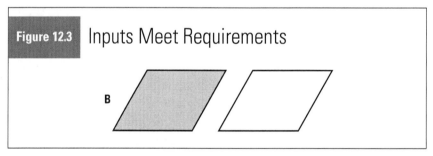

Figure 12.3 Inputs Meet Requirements

B

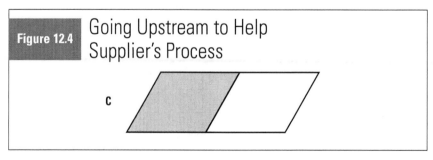

Figure 12.4 Going Upstream to Help Supplier's Process

C

As you become more skilled in process improvement, you can use your capability to improve your supplier's upstream processes. World-class organizations send teams of process experts to their suppliers. Sometimes the savings from the process improvement are passed along as price breaks. In addition, some of the cost savings can accrue to the suppliers as well. This creates a win-win for both partners.

Another option is to use your process excellence to help your customer. For example, GE Medical, which sells imaging equipment, will work with their customers to improve their processes for using newly purchased GE equipment. In addition, the organization sells its process capability by training customers in Six Sigma. GE took a capability, packaged it with a product, and now sells both.

Going upstream to help your suppliers improve its process is illustrated by the C in Figure 12.4. However, the first step of the journey to process improvement is to fix your own processes. When that's been done, then you can you branch out to both suppliers and customers.

SUPPLIER REPRESENTATIONS

If you consider your relationships with suppliers to be at arm's length, then you might prefer graphic A in Figure 12.2. It represents the option of choosing a supplier from an approved set of vendors each time you make a purchase. You list specifications in a formal, negotiated contract that's typically awarded to the lowest bidder. The supplier drives the truck to your loading dock with the product, leaves it on your dock, and you pay the negotiated price.

Graphic B in Figure 12.3 represents a supplier relationship with a measurement and feedback mechanism. In a B relationship, both the company and supplier work from a shared list of specifications. Performance measures are frequently discussed, and both entities work together to increase performance.

If your worldview is more like Honda Motor Co.'s, your relationship with suppliers might be depicted as the C in Figure 12.4. The relationship is nurtured, advice is offered; the interaction exists beyond delivery and payment. Honda was faced with "poor quality" from one bumper supplier. The U.S. firm achieved a defect rate of three out of 20,000, which it considered excellent. However, Honda expected *no* defects. It sent a team of quality engineers to improve the supplier's processes so that it now achieves this requirement. Both Honda and the supplier benefit significantly from this relationship.

Graphic C might also represent the relationship between Wal-Mart and its major suppliers, in which computer systems link the company's cash registers to the supplier's inventory and delivery system. Graphic D in Figure 12.5 represents vertical integration, where a company owns its suppliers to ensure a steady supply of critical materials. Graphic E in Figure 12.6 represents outsourcing.

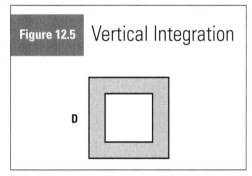

Figure 12.5 Vertical Integration

D

INCREMENTAL IMPROVEMENT

The preceding chapters outlined the process improvement approach to use for gains of 20 percent or more. What about incremental improvements? They can be achieved by following these six steps:

1. Identify the problem.
2. Pick the appropriate lens, such as quality, timeliness, or frustration. Gather the appropriate data.
3. Use either the task-procedure flowchart or the functional-activity flowchart to map the existing flow of work or information.
4. Ask those who experience the problem to analyze the flowchart. Have this team brainstorm solutions.
5. Evaluate and/or test the solutions.
6. Pick the solution that makes the most sense, implement it, and institute controls to maintain the solution.

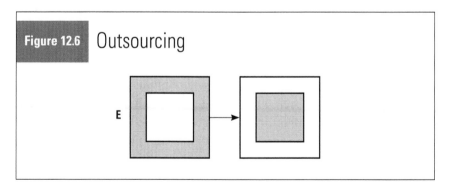

Figure 12.6 Outsourcing

E

Chapter 13

Becoming a Process-Focused Organization

Process management comprises of end-to-end documentation, improvement (from radical to continuous), and management of organizational processes. Decisions are data-driven and based on customer satisfaction metrics, quality, timeliness, and cost. The responsibility of monitoring process performance and facilitating process changes belongs to a process advisor or manager. Administering processes is dramatically enabled by business process management technology, which will be discussed in more detail in Chapter 15.

REALIGNING AROUND PROCESSES

Successful process redesign efforts in one area will precipitate change in other parts of the organizational system. In some cases, these changes are required for a particular process improvement to be implemented. Sometimes, process improvement and redesign might propel an organization into full-scale change, such as moving toward a matrix or, ultimately, an F-type work management style.

To completely align around process, your organization must consider the following areas.

Interpersonal

- Uninterested and unhelpful department heads must evolve into leaders who see themselves as links in a chain to create and deliver value. Chapter 14 discusses ways to encourage cross-departmental process management.
- Do department heads and process owners respect each other? Is there enough mutual regard that they consider their actions' effects on each other without being prompted by policy or structure?

■ Is there an informal network of relationships that complements rather than undermines the formal matrix structure?

Conceptual

■ Supervisors and managers must move from firefighting to structured, team-based problem solving using process improvement tools.

■ The organization needs a vision statement and strategy to provide context and direction as it becomes more process focused. This should lead to horizontal organization as opposed to a vertical separation based on functional units.

■ The business strategy should be linked to processes through mechanisms such as the balanced scorecard.

■ Data capture and reporting must move from individual departmental performance to process performance highlighting critical customer requirements.

■ Beliefs and assumptions regarding the root causes of problems must focus on processes rather than people.

■ Process methodologies such as lean, Six Sigma, reengineering, process improvement, and design principles should be used throughout the organization.

■ Do the organization's senior executives "think with process?" That is, do they translate plans into process performance requirements rather than functional assignments?

■ Do they view process capability as a strategic asset that must be cultivated and leveraged?

■ Do they balance the company's vertical functional organization with a horizontal process structure?

■ Do they allocate resources according to process requirements?

■ Is there a widely shared understanding of process management that draws attention to the horizontal flow of work rather than to vertical hierarchies of control and communication?

■ Can people use process terminology in everyday work encounters without having to provide a dictionary?

Cultural

■ The organization's values must shift from individual recognition to process excellence.

■ Pictures, graphs, and stories should highlight process improvement successes.

- Are there strong values about coordination within and across process teams?
- Are there strong norms against building fiefdoms or erecting boundaries?
- Are the organization's cultural heroes those who find process solutions rather than rebels or cowboys who do without a process focus?
- Are errors viewed as opportunities to improve processes rather than evidence of personal failure?

Structural

- A process advisor or owner is added to the process team.
- Managers and supervisors who are no longer required to make many of the decisions they used to must switch roles to become facilitators and coaches.
- A formal, seniority-type reward system must change to one based on knowledge and results. Individual rewards should be replaced by team- and process-based ones.
- Changes in job descriptions should enhance multiskilled and cross-functional capabilities (i.e., generalists versus specialists). Also, the structure must accommodate the compensation for skill and knowledge.
- Changes in traditional career paths should include more horizontal career moves rather than corporate ladder climbing.
- The budget's form and function should change. Activity-based costing will help overcome problems with managerial accounting so that true profitability by product, customer, or market can be calculated.
- Policy statements should be created and distributed that read, "No changes in the process can be made without the prior review and approval of the process advisor."

Technological

- Software should be used to model, test, and improve processes. (For more about this, see Chapter 15.)
- Is the organization's information infrastructure designed to make process information available to all?

Individual

- All management levels should have training in Six Sigma, lean, reengineering, process improvement, and design principles.

- Are there enough employees capable of doing process characterization, simulation, and improvement?
- Do all employees understand that learning process analysis is a key component of their professional development?
- Is the organization's hiring process designed to find process awareness among candidates?
- Do promotion strategies weed out people driven to power and control and favor those inclined to support process flows across organizational segments?

Political

- Career advancement opportunities should be available only to those who successfully use process methodologies and tools.
- Are people who use company problems to enhance their own personal agenda or power quickly confronted and weeded out?
- Is the organization's well being the primary driver for discussion and decision at all levels?
- Do senior executives avoid forming alliances to defend their own positions and instead respond openly and candidly to issues facing the organization?

THE PROCESS ADVISOR'S ROLE

In most organizations no one oversees the performance and improvement of cross-departmental processes. Management books often assign the title "process owner" to this role. However, "owner" implies authority, which is usually missing in organizations that include this position. "Process advisor" or "process consultant" are more accurate, in that they reflect this reality. Usually, authority pertains to resources, staffing, and prioritizing projects.

The process advisor or consultant's role is to monitor the performance of a process and continually improve it. This is accomplished by using measurements and feedback. Typical measurements include quality, timeliness, customer satisfaction, and cost. The process advisor should keep a process dashboard of key indicators and regularly share them with everyone who works in the process. This dashboard could also be prominently displayed for all to see.

In addition, people who work in the process—e.g., supervisors, management, and department heads—must have their performance, bonus, and evaluations tied to this dashboard. In this way, goals and measurements can be aligned.

As part of the culture of continuous improvement, problems in a process should come to light through metrics, worker comments, or customer issues. When they do, the process advisor's job is to assemble key team members to launch a process improvement effort. Generally, this would involve data analysis, root cause analysis, creating an improvement plan, implementing it, and finally monitoring the improvement.

The process advisor should "walk the process" regularly to chat with workers, observe individual tasks, and check conformance to procedures. If there are multiple problems in the process, this walk-through should happen often. When the metrics indicate process stability, the walk-through can be less frequent.

The policy statement, "No changes can be made in the process without the prior review and approval of the process advisor," can help provide change control. Without such a policy, department heads, managers, or supervisors could make changes in the process without fully understanding the effect on other departments.

Characteristics of a Successful Process Advisor

- Knows the process extremely well
- Doesn't have a vested interest in any one part of the process
- Is effective in influencing management
- Is well respected by department heads
- Knows the tools of process improvement (e.g., lean, Six Sigma, design principles)
- Is an effective facilitator and team leader
- Can perform or facilitate simulation, role playing, and practice of new process designs or changes

Working With Department Heads

Most organizations are functionally designed. Department heads control resources, people, priorities, and decisions within their respective areas. Thus, a process manager really has no control except what he or she can exert through influence.

A process owner can work with department heads by:

- Understanding the department head's priorities
- Giving feedback about process performance metrics

- Bringing department heads together to discuss issues, priorities, and resources
- Helping the department head when possible
- Communicating regularly with the department head

THE PROCESS OWNER'S ROLE

When an organization has transitioned to an F type, the authority over resources, personnel, and prioritization moves from the department head to the process owner, a person who focuses on the whole as opposed to just the pieces. It's through the seamless performance of the entire process that value is efficiently created and delivered to the customer. In this case, value refers to a transformation of the product or service in a way in which the customer would be willing to pay for. Efforts at optimizing the pieces invariably lead to suboptimizing the whole.

There should be a process owner for each of the cross-departmental processes listed below:

- Order to delivery
- New product or service development
- Strategy implementation
- Customer service

These four processes are the main vehicles for creating value and bringing in revenue to the organization. Other processes primarily support these four.

The department head's primary function is developing people, putting in place technological enhancements, and ensuring proper use of assets in their particular areas. The department head becomes a coach whose job is to work closely with the process owner; however, ultimate decision making rests in the process owner's hands.

Should conflicts arise between process owners, the decision-making process should be driven by organizational strategy. For instance, a process owner for order to delivery wants a key person in manufacturing to work in his process. However, the new product-development process owner wants that same manufacturing individual to work in her process. How does this conflict get resolved? The two process owners should meet with the manufacturing coach to discuss the problem. A critical criterion would be the organization's strategic goal. If it plans to replace 50 percent of its current product line with new products within five years, then it might make more sense for the manufacturing employee to work in the new-product development process. Resource allocation and prioritization should always be driven by strategy.

In the previous example, the manufacturing coach might point out another key manufacturing employee who would do an excellent job in the order-to-delivery process. Or, the manufacturing coach might be asked to quickly train another employee for order to delivery.

For processes that are contained primarily in one department, the choice for process owner is fairly simple: It's the department coach. However, for organizations with work management styles other than F type, the process owner should be the department head. For these organizations, the cross-departmental processes will be more difficult to manage and improve.

Similar to the role of process advisor or consultant, the process owner would monitor key metrics, regularly walk the process, and perform process-improvement initiatives when needed.

Characteristics of a Successful Process Owner

- Has worked in most, if not all, the departments spanned by the process
- Doesn't have a vested interest in any one part of the process
- Is well respected by the various department coaches
- Knows the tools of process improvement (e.g., lean, Six Sigma, design principles)
- Is an effective facilitator and team leader
- Can perform or facilitate simulation, role-playing, and practice of new process designs or process changes
- Understands the organization's strategy and how it applies to the process that he or she manages. Can link strategy to a balanced scorecard approach that ties into process metrics.
- Works well with the other process managers, CEO, and COO

VALUE STREAM MANAGER'S ROLE

The following excerpt is from "Value Stream Manager," by James Womack, published online by the Lean Enterprise Institute (*www.lean.org*):

> "You may have already noticed that tracing the value stream for a product family will take you across organizational boundaries in your company. Because companies tend to be organized by departments and functions instead of by the flow of value-creating steps for product families, you often find that—sur-

prise!—no one is responsible for the value stream perspective. (It's no wonder we have focused too heavily on process-level *kaizen*!)[1] It is astoundingly rare to visit a facility and find one person who knows the entire material and information flow for a product (all processes and how each is scheduled). Yet without this, parts of the flow will be left to chance—meaning that individual processing areas will operate in a way that is optimum from their perspective, not the value stream's perspective.

"To get away from the isolated islands of functionality you need one person with lead responsibility for understanding a product family's value stream and improving it. We call this person a value stream manager, and suggest that in this capacity they report to the top person at your site. This way they will have the power necessary to help change happen."

This excerpt is from *Learning to See*, by Mike Rother and John Shook (Lean Enterprise Institute, 2003):

A value stream manager is responsible for increasing the ratio of value to nonvalue and eliminating waste in the overall supply chain from start to finish; for defining a product family; and for ensuring that the value stream meets or exceeds customer requirements.[2]

Primary Responsibilities

A value stream manager's scope of responsibility plays out on at least two levels. First, there's the plant level, where the value stream manager looks after the value stream between the four walls of the plant and perhaps takes into consideration inbound and outbound logistics to and from the site. Then there's the value stream at the enterprise level. Not much has been written on this to date. At this level, the value stream manager is responsible for eliminating waste throughout the entire value stream, which often spans several independent organizations. This can be difficult due to the volatile issues regarding trust, privacy, and transparency in each organization.

The value stream manager is responsible for the following activities:

- Defining the product family by conducting product-routing analysis and appropriate groupings[3]
- Ensuring that a current-state value stream map is created of the end-to-end value stream(s)

1. There are traditionally two types of *kaizen*. The first is individual *process kaizen*, where the team in the work unit improves individual processes within their unit. The second is *flow kaizen*, where strategic processes are improved in the value stream to give an overall system improvement.
2. For a discussion on the principles of a lean enterprise, see page 277 of *Lean Thinking* by James Womack and Daniel Jones (Free Press, 2003).

■ Conducting fact-based analysis of the current state map(s)

■ Preparing an ideal-state map showing what the value stream could look like over the long term

■ Preparing a future state map that uses lean techniques to eliminate waste and improve process value in the short to midterm

■ Creating a plan to achieve the future state

■ Leading the implementation of the plan

■ Leading and mobilizing people (including customers and suppliers) inside and outside the value stream to enable the required changes

■ Leading day-to-day activities within the value stream to ensure that current commitments are achieved while improvements are made

Personal Attributes

A value stream manager must be able to step back and view the stream from a broad perspective. He or she must understand key system constraints and quickly spot critical process issues. This person should have a good understanding of lean thinking or, alternatively, be willing to work closely with a *sensei* to get this knowledge.[4] A value stream manager must focus on improving the value created by the whole system, not on optimizing parts of the supply chain.

This person should have exemplary leadership abilities and be able to motivate individuals in the value stream to change—even if his or her area doesn't receive the benefits. A value stream manager's decisions must be based on data rather than opinion. It's important be open to improvement ideas from employees and understand the working culture within the value stream. He or she should be able to create and manage a value stream plan. Knowing how to communicate with senior executives to achieve buy-in to major changes is also important. Can this person create a compelling case to show why change is required? He or she must be able to interact with customers and suppliers to ensure that win-win changes are made while increasing value.

Selecting a Value Stream Manager

How do you select the right person for the position of value stream manager? Should it be the current manufacturing manager? How about the logistics or human resources managers?

---

3. Product routing analysis is sometimes completed using a product family matrix. See page six of *Learning to See*, version 1.2, by Mike Rother and John Shook (Lean Enterprise Institute, 2003).

4. *Sensei* is Japanese for "teacher." In this case, a *sensei* is an expert in applying lean techniques. A learning instructor is called a *sempai*, a term traditionally used in karate for students who have nearly achieved their black belt status.

The candidate's personality should be the most important factor in the decision. The technical aspects of the job can be learned later if the right attitude and personality are there already. The person must be the type who sees the big picture. The value stream manager must have an extreme desire to improve: What was done before is never good enough for the future. Can the person convince and motivate others to make changes for the organization's good—even, perhaps, to the detriment of his or her own subprocesses?

The individual must understand that the core value on the work floor isn't the technology but the people. Therefore, the value stream manager should be the type who treats people as valued assets. He or she should be a good communicator, able to communicate the improvement process and gain credibility by sticking to it. A value stream manager must build and maintain employees' and executives' trust. He or she must be comfortable with taking calculated risks and living with the mistakes that sometimes occur as a result.

Next in importance is knowledge of lean techniques. Preferably this knowledge is grounded in actual experience in another organization or in a related value stream within the same company.[5] Without this knowledge and experience, mistakes and errors will be made more frequently, and progress will be slower. Therefore, an inexperienced value stream manager must be willing to work closely with and learn from an advisor who has the required knowledge, background, and experience.

Finally, the person should be very knowledgeable about the material and information flows in the value stream. He or she must have access to the people who are experts in these flows. This isn't just knowledge of the manufacturing processes and techniques. It includes the logistics processes, including both inbound and outbound materials. Real estate issues often enter the picture. One of the benefits is usually a reduced requirement for floor space. What will you do with the freed-up space to reduce operating costs?

The person must be in touch with marketing and sales departments to stay informed about future sales plans and requirements. He or she must know what satisfies the organization's customers. This industry knowledge should be recognized as both a good and bad thing. A detailed knowledge of the processes involved is very beneficial, but beware of the person who says, "We've already tried that before, and it won't work."

---

5. Many companies implement lean techniques on one model line first and then move to the next product family.

THE EXECUTIVE'S ROLE

Once a value stream manager has been selected, his or her superior should realize that in the beginning this person will need the support of top management to succeed. Individual process managers within the value stream must know that the value stream manager has the authority and responsibility to make changes within the stream. These individual process managers must participate willingly for the redesign to work. The senior executive can help by visibly supporting the value stream manager's direction and providing the tools needed to ensure success. Top management can also help with converting or removing resistance at the process level.

A second role of the executive is to shield the value stream manager during major changes. He or she will have enough to worry about without wondering where the next broadside might come from. Old-style measures might slip or prove ineffective while change is underway. For example, what would happen in your organization if point velocity was suddenly reduced due to a *kaizen* in the area—even though system lead time was improved?[6] The executive must run interference with the CEO, board of directors, or any higher level that can interfere with progress. Once the redesign is underway, the value stream manager must stay in close touch with executives and monitor their commitment to the project. Then he or she can in turn start protecting associates on the work floor.

This isn't to say that executives should sit back and not expect results. Naturally, they'll be impatient for bottom-line results but should understand that change sometimes means one step back for every two steps forward. They shouldn't dissuade the value stream manager from taking calculated risks but instead keep in mind that perfection isn't achieved on the first try.

Evaluating Performance

The value stream manager should be evaluated on the achievement of his or her plan. At the beginning of the year, and periodically throughout it, the senior executive should review the value stream plan with the manager to assess progress. Obviously, this can't be accomplished if the current state, future state, and implementation loops haven't been properly documented.[7] The senior executive

---

6. Point velocity is the speed through one process or machine. Often, achieving a target point velocity is rewarded, even though inventory accumulates at the next process downstream. What you really want to achieve is overall system velocity.

7. For a detailed description of value-stream loops, see page eighty-six of Learning to See, version 1.2, by Mike Rother and John Shook (Lean Enterprise Institute, 2003).

should recognize that all plans are fluid and can change over time as better ways are found. Therefore, he or she should be flexible during this evaluation process.

The value stream manager should also be evaluated on softer issues, such as leadership style, support of employee's suggestions, plans for dealing with excess labor, etc. The value stream manager must produce succession plans and developmental assignments for his or her subordinates in today's flatter organizations.

During performance and development planning, one of the key questions facing organizations that appoint value stream managers is how to take a value stream organizational approach while still building functional expertise. Moving people back and forth between functional careers and value stream management every few years can be the answer. For example, a person from engineering might be selected as the value stream manager and then returned to the engineering department in a more senior position three years later to upgrade his or her engineering skills.

New measurements might be required to ensure that progress is made in areas that support the strategy. Old measures should be scrutinized closely to ensure that they don't reinforce behavior that's contrary to the organization's new goals. (For example, is point velocity the key target for individual departments?)

At the start of the assignment, the value stream manager might take a great deal of time to firefight and deal with daily production issues. The percentage of time used on daily issues should drop, and the focus must definitely shift to longer-term value stream improvement as processes are improved and become more reliable. The executive should expect to see a declining firefighting trend in the value stream manager's routine. This should be a consideration in the staffing process. Sometimes the best firefighters enjoy what they do and get a great deal of satisfaction from solving daily problems. To maintain that satisfaction, they can sometimes also be the arsonists. This trait isn't appropriate for a good value stream manager.

Chapter 14

Building Cross-Department Process Management

M aking process and process management an understood and practiced part of the organizational culture can push against a common theme: to develop hard boundaries between departments. Building silos and fiefdoms is more common than building cooperation. This chapter explores the nature of greater interdepartmental cooperation and how leaders can create a smooth transition to process management.

THE NATURE OF INTERDEPARTMENTAL COOPERATION

The changes discussed in Chapter 13 can be challenging for any organization. As it moves from a traditional or involvement work management style, the roles of the manager and individual contributors shift. Staff increasingly works with their peers in other departments rather than taking direction only from their managers. As the organization moves into the process, cross-functional, and finally matrix work management styles, the process advisor's role starts to encroach on the manager's traditional roles and responsibilities.

Part of the task is strategic or tactical, but the real obstacle is cultural. The first change organizations must accomplish is getting department heads and staff to work *with* each other rather than just next to each other. This requires people to think differently, to value differently, and to behave differently. The underlying theme during this phase is creating cooperation across departmental boundaries. Process definition will accelerate that concern because most processes push right through departmental boundaries. Although some processes can be contained within an existing silo, most important processes will cut across them, from customer acquisition all the way to customer satisfaction.

But despite these pressures for greater cooperation between departments, there seems to be an almost unconscious drive for greater separation and independence. Humans are, by nature, territorial. Defining and defending our own turf is an instinct inherited from our tree-dwelling ancestors. Evolution has to some extent civilized that drive; though it's still there, it takes other forms, such as thinking in terms of "us" versus "them." The people you work with constantly will eventually begin to seem like your "tribe," while those you see only occasionally become "the other tribe."

This primitive drive was once essential to our survival as a species, but it now represents a significant threat to business enterprises. Organizations that hope to thrive and flourish in today's complex, global economy must learn how to act in a coordinated fashion, marshaling diverse resources across dispersed geographies to provide a timely, cost-effective answer to customer needs. They must innovate and execute across hundreds, if not thousands, of co-workers and in an unforgiving, competitive environment.

Companies that fail to get past this first hurdle toward stronger process focus will find themselves strapped by a fatal array of problems, such as:

- Executing strategic initiatives "falls through the cracks."
- Installing enterprisewide data systems (e.g., SAP, Oracle) gets massively bogged down and often stimulates political infighting.
- Product development cycles stretch out.
- Fixes in an upstream department negatively affect downstream departments.
- Products are delivered with significant gaps (e.g., poor documentation, weak collateral materials, poor internal orientation or customer training)
- Redundant demands are made on space, corporate services, etc.
- Key resources are hoarded for local agendas.
- Departments raid each other for talent.
- Information stops at departmental boundaries, forcing duplicate entry and errors.
- Customer service is disjointed and unresponsive.
- Effort is wasted defending one's own department.
- People feel isolated and alone in their work.
- Executive credibility is tarnished.

In attempts to turn the tide, organizations routinely "put more skin in the game," such as team-building weekends, planning retreats, training in communication, cross-functional task forces, pleading, yelling, arguing, and any other technique human resources can come up with—usually to no avail.

The reason that greater cooperation is so elusive is actually a clue to its essential nature. Cooperation isn't something that can be created solely by policy, structure, or executive demand. It's embedded in the decisions people make to return a phone call, invite someone to a meeting, or put someone else's priorities higher than his or her own. These decisions are made minute to minute, out of the view of executives, supervisors, or even peers.

Moreover, people make these decisions by the simplest of logic: i.e., Will it benefit me? Will it benefit the company? Will it be effective? Or will it be a waste of time? The challenge of creating stronger interdepartmental cooperation is changing peoples' perception of benefit and likely efficacy.

DEFINING DIFFERENT LEVELS OF INTERDEPARTMENTAL COOPERATION

The first step toward the goal of greater interdepartmental cooperation (IDC) is to break it down. Too often cooperation is viewed as a global good or a uniform moral value. In fact, cooperation comes in a variety of flavors. Each level of cooperation is more demanding than the last, so it makes sense to strive only for the level absolutely required. Table 14.1 is a summary of the six different levels of cooperation. There are several implicit assumptions behind this taxonomy:

- A particular pair of departments might be on one level in terms of their attitudes and behaviors, although the work actually requires a distinctly higher level.
- The levels are cumulative, that is, skills learned in level *n* are required for level *n*+1, plus a little more.
- A natural progression occurs from level *n* to level *n*+1, but it's a significant challenge to jump more than one level at a time.

Notice in Table 14.1 that interdepartmental cooperation prior to the thick line separating levels three and four is based on an occasional or transitory need. That is, departments can come together to solve a problem or even jointly manage a project but then fall back to their independent ways at the conclusion of the effort. But once they take on joint interface management or a higher level of cooperation,

	Table 14.1	Levels of Interdepartmental Cooperation	

	Brief description	Examples
Level 0	**Strict independence:** Groups are fully separate and distinct; there's virtually no need for coordinated action.	■ A group of therapists ■ Hairstylists in a salon ■ Many professional practice groups (lawyers, CPAs, etc.)
Level 1	**Information sharing:** Groups need information on the others' activities to fully perform their own charters. Work activities are independent except for the occasional need to share data.	■ Senior citizen residence center providing information to other divisions about an upcoming transfer of residents from independent living to assisted living to nursing care ■ Regional offices passing financial performance data into central office to track performance against plan
Level 2	**Joint problem solving:** Groups must periodically resolve problems together for the most effective solutions. No one group has all the information and/or resources to affect a complete solution.	■ Newspaper departments wanting to leverage their sponsorship of an upcoming wine festival with complimentary ads, news coverage, and related human-interest stories ■ Installation of a new software package in a credit union has discovered design problems as well as unanticipated training needs; groups need to share information and jointly design the best package of delivery services to satisfy the client
Level 3	**Joint project management:** Groups must commit to joint outcomes, sharing resources and coordinating timelines, as well as to longer and more complex interconnections than simple problem solving. The need for cooperation ceases when the project goals are achieved.	■ Mounting a theatrical performance, requiring coordinated delivery of actors, costuming, lighting, and sets ■ A startup, delivering its first product, requiring coordination of engineering design, manufacturing, documentation, training and marketing ■ Fast-track commercial construction
Level 4	**Joint interface management:** Groups with a high frequency of communication can focus on managing the interface between their departments. Work is still considered as departmental, but they acknowledge the need for smooth handoffs. There may be little or no understanding of where products come from or how they're used.	■ Installation department passes client information to the customer service group. ■ Purchasing and warehousing are constantly talking about purchases and available inventory. ■ Sales and legal frequently work together on contracts. ■ Warehousing passes parts into manufacturing on a predetermined schedule with only minor variations.
Level 5	**Joint process maintenance:** Groups must cooperate continuously to monitor and improve key work processes. The process is problematic, not only the outcome. The need for cooperation is ongoing.	■ Managing engineering change requests ■ New product development process ■ New product launch ■ Customer requirement definition

	Brief description	Examples
Table 14.1	**continued**	
Level 6	**Optimization:** Groups must calibrate their actions to provide the greatest outcome for the company. Some groups may suboptimize for the greater benefit of the whole. Over-performance by one group distorts or compromises other parts of organi-zation. Groups must be released from demand to maximize their individual budgets.	■ A tool shack at a large construction site uses suboptimal repair and distribution strategies to minimize wait times for tools and workers. ■ Engineering "loans" some technical staff to an overburdened manufacturing support function. ■ Warehousing keeps more than minimal inventory to expedite production schedules. ■ A sales group refrains from contracts that strain design capability and/or production capacity. ■ Audiovisual departments at universities incur operating losses to avoid making individual departments buy their own AV equipment.

their engagement is permanent. It's appropriate to create substantial systems and permanent rewards to support IDC beyond that point.

Characterizing cooperation more precisely at a variety of levels enables an entirely different kind of conversation. It's then possible to distinguish between the current state versus the desired state. You can speak more directly about how to move a pair of departments to the next highest level, or up two or more levels.

Table 14.2 suggests some of the conditions that could force a pair of departments to adopt a more demanding level of cooperation.

ASSESSING THE NEEDED LEVEL OF IDC

The current level of IDC can be quite different than the level required by the work. Read down the "forcing work conditions" column of Table 14.2 to determine the needed level of IDC for a given situation.

Assessing the Context

Cooperation is the result of minute-to-minute decisions people make during their work day. There isn't much leverage in structure or policy; the most useful hooks will be in personal or interpersonal interactions, group dynamics, or culture.

Table 14.2	Work-Required Level of Interdepartmental Cooperation	
	Forcing work conditions	**Forcing environmental conditions**
Level 1: Information sharing	■ No one group has all the needed information for successful performance. ■ Although work steps are self-contained within a department, information needs cross boundaries	
Level 2: Joint problem solving	■ Solving an important problem requires more skills or resources than any one department can provide. Once the immediate problem is solved, the groups fall back into separate operation.	
Level 3: Joint project management	■ Joint action is required by the mutual interdependence of tasks across departmental or divisional boundaries as well as the shared commitment of resources. ■ All groups involved are accountable for schedule and budget on deliverables requiring coordinated effort.	■ Pressure for a faster time-to-market forces concurrent (rather than sequential) work.
Level 4: Joint interface management	■ Departments with a high volume of interactions across a variety of work activities have a pressing need to improve the efficiency and accuracy of handoffs. ■ An ongoing concern, as opposed to the time-limited concern with a single project	■ The frequency of errors or dropped handoffs begins to threaten the company's competitiveness. ■ Customers complain of the time required for approving sales contracts, negotiating product specs, or other multiple-department activities.
Level 5: Joint process maintenance	■ Key work processes span several functions or work groups ■ Without coordinated effort, the work processes easily erode and handoffs routinely stumble. ■ Anticipation of repeated need for the process makes process redesign and/or maintenance worthwhile.	■ Major customers might force attention to better process management as a condition of sale. ■ Competitors who have emphasized process excellence pose a compelling threat due to their faster, better, cheaper delivery. ■ Regulatory constraints may force the company to maintain carefully documented and enforced work processes.

	Forcing work conditions	Forcing environmental conditions
Level 6: Optimization	■ Strong interdependence of functional activities requires that each group's activities and volume be coordinated with every other group's activities and volume. ■ Any one group that over-functions might threaten the balance of the whole and compromise the quality of the final product.	■ Complex technologies and/or work processes create fragility of overall operation ■ Delivering competing products to the market-place forces an integrated strategy across divisions to preserve credibility in front of skeptical customers.

Table 14.2 continued

I recently did some research into cooperation at several organizations. The key issue was identifying those dimensions that were critical for more advanced co-operation. What proof did people need to see to believe that supporting another department would be worth the effort? What would tell people that any efforts to cooperate would be nullified or reversed? The interviews, survey data, and observations, together with my consulting experience, defined a number of key variables. Each of these have been characterized in terms of the worst case, best case, and a more neutral case between the two requirements.

Read through the table, perhaps with a specific situation in mind as it relates to work or information passing from one department to another. Work through each row and determine which scenario best captures the current state of affairs for the groups with which you're concerned. Feel free to modify or blend the descriptions to arrive at a clear statement of your current situation. Then read the following suggestions for using the exercise to set up a significant improvement in interdepartmental cooperation.

Table 14.3 is actually the backbone of several powerful practices to enhance co-operation between departments. It's designed to highlight awareness of the various themes that support a shift to higher levels of interdepartmental cooperation. The basic strategy is to make the current situation visible and open to discussion. Once the themes are out on the table, the players involved can start to create the supports needed to move ahead. For example, if the group is extremely poor on decision making, then an organizational development consultant might negotiate a structured decision-making process and then guide the group through it meticulously.

		Improving Interdepartmental Cooperation
Table 14.3		

		Worst-case scenarios
A	**Density of interpersonal relations**	There are few (or no) personal connections between departments. Individuals relate from behind job definitions and functional loyalties. There is little or no awareness of the others as unique individuals.
B	**Trust**	There is little or no trust between the groups involved. They are more likely to avoid each other than engage. Anyone attempting to bring about change is quickly ignored or marginalized.
C	**Rewards**	Individuals and groups are rewarded for achieving goals that might jeopardize the goals of other individuals or groups. Rewards reflect individual performance even if team contribution is weak.
D	**Cultural differences**	The two groups involved represent distinctly different cultures. Events are interpreted through very different frames, so common understanding is difficult at best.
		For joint problem solving and beyond
E	**Decision making in meetings**	Decisions are never clearly made or recorded. What seems like a decision is more likely a way to close off a frustrating debate. Whatever decisions are made, they quickly unravel in political wrangling after the fact.
F	**General interpersonal skills**	Individuals are clumsy at even basic interaction. Conflicts quickly escalate, and few people, if any, can soothe situations and pave way for resolution. Virtually no one can talk about communication patterns when needed.
G	**Sophistication of group dynamics skills**	Key players are oblivious to the need for process planning. Focus on the task is easily undermined by inadequate planning about facilitating information exchange, involving players, and problem solving, decision making, or handling conflict.

Neutral scenarios	Improved scenarios
There are some relationships across departmental boundaries. Except for times of real stress, people can relate to each other as unique individuals as well as within their job categories.	There is a rich network of interpersonal relationships, so that even under stress, people can relate to each other's unique qualities as well as their job category.
Although there is enough trust to engage, it is still limited; the two groups are willing to talk through issues. Although differences are unavoidable, they are willing to negotiate enough agreements to allow joint action.	The two groups trust each other, assuming each other's best intent when there are disagreements. When frictions emerge, the groups move quickly to repair the basic relationship.
Individuals and groups are partially rewarded for supporting the goals of other individuals or groups. Rewards primarily reflect individual performance, but poor team contribution is a limiting factor.	Individuals and groups are rewarded for an organizational outcome as much as for achieving their own goals. Rewards reflect a balanced mix of individual performance and team contribution.
Although the two groups have some significant cultural differences, they also identify themselves as part of an overall culture. Major cultural symbols are shared, allowing for some common understandings.	The two groups are merely subgroups of a common culture. They share enough values and symbols that clear communication is possible, even if there are disagreements.
Decisions are clearly made and captured. Planning for implementation or deciding on accountability is uneven. Decisions often unravel in the face of implementation problems. Decisions are sometimes reversed without reference to the originating meeting.	Decisions are understood to be a key outcome of meetings. Once made, they're clearly identified and captured. Implementation and/or accountability is negotiated before the meeting is closed. Reversals are taken back to the originating meeting for reconsideration.
People are fairly competent at straightforward expression of ideas and preferences. Emotionally loaded encounters are volatile or avoided. Conflicts that do erupt are addressed, but may leave relationships damaged.	Communication about straightforward or emotionally complex topics is generally successful. When conflicts arise, they are resolved and relationships are repaired. People can discuss communication patterns when needed.
Key players understand the need for process design but are only infrequently able to react appropriately without significant consulting input. When process arrangements become inadequate, it is difficult for the group to name the problem and negotiate a different process. Important actions are often taken without concern for how they might compromise relationships.	Key players and a critical mass of others understand the need for process design and implementation. Important meetings are well orchestrated to be both effective and engaging. When processes are stumbling, people are willing to cite the process and negotiate better ways of working. Important decisions are approached with an eye to how they might affect important relationships.

Table 14.3	continued	

		Worst-case scenarios
H	**Value on cooperation**	Cooperation is viewed as the strategy of those with little political clout and/or personal weakness. Offers to accommodate others or pursue a compromise are taken as a sign of weakness.
I	**Goal compatibility**	Goals of different groups are clearly contradictory; every group's success implies another group's failure. Conflicts over priorities swiftly rise to the highest executive levels because no one is confident about what they would decide without asking for a judgment. Groups are openly competitive in front of customers.

	For joint process management and beyond	
J	**Readiness for change**	Change is viewed with suspicion and resistance. Previous change efforts have exhausted the groups' openness to new efforts.
K	**Structure vs. process orientation**	People think of work solely in terms of departments, procedures, and job descriptions. Horizontal work processes are only viewed as "hand-off" problems. Attempts to define work processes inevitably degrade into individual job responsibilities.
L	**Senior support for cooperation**	Competitiveness between groups clearly derives from friction between senior executives. Local efforts at cooperation are considered foolish, given the inevitability of executive-level sabotage.
M	**Goal clarity**	Goals are unclear or only financial in nature. Groups constantly fight over interpretation of goals or adequacy of plans. Attempts to clarify goals only prompt more political infighting.
N	**Quality of vision**	Departments pursue immediate and short-term objectives (e.g., sales volume, profit, market share) without a clear sense of the larger organizational direction. Employees frequently wonder how their jobs fit into the overall corporate picture.

Neutral scenarios	Improved scenarios
Different interests are viewed as a common feature of business, and compromise is viewed as an unfortunate necessity to maintain momentum. Although people are willing negotiators, they may all be somewhat dissatisfied with outcomes where everyone sacrifices somewhat.	Cooperation is viewed as essential for success, both individually and collectively. Overly competitive or stubborn behavior isn't tolerated. Rather than accepting compromise, conflicts are pursued until new, more creative solutions that satisfy all concerned are finally crafted.
Although goals are in conflict to some extent, the need for trade-offs is acknowledged. Negotiating for joint outcomes is supported. Senior executives are only involved in the most complex debates because many understand what their judgment would be without asking. Best value for customer is a dominant theme in resolving conflicts.	Goals are congruent or independent. Groups only have to deal with joint resource needs. Senior executives are articulate enough about priorities that managers and directors can typically speak on their behalf without having to secure advance approval.
Change is viewed as difficult or painful but also as a necessary feature of business. The groups participate willingly but without enthusiasm.	Change is viewed as a constant. It's embraced not only willingly but with some enthusiasm. Employees view change as an opportunity or an adventure.
People think of work as a mix of (vertical) structure and (horizontal) process. Resources and work control are still vested primarily with department heads, but process owners are informally identified and have some authority. Performance reviews reflect inputs from both sources.	Work is viewed primarily in terms of processes, with departments expected to support processes through developing skilled staff in specific areas. Process owners are formally identified and have substantial control over resources and rights to resolve work issues.
Although cooperation is viewed as a strength, there is a contravening value on competition, individual accountability, or strong resource constraints that eventually pits groups against each other despite their best efforts.	Senior executives treat cooperation as a strong value and regularly confront their own tendencies to compete unnecessarily. Senior executives are reasonably thorough in creating structural supports for cooperation.
Although there are significant gaps in goal clarity, there is at least a willingness to discuss the issues and move toward greater clarity. Goals are often not very durable, shifting easily under the rationale of "market responsiveness."	Basic goals are clear, but there's enough room for creativity or strategic options that they remain inviting. There's a vigorous debate about how to best articulate strategic goals. Adjustments are made in response to fundamental changes in the market, not short-lived fads.
Departments or divisions have sense of local direction, but there's no integrating vision for the organization overall. Employees understand their roles in achieving at least the smaller objectives.	Overall organizational vision is articulated and institutionalized; employees act in ways that support the overall vision (even if it means that their work is suboptimized) for the company's greater good.

Or, if a group has little trust, a respected and neutral party might be a valuable aid in capturing agreements and highlighting each completed one.

Table 14.3 can be used in the following ways:

- Have the heads of two departments highlight the paragraphs they believe are the most accurate for their situations. Review their assessments together and look for areas where they agree or disagree on the current state. Get agreements on what group process supports they might need to move ahead to greater cooperation.

- Have members of two departments highlight the applicable paragraphs individually and then collectively in a workshop format. Help the group see the possible structural or systemic causes of their worst-case dimensions and negotiate for some next steps.

- Have a key person sitting atop the two departments identify the most applicable paragraphs for the current relationship between the departments. Use his or her assessment to determine what kind of intervention would fill in the gaps for the two departments.

In each of these strategies, the process is different only on the surface. The underlying goal is to make interpersonal dynamics or group processes more visible and negotiable. Most important features of inter-group relations degrade precisely because people aren't fluent in talking about process issues or negotiating a different process to meet new challenges.

It's often useful to assess different levels within the focal departments. Department heads often believe their relationship is more advanced than how it's reported by staff. Department heads, for example, might consider their groups capable of joint process management, although their staff reports that even joint problem solving is awkward.

Again, it's useful to get those differing perceptions out into the open. It's not a question of who's right or wrong but simply that people perceive the same situation differently. The difference is made visible, and, therefore, discussable. Rather than push for convergence around a single point of view, it's more useful to think of ways to accommodate both viewpoints.

Table 14.4 provides some general suggestions for addressing the worst-case situations.

Table 14.4		Addressing Worst-Case Scenarios
		Recovering from worst-case-scenarios
A	**Density of interpersonal relations**	Use every joint activity as an opportunity to get to know each other. Start with lunch, and mix up the seating arrangements. Have people put their favorite sport under their name on their nametag. Have everyone introduce themselves by sharing something no one at work knows about them. Celebrate birthdays as a group. Use anything that highlights the personal features of the lives of the participants; make them into individuals rather than just job titles. Use nonwork dimensions to soften functional distinctions.
B	**Trust**	Trust is built in small steps. Highlight agreements, and be meticulous in checking that they are doable. Start each meeting by reviewing agreements and noting each time someone follows through. When agreements are broken, explore for extenuating circumstances and push for agreements to be honored in the future.
C	**Rewards**	Push for greater alignment in rewards. People should be rewarded for supporting each other rather than ignoring each other. For example, part of their compensation could be contingent on the success of the other group. Bonuses could be determined by cooperative efforts entirely. Performance reviews must include efforts that support "the other side," even if it compromises the goals of the home department.
D	**Cultural differences**	Build a new culture, acknowledging and honoring the most significant features of the two separate cultures. Adopt signs and icons that make the shared culture visible. Find some external activity (e.g., company baseball team, a charity event, soccer games) that everyone can orient to as a group.
E	**Decision making in meetings**	Negotiate a decision process within the group. Assign one person (possibly a neutral facilitator) who will march the group through the process. Keep track of decisions made (for example, write them in longhand during the meeting, and make copies for everyone before they leave). Normalize the fact that decisions might require revision, but go after anyone who routinely undermines the group's decisions. Make sure changes are brought back to the group for collective reconsideration.
F	**General interpersonal skills**	Structure the exploration of conflict. For example, have people write down the pros and cons of a situation and explore them with someone else in the group, just to enhance the clarity of their concerns. Then get the conflict "up on the wall" so people can stand side by side and work on the problem that's "up there" rather than point fingers at each other face to face. Use a similarly structured process for any other difficult interaction.

	Table 14.4 continued	
		Recovering from worst-case-scenarios
G	Sophistication of group dynamics skills	Have a group-process expert lay out the "game plan" for each activity. Ask for the agreement and support of the players. If the process starts to bog down, stop the action and review the process. Suggest some alternatives and then restart. Have a neutral party interview with everyone beforehand to ask if there are any strong personalities that routinely obstruct group meetings. Plan ahead for how to neutralize them; for example, someone who dominates the discussion can be centralized by having people work on their own or in groups of two. Then every group puts its main idea up on the wall before anyone is allowed to rebut any particular statement.
H	Value on cooperation	Make sure someone with clout and credibility can underscore the need for cooperation, not just as a nice idea but also as a strategic necessity. The two department heads should always sit side by side and speak with one voice. If they have disagreements, resolve them privately. Their staunch refusal to collaborate must change, even if that means reminding them that their positions aren't permanent, despite substantive contributions they've made in the past.
I	Goal compatibility	The department heads as well as the senior executive team will have to re-solve the goal conflict. The new, joint goals must be reflected in resource allocation and rewards. If senior leaders can't resolve the conflict, the effort will fail.
J	Readiness for change	Acknowledge the group's suspicion or cynicism. Break up the overall ef-fort into smaller, more palatable chunks. Develop the group's criteria for a successful change, and make sure those criteria are met.
K	Structure vs. process orientation	A process orientation represents a significant mind shift; it won't come easily or immediately. Capturing processes with "swim lanes" allows peo-ple to keep some link to their functional perspective and at the same time see the entire process and how it relates to other areas. Problems with smooth, error-free hand-offs are often the stepping stone to a process perspective. Providing rich feedback from the customer of the process is another impetus for working on a smoothly flowing process rather than just "doing the job."
L	Senior support for cooperation	The best approach is to confront executives with the cultural conse-quences of their conflict and let them decide how much they want greater coordination across departments. Be prepared to offer support for any attempts to improve their relationships; it probably won't happen easily if it hasn't happened already. The next best approach is to have someone act as a buffer between the senior executives and the coordination effort. He or she will need a clear charter from the senior managers and the courage to remind them of their commitment when they start to interfere.

		Recovering from worst-case scenarios
M	**Goal clarity**	Once again, the best solutions require senior executives to address the goal disparity and craft a common goal that can unite the warring departments. You might need to draft some possible goals and present them to the executive team for selection.
N	**Quality of vision**	Vision is always the responsibility of senior executives. If they haven't provided a clear vision in the past, they can't expect substantial improvement in interdepartmental cooperation. If they open to the possibility, the departments involved might be able to identify the vision that would justify their greater cooperation.

Table 14.4 continued

MOVING TWO STEPS AT A TIME

Sometimes the need for the increased performance from better cooperation is so great that an organization is compelled to jump two or more levels at once. Obviously, it's a more manageable shift to attempt one level, but sometimes that's not possible.

If the need for greater cooperation is so strong that groups must make a two-step jump or greater, these guidelines will increase the chances for success.

■ *Make sure that senior-management support is informed and authentic.* Senior teams often underestimate the importance of their support for such aggressive ventures. In particular, they must know that the level of cooperation exhibited by their behavior will be the upper limit of any effort at greater cooperation further down in the organization. If the senior team is competitive and manipulative with each other, it can hardly expect anything better from the staff. And staff will be looking to the team to decide if a call for much greater cooperation is genuine and likely to succeed. If the senior team is lackluster in its attitude, the staff will be, too. If the senior team is sporadic in its support, the staff will be, too. If the senior staff clearly recognizes the need for more cooperation and acts consistently with that need, then others will follow suit.

■ *Work first with the heads of the two departments.* Department heads can't afford to stumble. They must speak with a unified voice, demonstrating the spirit and the letter of whatever charter calls them to work together more closely. The symbolic meaning of their behavior is both a critical resource as well as a potential stumbling block. If they sit on opposite sides of the table at joint meetings,

CASE STUDY: REACHING CONSENSUS IN A TRADITIONAL ORGANIZATION

A software company held an annual planning event that had become legendary for its rancor and predictably bad outcomes. The company's sales divisions penetrated different market segments: Windows computers, UNIX computers, and networks and mainframes. Each sales group was asked to come to the meeting with its three top priorities for future software development. The meeting was chaired by the engineering department, which was overburdened with conflicting demands for development trajectories as well as support for previous versions of the software. The annual planning meeting was engineering's attempt to get consensus on a sustainable program. It was usually an unmitigated disaster.

Each sales group would show up with its "three top priorities," but each proved to be the tip of an iceberg. The three requests usually turned into dozens, each supported by a compelling argument based on estimated sales if only the group could get the "few obvious improvements" presented at the session. After all the sales divisions made their presentations, the engineering department faced a list in excess of 100 changes. Then the fun began.

In previous years the meeting usually disintegrated into a heated debate that never converged. Frustrated, the CEO would step in and take back the decision about development priorities. Knowing the CEO would eventually be drawn into the fray, the sales groups made presentations that were aimed more at convincing him of the merit of their requests; they cared little for either convincing others in the room or listening to their positions. There was little, if any, interest in either negotiation or sacrifice for the good of the whole. Anticipated sales numbers were routinely "optimistic" (i.e., inflated). Once a relatively new manager offered to take something off his request list, but the other managers just rolled their eyes and made side comments about the fact that "He was new." Clearly, they thought he would be "wiser" in the future.

The organization as a whole was fairly traditional in structure. Work was defined by jobs and departments, with little appreciation for horizontal work flows. Cooperation was at level one: information sharing (see Figure 14.1). When a significant problem required cooperation to solve (a level-two task), employees' skills and attitudes fell short of the process. Everyone assumed that working together to enhance the "software development process" was an event that would take years to accomplish. Thus, the first step was to bring these groups along to level two, knowing that the shift had to be achieved within the context of a traditional organization.

Because the lack of cooperation was mostly among the sales divisions, the consultants started there by bringing the department heads together to reflect on their current context. Each one took a copy of the worst-case versus best-case scenarios described in Figure 14.3. They highlighted the paragraphs that were closest to their assessment of the situation. Despite their antagonistic stance during the planning meetings, there was a surprising consensus in how they perceived the mess they were in.

Given their assessment, several strategies were relatively clear. Although some relationships existed across the sales divisions (mostly due to job shifting), the level of trust was too weak to support an effort to deal with the problem through face-to-face interaction. Company rewards would most likely seduce them away from any cooperative efforts. Their capacity for handling conflict—which was inevitable—was equally minimal.

Because their group dynamics skills were poor, the need for an external facilitator as well as careful planning was obvious. The department heads would most likely resort to backroom politics if they were left to address the issues on their own. The company's values made cooperation suspect. Anecdotal comments suggested that most managers viewed collaboration as a sign of weakness and even linked it to lack of masculinity.

The bulk of the responsibility for initiating change fell on the CEO. He needed to acknowledge his shortcoming in defining the required outcomes earlier, and in linking them to the company's overall success. He also needed to clearly state the absolute necessity of a workable plan for software development that respected the finite capacity of the engineering department and maximized the benefit for the *company as a whole rather than the isolated benefit of each sales group.*

The next step was somewhat counterintuitive. The CEO announced that he wasn't going to step in at the end and resolve conflicts as he'd done so often in the past. Instead, he'd leave this to the discretion of the department heads, although he would hold them accountable—collectively and individually—for the quality and timeliness of the final decision. In his stead, the CEO introduced the external consultant, who was available to the department heads to help map out a different procedure for the annual planning meeting. It was clearly understood that the consultant worked for the CEO and would report to him about the effectiveness of the implementation.

The map for the meeting was fairly straightforward to design but tough to implement. The three department heads would sit side-by-side rather than as widely separated as possible, which was their usual preference. They would speak from a single script and announce with a unified voice that the group was to come up with a single priority list. Failing that, they would resort to a relatively random procedure for selecting requests from each group in turn until the available development resources were exhausted. Because no one would benefit from the default procedure, this proposal focused interest on how to work things out more deliberately.

The criteria for choice were clarified. Compatibility with existing software would be determined by the engineering department. Anticipated revenue would count heavily, but the estimates had to be defensible. If projected sales weren't realized during the coming years, the group's credibility would be downgraded for future planning sessions. Thus, each group had a vested interest in offering more reasonable estimates. Finally, the department heads would present a summary of the overall strategic direction of the company that was reviewed by the CEO and would determine which market segments might have some priority over others. The UNIX market, for example, was highly volatile and might drop out of the company's strategic vision if it failed to show the rapid growth of previous years.

The CEO had one more important role to play. The bonuses of the three department heads had to be interlinked. For starters, he decided that 20 percent of the bonus of each department head would depend on the sales success of his or her peer departments. This merely reinforced the needed attitude of cooperation. It also encouraged them to look for opportunities to cross-sell, which had previously meant simply giving away rewards and bonuses to another department. If the 20-percent figure was insufficient, the CEO made it clear he would consider moving it to 40 percent or higher until he saw the level of cooperation he wanted. The generally macho culture strongly pushed for maintaining independence and control, but the thought of having their fate in the hands of others was enough to get the department heads' attention and motivate them to attend to new ways of doing business.

The next planning session was hardly a fairy tale ending, but people did sense that the winds had shifted, and sales staff began trying to figure out the new rules and how they could succeed under the new regime. The CEO had to be coaxed and cajoled more than once to keep out when conflicts failed to resolve quickly. Reminding him of the rabid conflicts of previous years was usually enough to squelch any temptation to return to his earlier managerial habits. The department heads needed a practice session to get their presentation down. But the mere act of designing the planning session together created new relationships among them. The facilitator brought not only a wealth of options they'd never considered before (e.g., new group-process scenarios, conflict management strategies, and better decision-making tools) but also a constant reminder that the CEO was watching, and waiting.

Perhaps the most rewarding outcome was making a dent in the high-testosterone culture that defined cooperation as weakness. Everyone had experienced a compelling example of the benefit of working together. "Working together" was redefined as a challenging and complex undertaking, something only a "real man" would be able to master. The former belief in stubborn confrontation had been redefined as "petty squabbling," something more typical of children. Some of the star achievers in the organization made a public commitment to cooperation. They acknowledged that it was a new and sometimes puzzling effort but the value was undeniable. Numerous similar ventures will be required before cooperation becomes a widespread value in the company, but each venture has proved easier than the last. And for major organizational changes, that's a great outcome.

it will convey a message quite different than if they sit side by side at the head of the table. If their statements are clearly jointly authored and delivered together, they will communicate that the effort is sincere. If they speak from obviously separate notes, then that will reveal they haven't worked together even in the simplest ways. Their respective staffs won't any better.

■ *Buffer the effort from possible contamination from other departments.* A dramatic shift in the operation of two departments will undoubtedly send ripples through the rest of the organization. Changes in behavior can disrupt the lives of those in related departments enough to provoke defensive responses. If the two departments involved are making strides, the departments around them might set up subtle roadblocks. Even if the interference is only minor, other departments might find the new behavior threatening to the culture they've come to know.

CONCLUSION

Greater cooperation between departments has been elusive precisely because organizations are structured along functional and hierarchical lines. Without fully intending to do so, companies develop vertical lines of authority that imply horizontal blocks. Dotted-line relationships and other mechanisms are fairly pallid against the vertical structure typical of most organizations.

As the work world becomes more complex and markets more global, and as customers begin demanding smoother, more integrated products and services, the costs of the functional and hierarchical organization have become unbearable. Tomorrow's successful organizations will be those that can work as one team with information and activities integrated across departmental boundaries. In fact, they'll be the companies that have almost no boundaries at all.

Successful companies in a process-dominated business world will be the ones that think in terms of horizontal workflows rather than top-down controls. Employees will see their teammates as people who work in the same process, rather than in the same department.

Note: The author gratefully acknowledges this chapter contribution by Jerry Talley, Ph.D. Talley spent fifteen years on the Stanford University faculty, teaching in the Department of Sociology. He continues to lecture widely at Stanford, DeAnza, and Santa Clara universities. During the early 1980s, he began his organizational consulting career, starting with organizational assessments to identify complex company problems. Based on the knowledge gleaned from more than 250 corporate engagements, he expanded his practice under JLTalley & Associates, a consulting venture providing advanced problem solving, improved decision making, process improvement, and implementation of strategic plans. Descriptions are available at *www.JLTalley.com*.

Chapter 15

Using Dynamic Simulation in Business Process Management

W hen the Wright brothers built their airplane, their design could be captured adequately on a few sheets of paper with static drawings. When Boeing built the 777, it replaced paper drawings with computer-aided design (CAD). Had the Wright brothers had 21st-century CAD tools and the knowledge to use them, their first plane would have flown sooner, farther, and much more safely.

CAD technology provides four very powerful advantages over static representations for designing and improving not only 777s but also business processes (see Figure 15.1).

First, information about the current status of any modeled process can be available to anyone instantly. The technology ensures that information in a properly managed CAD repository is the most current version. Moreover, the repository isn't limited to drawings and text. It can contain anything that can be recorded, and that information can be cross-referenced simultaneously with other information in multiple ways.

Figure 15.1	Computer-Aided Design Provides a New Approach to Business Process Management

- Shared, reliable, and complete memory ("We all know what we each know.")
- Shared complex concepts
- Alternative views of the same elements
- Visual language to capture and measure process dynamism

214 Process Mapping, Process Improvement, and Process Management

Second, complex assemblies of information can be constructed and maintained as components and used as subsystems wherever required (e.g., a process titled, "How we handle complaints from class A customers.")

Third, multiple perspectives of the same elements can be maintained so that all the elements in one perspective are always identical to those same elements seen from another perspective. If, for example, from the workflow perspective, a role description is changed, then instantly anyone looking at that role from another perspective, such as reporting authorities, will see the consequences for that perspective (e.g., for supervision).

Fourth and perhaps most important, CAD diagrams can be dynamic. When a workflow process diagram is changed, the system doesn't merely draw new boxes on a diagram; it simulates the consequences of that change to the whole workflow system and its outcomes. Then it informs both the workflow manager proposing the change of those consequences, along with everyone who would be affected by them.

Commercial CAD systems that include dynamic process simulation have been around for more that twenty years, as Figure 15.2 indicates. During the 1970s, office automation spurred on the first generation of business process analysis (BPA) tools—known as "computer-assisted systems engineering" or CASE tools. When the reengineering movement for business process redesign emerged during the 1980s, the information technology industry began developing CAD-based BPM tools that focused more on capturing and representing user descriptions of complex business processes. The advent of enterprisewide packages that covered

---

Figure 15.2 Computer-Aided Business Process Management

Information technology (IT) has encouraged business integration and is a source of business process management tools such as CAD.

- 1970 to 1985—"CASE" BPM tools invented to manage the IT infrastructure
- 1985 to 1995—BPM tools extended to "reengineer" core business process
- 1995 to today—BPA tools are now powerful enough not only to record and make easily available all that everyone knows about business processes, but also to simulate complex business processes such as management (i.e., design, evaluate, and implement whole lines of business).

everything from finance, to customer relations, to manufacturing, has allowed new approaches for documenting, redesigning, and communicating ever more complex ways of doing business. Today's tools are fully adequate to capture as well as simulate business processes to whatever level of detail is useful.

Business process analysts haven't evolved as quickly as their tools, however. Most are still capturing, representing, and disseminating process changes through static media. Whiteboards, Visio, PowerPoint, Word and Excel are the dominant tools of most of today's business process design teams.

Such media are particularly useful for process redesigns that aren't bigger than a "headful." That is, so long as one person or a small team can completely understand the process to be changed and its consequences. Still, even in these situations, dynamic simulation tools, which can quickly and inexpensively identify risks and provide defensible measures of expected benefits, typically reduce the effort required and produce a more insightful and useful result.

Turn to CAD tools whenever speed of response, reduced risk of failure, or coping with complexity is required. Figure 15.3 summarizes the benefits of using dynamic simulation for business process mapping and analysis. These powerful tools exist; the challenge is to develop the business art of using them.

What follows is a discussion of that emerging art and the forces behind it.

Figure 15.3 **Benefits of Simulation-Based Process Mapping**

- Using computer simulation to develop and evaluate prototypes, dynamic simulation enables an organization to combine the analysis of business opportunities with a redesign of business processes.
- "Runable" prototypes capture the current "as is" process, as well as future "to be" processes. They measure benefits and risks as well as costs of proposed changes.
- Because the as-is prototype is dynamic, it can generate performance measures that can be validated against actual performance. This enables comparison of the to-be prototype against hard data, rather than relying only on its face value.
- Using prototypes, a management team can bring together the ideas of all those involved across multiple organizational levels.

THE MARKET NEED FOR BPM SIMULATION TOOLS

An Internet search for "business process" and "simulation" produces more than a quarter of a million hits. Today, at least 100 software suppliers offer one sort of business simulation or other. Although this market is highly fragmented, it's beginning to consolidate. IBM and Microsoft are two of the 800-pound gorillas in this domain who are making their presence known.

Two primary market needs drive this growing supply of new tools. First, business processes are becoming more complex, especially as they integrate information technology (IT) systems. Increasingly, best practices such as lean manufacturing require organizations to examine all processes simultaneously from end-to-end of their business lines. Mapping complex processes with static tools such as Visio typically results in very complex maps that the mapmakers must interpret. Often these are difficult to validate and hard to use when designing alternative processes. Conversely, maps created by process owners and team members using dynamic simulation tool sets capture all the complexity but reveal only as much as is necessary for the specific analytic or design task at hand.

Second, simulation-based tools can create a safe testing ground for experimenting with alternatives and communicating new ways of working. This is possible because, unlike static maps, simulations "run"—i.e., they produce behavior, and you can measure it.

In addition to these two primary market needs, regulatory forces are encouraging the development of simulation tools for capturing and improving business processes. A number of regulatory bodies require process improvement documentation. Three rather different sources of such regulation deserve note:

- Continuous process improvement methodologies characterized by such standards as ISO 9001:2000 not only call for documentation and improvement of business processes but also documentation and improvement of the improvement processes themselves.
- The Sarbanes-Oxley Act of 2002, the new federal financial reporting rules, requires that the CEO and CFO sign off on the accuracy of both the company financial statement and the process that produced it.
- Subsequent to the World Trade Center disaster of September 11, 2001, more companies are expected to have, and prove that they have, flexible and effective continuity and disaster-recovery processes.

Figure 15.4	Business Process Resources

- Business process trends advisor:
  www.bptrends.com
- *Business Process Management: The Third Wave*, by Howard Smith and Peter Fingar (Meghan-Kiffer Press, 2003)
- Business Process Management Group:
  www.bpmg.org
- BPML4WS is an acronym that stands for business process modeling language for Web services:
  www.bpmi.org/downloads/BPMLBPEL4WS.pdf

Another market force worth noting is the increasing demand of dynamic business process analysis tools and techniques associated with advances in back-to-back process integration among companies mediated by the Internet. This demand for inter-company process integration is already leading to the development of a standard notation for describing business processes (i.e., "business process modeling language" or BPML). The BPML movement is driven by major suppliers, including IBM, and has already been adopted in many process simulation products. Proponents of the notion that Internet-based business integration will radically transform the structure of business are coalescing into groups such as the Business Process Management Initiative (BPMI) and the Workflow Management Coalition (WfMC).

All this activity has become known as the business process management movement. Some resources for exploring this movement are shown in Figure 15.4.

BENEFITS OF DYNAMIC PROCESS MODELING TOOLS

The chief attraction of these new tools is that they offer the potential to make business process "knowledge management" a practical reality. Examples of how they're used to do this are presented in "Application Domains" later in this chapter. Six features in particular enable dynamic mapping tools to provide "better, faster, and cheaper" business process management.

Multidimensional Information Repository

The leading dynamic process simulation suites are built on relational databases capable of an unlimited variety of associations. This provides the ability to store and reference any kind of information that can be digitized (including diagrams, video clips, and Web references). A sample list is shown in Figure 15.5.

With proper controls, such an information base can be maintained so that it's always up to date and guarantees users are looking at the most current and authoritative data. More important, it enables process knowledge managers to build, store, and easily access as many different sorts of associations among knowledge elements as are useful. Another indexing dimension can be added at any time with little additional effort.

Such databases allow fast, high-quality manipulation. They can guarantee that only a properly authorized agent may change a given element of the content. They also ensure that any element affected by a change in some other element immediately shows that effect, and can even report that effect immediately to all those who've asked to be informed.

Figure 15.5 | Elements of Computer-Based Business Process Analysis

The repository can include any information that can be recorded, e.g.,

- Events, activities, and products (i.e., work process)
- Timelines, deadlines, and time periods
- Original locations
- Training programs
- Issues (e.g., free text)
- Beliefs or assumptions
- Requirements
- Goals
- Hierarchies
- Strategy maps
- Data elements
- Video clips
- Web references
- Associations between elements (user-defined)
- Any element can have multiple, user-defined properties

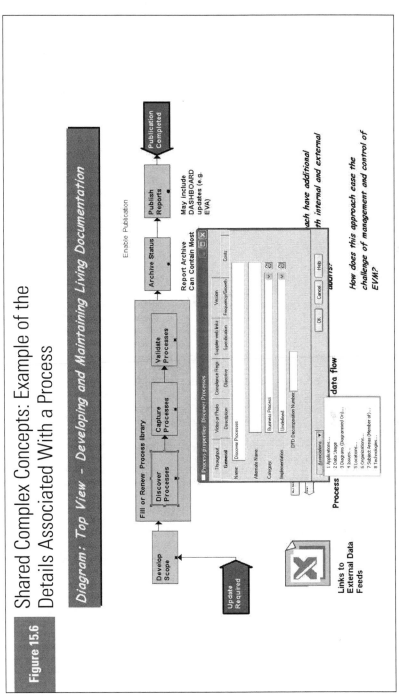

Figure 15.6

Shared Complex Concepts: Example of the
Details Associated With a Process

Diagram: Top View – Developing and Maintaining Living Documentation

Note: The screen shots shown in this chapter were produced using "Corporate Modeler," one of the leading modeling tools now in its tenth edition (CM10) from Casewise Corp. See *www.casewise.com*.

Figure 15.7 Coordinated Alternative Views of the Same Concepts

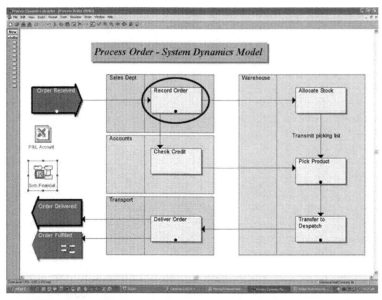

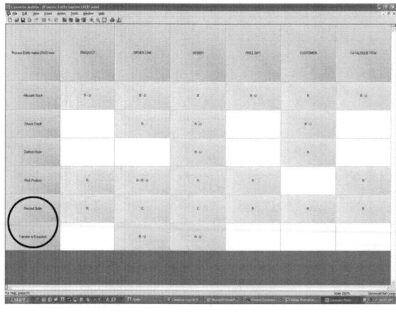

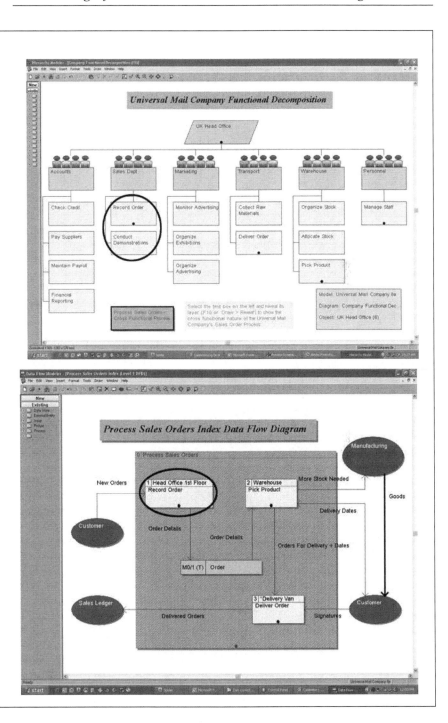

Display Complex Concepts

Dynamic process simulation suites enable process analysts to group information elements in a variety of overlapping ways. For example, in Figure 15.6 a cluster of elements define the process called "Discover Processes" for a particular organization. The process box labeled "Discover Process" (in the smaller circle) is shown in its position in the overall process flow across the top of the window. The expanded view in the large circle shows the details that make up the "Discover Processes" process. In this case, the process management team decided that each subprocess will have eleven different types of information associated with it, which are ranged as menu tabs across the top of the exploded process in the large circle. These include a video clip and compliance regulations. The process analysts have also decided that each process will have eight different associations with other elements wherever they may be in the process model. These predefined categories include associations with specific issues, organizations, or locations. Should the need arise, the team can add a new association category (e.g., with a process sponsor or primary customer).

Multiple Coordinated Views

Dynamic simulation tools support the construction of alternative views (such as maps or matrices) of the same process from distinct perspectives while preserving consistency. In Figure 15.7, the relationship between the process "record order" and other processes is shown from four perspectives. Proceeding clockwise, they are: (1) process flow, (2) functional reporting, (3) data flow, and (4) data elements usage and responsibilities. Note that if any characteristic of the process is changed in any of these perspectives, then that change and its consequences are immediately available in each of the other three perspectives.

Most of the leading process simulation tools contain not only a set of predefined perspectives, such as process flow and data flows, but also a generic mapping tool that allows process managers to build unique or highly tailored perspectives.

Dynamic Simulation

The fourth and most novel feature of dynamic simulation tools for capturing and manipulating process knowledge is that they're dynamic. One critical piece of information is necessary to create dynamic process diagrams, however, and that's throughput. A process team must identify how much, or how many, per unit of time and with what variation pass through each process step.

Figure 15.8 shows a tool supplier's approach to documenting throughput. Although only the amount of service time and its distribution is required, it's often useful to track other throughput elements such as batch sizes or number of servers available.

With throughput information, it's possible to produce not only static maps but also those that can be run. These latter substantially reduce the challenge of validating that they're accurate and complete. Static maps, whether they're "as is" or "to be," can only be validated by a walk-through inspection, which can be time-consuming and tedious, especially with complex processes.

In contrast, dynamic maps facilitate validation in three ways. First, users can establish consistency rules and set up the program to monitor whether they're followed. Such rules might range from simple (e.g., each off-page connector has a corresponding on-page connector somewhere else) to complex (e.g., an "inclusive or" that splits a task into two parallel tasks is followed by an "inclusive and" to bring each case together again further along in the process.) Figure 15.9 shows how the violation of such a rule is noted and how the tool indicates where a violation was detected.

Second, because a dynamic map produces behavior and corresponding measurements when it's run, the model's as-is performance measures can be examined and compared against reality. A to-be map's performance measures can be compared to the expectations of process owners and participants. Presumably a simulation that produces the same behavior as the real process being simulated is more valid than one that doesn't. Figure 15.10 shows that after 159 orders have been received, only thirty have been delivered, and there's a backlog of 112 unprocessed orders at the "record order" point. Does this backlog behavior match reality?

Figure 15.11 shows some of the types of behavioral data such simulations can produce. For the process being simulated, notice that while the average touch time to complete an order is 4.2 hours, completion takes an average of 33.81 calendar hours.

Third, a simulation can substantially improve on a visual walkthrough by exhaustively identifying each and every path through the process and the behavior associated with it. The team doing a walkthrough can refer to the simulation to be sure that all the alternative paths and cases that a given map represents are checked. A simulation can also help the walkthrough team by identifying performance measures between any two points on the map.

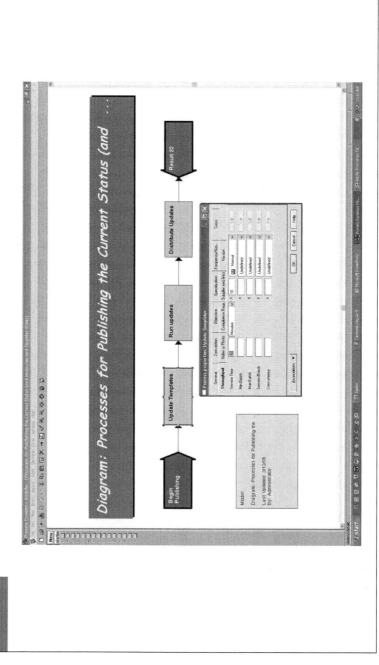

Figure 15.8　Throughput Is Required for Simulation

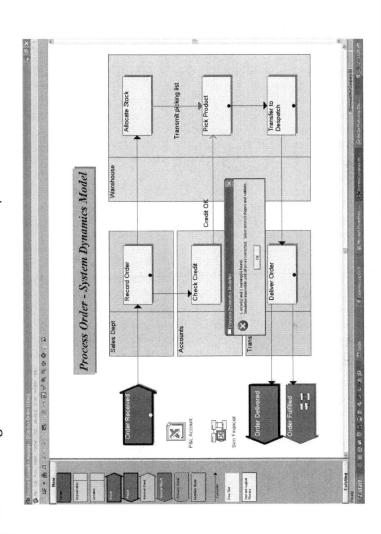

Figure 15.9 Run the Diagram to Determine Consistency

Figure 15.10 Run the Diagram to Generate Performance Measures

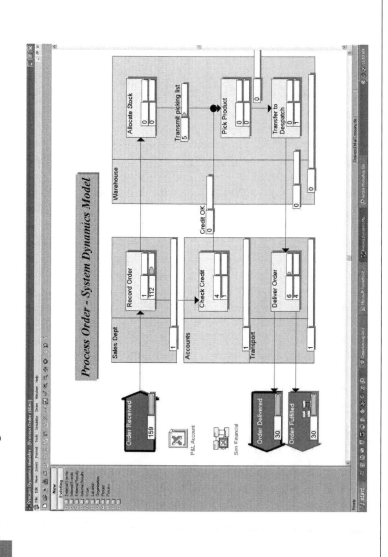

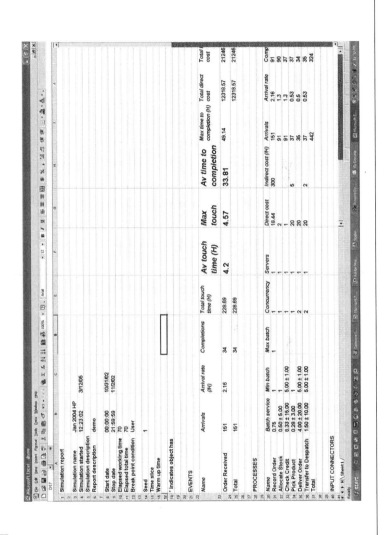

Figure 15.11 Reporting Dynamic Behavior

Publishing

Process mapping tools contain automatic publishing features. Once a publication template has been set up for print or Web distribution, the task of producing an update of the most current process information and maps is automatic. With very little overhead burden, this permits an organization to make available the most current documentation of all processes. One standard way of maintaining process documentation with these tools is through a company intranet Web site. This site is updated automatically as often as processes are updated. In this way, the process in practice and the process as documented can be kept synchronized.

Configuring Workflow Applications

Many dynamic simulation process analysis and modeling suites contain export functions that enable a tested to-be model to automatically transfer to, and set up in, the company's IT workflow application. This eliminates much, if not all, of the work required for IT experts to translate a new business process from model into application requirements before configuring the IT application. Today's dynamic business process simulation suites are making a reality of the automatic workflow programming dreamed of by CASE tool suppliers decades ago.

CATEGORIES OF BUSINESS PROCESS SIMULATION TOOLS

A model is a tool for thinking. We use models every day; they're a basic feature of the way people think. Faced with buying groceries on the way home from work, for example, a person calls up in memory the model of the route home and the location of stores along the way. He or she considers which route and what stores will most likely yield the goods required and meet accessibility criteria.

Figure 15.12 identifies the two major characteristics of models used by people to improve their thinking and problem solving: the knowledge in their heads and the shared description used to communicate and build on that knowledge. It's important to realize that only part of a model can be externalized. Although analogies can be dangerous, it might be useful to think of a corporate model as an organization's game plan. The model (or game plan) is useful only to the extent that its users understand it and have the capability to act it out.

Figure 15.12 A Model Consists of Two Parts

- A team that's thinking about a situation (what's in team member's heads)
- A (shared) description that serves as a tool for thinking (what's in the computer and on paper)

Therefore, the limits of models are:
- The skill and ability of the modeling team to think
- The clarity and ease of use of the toolset used to facilitate thinking

A model that's so complex that its end users no longer understand it is both dangerous (i.e., likely to be wrong) and unlikely to be persuasive.

Figure 15.13 There Are Many Types of Models

- Soft models (e.g., simple static maps and text)
- Hard static models (e.g., multilayer static maps, text, and spreadsheets such as Microsoft Visio and Excel)
- Systems dynamics models (based on feedback control)
- Hard simulation models
  - ☐ Predictive (e.g., linear programming)
  - ☐ Descriptive (e.g., behavioral mapping)
- Heuristic (e.g., neural networks)

There are many types of models that are useful in business management, as Figure 15.13 summarizes. For a more complete explanation, see *Tools for Thinking: Modelling in Management Science* by Michael Pidd (John Wiley & Sons, 2003).

The type discussed here is particularly useful in describing, analyzing, and improving business operating processes in which people, rather than machines, are the principle players. With this goal in mind, descriptive business processes that map behavior deserve to be distinguished from the other modeling approaches shown in Figure 15.13.

Soft models refer to those we hardly think of as models. They emerge in conversations in forms ranging from napkin doodles to whiteboard drawings to carefully drawn Visio maps.

Hard static models are the next step up in complexity and include blueprints or company budgets.

In the area of business planning, "systems dynamics models" (not to be confused with models of dynamic systems) have been in use since the 1960s. This type of model is especially appropriate where complex social, political, economic, and technological forces interact in a system of feedback loops, and little is known except the direction of the feedback.

Heuristic models are just in their infancy. They're most easily thought of as self-defining models. In this category are computer programs that include neural networks, which are self-modifying—that is, they "learn." For example, a self-modifying program could be given a goal of identifying damaged apples coming down a conveyer belt and be told when it correctly identifies a bad apple or identifies a good apple as bad. The program is expected to modify itself so that it becomes increasingly accurate in its identifications and makes fewer type one or type two errors.

From the perspective of improving business process management, hard simulation models are most immediately useful. These are discussed further below.

HARD SIMULATION MODELS

As the size of the team using a model increases and the amount of detail that must be remembered and integrated rises, it becomes increasingly useful to have a more powerful, complete, and external record to share. At the executive team level, a business process model of six to ten core processes might be sufficient to facilitate a discussion. But as the executive extends its communication to a larger circle of management and eventually to frontline supervisors and staff, the detailed meaning of each core process, its interactions with other processes and with any other relevant component of the business requires an ever-expanding explosion of details. Hard-system models are expandable, usually computer-based descriptions of as much detail as a modeling team requires to discuss, and control, a particular system.

The psychological advantage of hard-simulation models is that they not only "work" in a way similar to the way that people think, but they also represent a process with more efficient language than the language of static maps, text, and spreadsheets. Just as a picture is worth a thousand words for representing what one has seen, so, too, is a dynamic description worth a thousand static maps when the object of description is a process with flows that change dynamically.

Hard Simulation Models for Games and Education

Business simulation games have been around for decades in the form of role-plays. In role-playing simulations, a group acts out the process in question and reflects on the experience. In recent decades, mechanical and digital devices have been added to make role-plays more interesting and realistic. The ground-based, flight-simulation trainers used to develop student pilots' control and navigation skills are a classic example. Today, such trainers are sophisticated, computer-driven team games in which a student crew inside the trainer tries to master the skill of flying, while the crew outside the trainer presents situations that will lead to a crash, all mediated by computing.

The advent of the spreadsheet has given companies the capability to play "what if" simulation role-plays with budget alternatives. Emerging process simulation suites are beginning to supply the equivalent of simulated "flight trainers" for business process management.

With the invention of Pong, the original video game, in the 1970s, computer game designers began exploring how to create simulated environments—first for play, and then for education and training. Today, most people have at least heard of simulation games such as Simearth and Simcity. More significantly, most college graduates of the past twenty years, especially those with degrees in math or sciences, have used one or more simulations as part of their education. Companies such as Management Simulations Inc. have twenty years' experience developing and delivering business management simulations for the education market.

Predictive Hard Simulation Models

In business environments, particularly in manufacturing and research, modeling tools have been developed for predicting how physical, chemical, and mechanical systems will behave. In manufacturing, simulation tools such as Extend (*www*

.imaginethatinc.com) and Witness (*www.lanner.com/products/why_simulation.php*) provide powerful guidance for projecting how manufacturing configurations will likely perform when built. In such tools, the known behavior of components is built into the model as a whole system, and the behavior of the system is examined using various parameters that are within management's control.

An important subset of predictive simulations is Monte Carlo simulations. In these, the analyst uses some basis, such as scenario thinking, to define the range and shape of the distribution of all parameters that might affect the outcome of the behavior he or she is modeling—for example, the outcome of a retirement investment program over the course of thirty years. Monte Carlo simulation calculates the size and shape of the distribution of outcomes, given the size and shape of the distribution of inputs. Many of the risks associated with a particular "to be" are revealed by running a Monte Carlo analysis of that model and using the range and distribution of parameters required to meet the business scenarios the organization has decided it must be prepared to weather.

Descriptive Hard-Simulation Models

Business process modelers of human behavior, especially managers, require a specific type of modeling tool that captures and describes behavior without knowing the underlying rule that drives it. This type of modeling falls in the social science tradition of classical behavioral modeling. Such models record what behavior is observed (the as is) or is expected (the to be) as well as the probability distributions of the various outcomes of that behavior, without attempting to ascribe a causal rule for the observed outcome.

For programmers, descriptive hard-simulation modeling takes some getting used to, although it will likely be obvious for social scientists. There are no "do loops" of "if then/else" statements in this type of modeling. Rather, statements indicate that activity X, for example, occurs with a frequency of A, and the distribution of frequency A is B because (and only because) that's what has been observed, or that's what knowledgeable experts say will happen. If the outcomes of activity X are N1, and N2, then builders of descriptive models record for each outcome their observed or expected frequency and its distribution.

HOW DESCRIPTIVE MODELING TOOLS HELP US UNDERSTAND MANAGEMENT PROCESSES

The features of descriptive dynamic simulation models can dramatically reduce the time it takes to capture and document a process and build a consensus that the description is complete. They do this by providing immediate analysis and feedback as the model is being built.

Enable Better and Faster Validation

Validation is speeded up by instantly revealing when the rules of consistency in process mapping have been broken. Dynamic models can be used to confront the process practitioners with the consequences of their description. No longer must the business process analyst figure out whether the description he or she has been given makes practical sense. By running the model, the analyst can simply present the resulting behavior. For example, if the model description indicates that process practitioners are putting fourteen eggs into every dozen carton, the analyst can simply ask the practitioners whether this is true and, if not, ask for help in locating the root cause of the problem in the model that's producing this impossible result.

Facilitate Faster, Safer Testing of "To Bes"

To-be processes or situations are evaluated more rapidly because the simulation can project their behavior and consequences with the same speed that consequences of changes in financial assumptions can be projected by a spreadsheet. Simulations provide several other advantages for evaluating to-be situations. When set in goal-seeking mode, simulations can be asked to identify which input variables have the greatest effect on the desired output variables. Similarly, simulations can be set in search mode and directed to find combinations of factors that will produce a particular desired combination of outputs.

Provide Defensible Benefits Projections

Dynamic models can also promote management understanding by projecting defensible benefits of proposed changes. Two points should be noted here. First, benefits are almost always a result of a complex interplay of elements. Financial spreadsheets can sometimes give a reasonable picture of this complex process, but they don't reflect all the interactions that must occur for the benefits to emerge. Dynamic simulations can provide such assessments, identify how much and what sort of benefit will occur, and where, as well as the cost in time, resources, and reconfiguration.

Second, and more important, dynamic simulation can indicate what else outside a given change effort must also change to turn the benefits into a bottom-line contribution. For example, if a new approach to customer service will produce a 40-percent reduction in the amount of service effort by company staff per year per customer, questions arise about how to convert this time savings into shareholder value: "Can we redeploy some service staff?" "To where?" "How fast is the customer base rising?" and, "Are there new customer services that we should price and add?"

SKILLS REQUIRED FOR DYNAMIC SIMULATION BPM

Mastery of Process Mapping

Dynamic process modeling tools presume, first and foremost, that the user is a skilled business process analyst. Just as a spreadsheet won't turn a naïve user into a skilled financial analyst, dynamic process modeling tools don't confer the skills of good process mapping and modeling described in earlier chapters of this book. The first skill needed by a financial analyst is *not the ability to manipulate Excel but to understand the principles of finance. The same logic holds true for the business process analyst.*

Mastery of a Tool Set

Acquiring an off-the-shelf tool set for developing dynamic models of business processes is a bit like buying a grand piano. You know it's capable of producing beautiful music, but only in the hands of a skilled pianist. The pianist has two distinct skills. The first is the ability to learn and reproduce music; the second is the practiced dexterity of playing the instrument. One can be a skilled composer and create brilliant symphonies without being a pianist, and vice-versa.

Using powerful business process modeling suites requires that users be skilled not only in process mapping and analysis, but also in the peculiarities of the tool set itself. Some savvy companies have been disappointed after acquiring business process simulation tools because they put them into the hands of staff who've never done process mapping and analysis before and weren't trained in the peculiarities of the tool set itself. Effective business process analysts are made, not born.

During the early stages of adopting dynamic simulation technologies, it's a good idea to keep the three main roles of process analysis—i.e., process owners and practitioners, business process analyst, and dynamic process modeling operator—distinct. Because business process models are based on descriptive rather than predictive logic, when these tools are acquired through the company IT department, business analysts, trained in the IT approach to capturing processes, tend to use the mapping tools in static mode. Having been trained in the predictive logic of computer programming, they don't understand how to build models descriptively. Business systems analysts without a strong social science background will likely find using the descriptive approach difficult.

Command of Statistics

Key to using descriptive models of human behavior are two classical challenges of social science: the need to understand and manipulate statistics (especially means and various forms of deviations from the mean) and a sound understanding of behavioral measures and the ways in which measures can be invalid or unreliable.

To extract reliable value from descriptive dynamic simulation tools, the team using them must therefore have solid backgrounds in three distinct areas: business process mapping, statistical analysis and the design and interpretation of social science measures, and operating a dynamic business process analysis tool set.

HOW DYNAMIC SIMULATION BPM AFFECTS PROCESS CHANGE MANAGEMENT

The Change Equation

Although much lip service is paid to the importance of persuasion and building commitment for successful process improvement efforts, in many cases little practical action is taken. Motivating for change often consists of an exhortation by senior managers that change is necessary, and the result will be good for business.

The key to the motivational side of change has long been known. It consists of three very simple components and their interaction, as shown in Figure 15.14.

Individuals who must change will do so willingly, even enthusiastically, when three emotional conditions are met. First, those facing a change must be substantially dissatisfied with the status quo. Simulation makes it much easier to identify and demonstrate the problems or limitations of the present way of doing things. It's is a powerful way to change a general sense of dissatisfaction into a focused recognition of a need for change.

Of course, dissatisfaction alone won't lead to change, no matter how disturbing it is, unless it's possible to imagine a better situation and believe that it will not only work, but also that the people required to change can make it work and will be a part of the new reality. Again, simulation can provide this specific vision and allow those involved to become accustomed to the future circumstance in a way that builds confidence and enthusiasm.

Finally, it must be possible to imagine the intervening steps that will enable the organization to make the transition without crashing in the process. Simulation can help by demonstrating the feasibility of intermediate steps and identifying in advance the vulnerabilities that could arise during transition. Transition simulations can help companies avoid the trap of imagining they can accomplish the transition yet continue doing all that they're currently doing. Transition simulations are particularly useful for identifying what current activity and resource consumptions can be stopped or at least put off until the transition is complete.

Figure 15.14 **Psychological Components of Change Management**

Simulation-based business process management meets the challenge of change design, evaluation, and implementation.

However, even when dissatisfaction is high, a compelling vision is clear, and the transition path is defined, change will only happen if the benefits to those who must make the change substantially outweigh the costs and risks. Dynamic simulations, because they "perform," can provide very specific measures and demonstrations of the likely benefits not only in terms of productivity and cost savings, but also in psychological terms such as convenience, reduced risk, and reduced causes of stress.

Adopting a Continuous Change Mentality

Another major concern must be addressed when managing a substantial change in organizational behavior. The new solution imagined at the start of the change will almost certainly need to be adjusted, often repeatedly, before the transition is complete. Expressed another way, today's process management challenge isn't to go from one stable state to another, but to go from today's unsatisfactory state to one of continuous improvement. This paradigm shift, to a world of managing continuous change in processes, is greatly facilitated by simulation.

Think of the Apollo 13 rescue mission. From the moment the first oxygen tank exploded, the challenge of keeping the crew alive required one adjustment after another. The crew was saved because they and the ground support team were expecting the next challenge and psychologically ready to evaluate and respond quickly to any change in circumstances. Moreover, they weren't merely responding but also projecting what might happen next and preparing for contingencies. This constant adjustment and contingency planning was greatly facilitated by a one-for-one simulation of the spacecraft and all its components and fittings available to the ground crew.

Simulation makes it possible to quickly and safely evaluate a continuous stream of changes and improvements. Following the Theory of Constraints also becomes possible—i.e., that success will go to those who can manage their businesses as one integrated whole, as a "critical chain" in which the challenge is always to identify the current and next weakest links and strengthen them.

The Emerging Role of Process Analyst as Facilitator

Dynamic business process management is changing the process analyst's role. First, this person no longer has primary responsibility for validating the process descriptions. As Figure 15.15 summarizes, from the advent of "Taylorism" in the 1920s through operations research during the 1950s and 1960s, to systems analysis associated with office automation in the 1970s and reengineers in the 1990s, the business analyst was responsible for gathering and interpreting descriptions of the situation. He or she determined whether the description was complete and made logical sense. If the description was incomplete or inconsistent, the analyst identified possible causes and returned to the practitioners to collect missing data or obtain corrections in the descriptions previously given. This put the analyst in a position of judgment. The analyst, not the practitioners, "owned" the map in the sense that he or she determined whether the map was valid.

Dynamic simulations can put the primary responsibility for model validity back into the hands (or, more accurately, the minds) of process owners and practitioners. Recall that a model is a tool for thinking. What's most important is that the process owners and practitioners are its primary authors. Therefore, rather than informing the practitioners who supply a description that they've made a mistake or failed to supply some critical information, the analyst might take what's given at face value and present it back to them to decide whether it's accurate and complete. If,

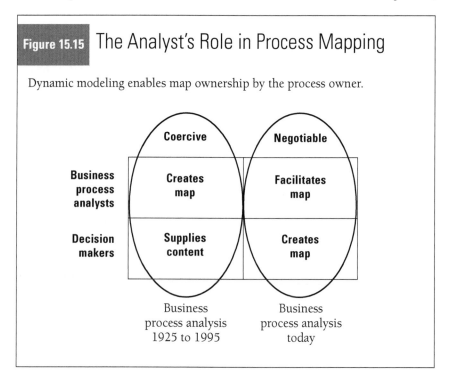

Figure 15.15   The Analyst's Role in Process Mapping

Dynamic modeling enables map ownership by the process owner.

	Coercive	Negotiable
Business process analysts	Creates map	Facilitates map
Decision makers	Supplies content	Creates map
	Business process analysis 1925 to 1995	Business process analysis today

for example, a simulation of the inputs results in the outcome that employees are putting in thirty-hour days, the analyst need do nothing more than point out that this is one of the model's behaviors and ask if it makes sense. Simulation makes it possible for process owners and practitioners to also be the primary owners of the simulation. That is, they can actively identify problems with the model and how to correct them. The simulation becomes truly their way to think about their situation.

This is important not only to ensure a more accurate model and build buy-in, but also to promote the simulation model as a tool for thinking. By actively participating in debugging the model, practitioners are practicing the art of thinking about their process. In fact, the debugging quickly shifts from an exercise in modeling to an exercise in the substantive task of improving the real business. The question rapidly shifts from, "How many hours do we really work?" to "What made us think that the we spent so much time on the component tasks that the total would add up to thirty hours per day?"

Put simply, with process simulation tools at hand, the primary role of the process analyst shifts from operations researcher to facilitator of clear thinking and communication among the extended team associated with the processes being simulated. The process owners themselves must sharpen their skills as their own operations researchers.

During the past fifty years, every senior line manager has had to learn to be his or her own chief strategist and chief financial analyst. By taking on the role of "thinking and communicating facilitator," the business systems analyst can now help the line manager become his or her own chief business process analyst.

Also, as analysts becoming less responsible for validating process descriptions, they're becoming more responsible for the psychological domains of communication facilitators and the social and/or motivational side of change management. Although the analytic skills shown on the left side of Figure 15.16 are still important, the primary skills called for in analysts are now more sales-oriented. They must help the team turn its understanding of current problems into gut-wrenching dissatisfaction. They must help the team create a compelling vision of its own. And they must assist the team to identify engaging transition steps that it believes it's capable of performing and that will lead to the desired future.

In the world of business process simulation, the label "business systems analyst" should be replaced with "business process management facilitator." This BPMF combines facilitation skills with social-psychological skills. The BPMF brings to

Figure 15.16	The Social Dimension of Change Management

Simulation powerfully addresses the social dimension of change management.

	Analytical	Social
As is	Discover	Understanding dissatisfaction
To be	Design	Motivating vision
Transition steps	Deploy	Engaging first steps

the team such skills as operations research, value-chain analysis, and business process-simulation tool operation only as required.

WHY PROCESS MAPPING IS AN ONGOING LINE-MANAGEMENT RESPONSIBILITY

The days of the functional department barons are drawing to a close. The 1990s saw the end of the independent departmental budget. The ubiquitous spreadsheet and the ease of rollup that it enabled, combined with the standardization of company financial databases, resulted in budget management becoming a true team activity where the financial interactions across departments and divisions are made evident. This forced line managers to become skilled and thoroughly knowledgeable about how their own budgets affect, and are affected by, the budgets of all other managers.

As the integration of business processes from end to end increases, it's becoming more important for a process manager to understand not only the options for improving processes in his or her domain but also how changes there affect, and are affected by, changes in processes elsewhere in the organization—including processes that might be many steps removed from his or her situation.

This can be accomplished by treating business process management as a team sport (For more about this concept, see *www.anclote.com/spanyi.html*). Just as the

---

Figure 15.17 Applications of Business Process Modeling

- Strategy planning and implementation (e.g., reengineering)
- Workflow management (especially in a back-to-back world)
- Monitoring and control processes (e.g., balanced scorecard)
- Compliance and CPI processes (e.g., ISO 9001:2000 and Sarbanes-Oxley)
- Continuity and disaster-recovery planning and implementation
- Education and training (e.g., effective knowledge management)
- Managing the information technology infrastructure and applications

---

spreadsheet and its rollup provide the playing field for the team sport of corporate financial management, the dynamic corporate model of business processes provides the playing field for companywide business process management and continuous process improvement.

Application Domains

Dynamic modeling of business processes substantially improves the ability of managers to deal with a wide variety of requirements and produce better results while controlling costs and effort. Figure 15.17 lists a subset of those applications that are briefly reviewed in this chapter.

STRATEGY PLANNING AND IMPLEMENTATION

Successfully implementing changes that are required by shifts in strategy can be accomplished when three conditions are met. As described above, those charged to undertake the change must identify the weakness of the as-is situation and be persuaded that change is absolutely necessary. They must design an alternative, to-be vision they believe will work and that will also provide compelling motivation. Finally, they must develop steps for transitioning from the existing to the envisioned state that will deploy their new vision while keeping the business running in the meantime.

Dynamic process simulation is a powerful persuader and validating tool in each of these three domains. An as-is simulation can enable a management team to identify, measure, and demonstrate the sources of weakness. Especially when faced by skeptics, simulations can persuade by allowing doubters to "see for themselves," to test their assumptions, and observe consequences.

In the challenge of implementing a new strategy, creating dissatisfaction with the as-is model can be rather straightforward. The performance of the as-is simulation can be compared to known benchmarks such as competitors' performances or best practices. It's also easy to show how much improvement is needed above the as-is situation to meet or exceed competitors' capabilities.

Simulation's role in overcoming the other two basic impediments to implementing a strategy implementation is even more significant. It's been said that enthusiasm is the feeling we get about a great idea just before we realize what's wrong with it. The problem with most strategic visions is that something's wrong with them. In almost every case, revising the strategic vision itself is one of the most important changes that occurs during implementation. Anticipating that unforeseen problems with the strategic vision are likely can cause most management teams to hesitate. Mid- and lower-level managers who know there are problems with the vision but who lack any effective way to communicate their knowledge fail to show enthusiasm and often actively resist the implementation.

Simulation greatly reduces this problem in two ways. First, it provides senior managers with a way to safely and quickly test the practicality of their vision in advance and demonstrate that it works. Second, by using this dynamic demonstration, they can create a dialogue with managers and practitioners at all levels. If, after observing the simulation, a mid-manager or practitioner realizes something hasn't been considered, it can be added. If this new knowledge is, in fact, disruptive to the vision, adjustments can be made. If it isn't disruptive, then the holder of that knowledge can be brought around to believe in the vision. He or she can be converted from skeptical resistance to active support by seeing that the proposed changes do work. Figure 15.18 demonstrates how this communication might work. Notice all the backlogged orders piling up at "record order." If this information is true, it might need correction, and if it's false, then the erroneous descriptive elements must be corrected.

One way to determine the answers to these questions is to gather experts on the record-order process and expand it to finer detail as shown in Figure 15.19.

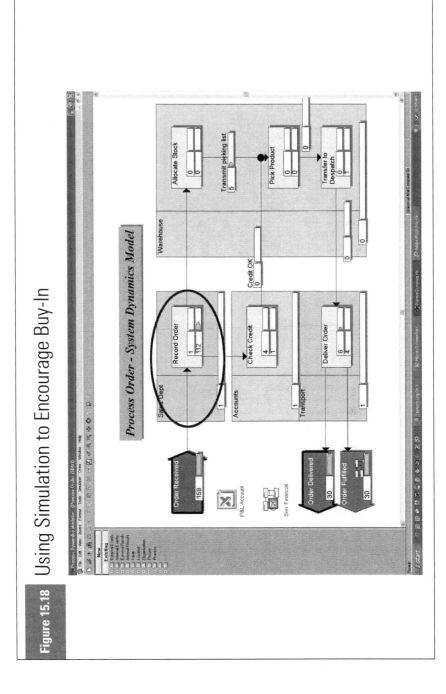

Figure 15.18 Using Simulation to Encourage Buy-In

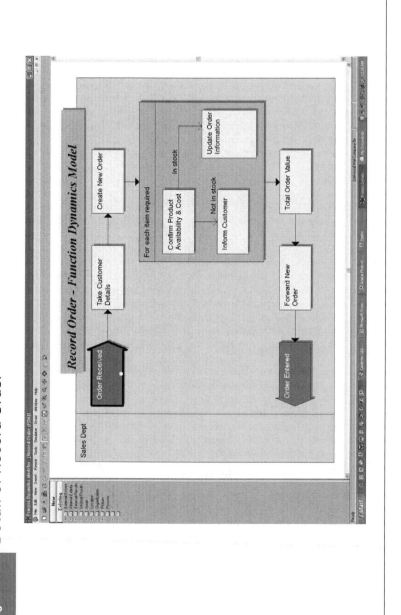

Figure 15.19 Detail of Record Order

Dynamic process simulations of to-be situations are persuasive for several reasons. They demonstrate that a proposed alternative can actually be made to work, and they can demonstrate the type, quality, and quantity of the improvement that the new way of working can be expected to produce. Conversely, such simulations can facilitate dialogue that can reveal weaknesses in a proposed alternative. They provide a way to draw out the knowledge in the heads of employees who weren't part of the process design team. Dynamic simulations can educate anyone who needs to know what some other member of the organization knows about a process or its consequences.

A dynamic simulation of a to-be situation can also be used to reduce the anxiety of change. It can show, in advance and very specifically, what will be people's new roles and even allow them to practice those roles in virtual reality.

The road from current reality to future vision is increasingly filled with twists, turns, and forks. In fact, to be has become a horizon that perpetually recedes as one moves toward it. This is what continuous improvement is all about. Many of the reengineering project failures of the 1990s occurred because they were designed as projects to be completed as designed. When the design proved faulty or the environment changed, the project derailed because continuous adaptability wasn't built into it.

Consider again, as an example, the Apollo 13 mission. Although the goal of this project was to land a crew on the moon, an accident shortly after launch changed that goal dramatically to bringing the crew back alive. The ground crew's one-for-one simulation of the spaceship became the "serious playground" for rapidly finding and testing workable alternatives to meet each new challenge.

Dynamic simulations of the organization—as it is and as it wants to be—provide similar support for rapid, safe, and cost-effective adaptability. As goals change, as problems with planned solutions arise, and as new insights into the company's conditions and capabilities become evident, controlled adjustments can be made. Conversely, such simulation capability provides an effective and efficient way to evaluate the likely effect of various circumstances to which the company believes it must be resilient.

The second great hurdle that slows and often derails implementations is a lack of clear and shared tactics for managing the transition. Again, simulation can be of great help by enabling managers of all levels to work through those tactics in detail in a virtual world. They can role-play in advance each of the transition steps, understand how something might go wrong, and practice how they would make corrections. The simulation becomes the company flight simulator. Among other things, it can allow managers and staff at all levels to practice doing their jobs in virtual space before they face reality. It can allow them to build, off-line and in advance, some of the new skills that previously could only be acquired by doing them.

WORKFLOW MANAGEMENT PROCESSES IN A BACK-TO-BACK WORLD

During the past twenty years, suppliers of IT software solutions have developed two classes of business process integration software: enterprise packages from companies such as SAP, which include customer relationship management and enterprise resource planning, and workflow integration packages such as IBM's Holosofx and Tibco's Staffware.

To successfully install an enterprise package, a highly detailed specification of the company's process must be developed and converted into systems requirements. This is especially true if the adopting company wants to be able to tailor the application to its processes rather than adapting its processes to the package. Only with a dynamic simulation can the analysis team be reasonably certain that it's captured a complete picture of the process that's already in place. Likewise, only with a dynamic simulation can the project team be reasonably certain in advance that the business process changes the organization wants to make when installing a workflow IT system will work and produce substantial value. The team knows this because the simulation runs, has been vetted by all parties affected, and produces the anticipated benefits in its virtual reality. Finally, as noted above, there will be inevitable calls for changes in mid-transition. Dynamic simulation can provide substantial additional control and safety to manage such changes.

The realm of workflow management has lagged behind the development and adoption of enterprise packages. However, with the rise of the Internet and, in particular, back-to-back dealings, workflow is coming into its own. The word "workflow" is used here in a technical sense and shouldn't be confused with the common meaning—i.e., flow of work. Workflow technology refers to computer and telecommunications hardware and software used to link a series of human activities with the activities of legacy systems (including enterprise packages) needed to integrate work processing from end to end of a line of business.

Setting up a home mortgage provides an example. Beginning with a call or visit by a customer and continuing through to the final retirement of the mortgage later, we can imagine a bank employee opening a case file. The workflow system prompts the filling out of the case initiation documents, provides help and even embedded training. The workflow system won't allow the application to be forwarded until all required fields are filled and might even run a check for some types of errors. The workflow application then routes the case to the next required activity, such as the credit check and keeps track for each next step.

This is where back-to-back potential begins to surface because the credit agency is likely another company, and both the mortgage-initiating company and the credit agency would like to modify their parts of the process as they see fit, yet maintain the interface as a fully automatic computer-to-computer exchange.

While managing the flow, workflow systems carry out a series of administrative tasks. They build a complete, thorough, and absolutely current case history of all transactions associated with each case, including a 100-percent audit file, and make it instantly available. Workflow systems monitor case progress and prevent cases from languishing at any one point by sending reminders or recommending an alternative action from a higher authority. Workflow systems develop the details of system behavior that allow the principles of both lean and Six Sigma methodologies to be applied to many types of office work.

Today's dynamic process modeling tools not only support the development and safe testing of workflow configuration requirements but also contain automatic export functions that will directly configure the workflow application with little or no human intervention.

MONITORING AND CONTROLLING PROCESSES

W. Edwards Deming once said, "If you can't describe what you're doing as a process, you don't know what you're doing." Despite the prevalence of the process prospective, it's surprising how much difficulty many managers still have with thinking about the activities necessary to execute their responsibilities as processes. Even in a pure craft-guild setting, where every product or service is unique, there are processes. Every management decision—and the overwhelming product of management is decisions—is unique, but the activities associated with making decisions, particularly within teams, is very much a process. Information must be gathered and sifted. Options must be identified and evaluated. Risks and consequences must be identified and weighed. Stakeholders must be consulted. All these activities are processes.

Some of the difficulty managers have in characterizing their activities as processes arises from confusing the concept of "process" with that of "routine." With the invention of algorithms in the 18th century, business has sought to reduce as many activities to routines as possible. Routines enable less-skilled employees to perform more complex tasks. They allow machines—beginning with the Jacquard loom and continuing to today's automatic teller machine—to execute increasingly complex yet precise routines.

As machines take on more routines of business, process management shifts its focus to the management process itself. The challenge is to improve the "meta" processes that define, implement, and continuously improve an organization's operational processes. These are increasingly becoming sets of routines, even while management activities are becoming increasingly eclectic.

It's important to recognize this distinction between design of process modeling and monitoring programs.

Monitoring systems such as the balanced scorecard are meant to provide information to guide two types of management adjustments: to operating processes (typically routines) and to management processes (typically sequences of unique decision making). Process simulation can contribute to each.

IMPROVING OPERATIONAL CONTROLS

As any Six Sigma Black Belt will tell you, the key to improving the quality of operational systems is to measure the right characteristics of the process and its outputs in the right way. But applying Six Sigma principles outside the factory can be difficult. By using a dynamic simulation, it's possible to test the usefulness of measures taken at various points, as well as their results applied at others. Two of the most common reasons why balanced scorecards fail are that the process used to reach a given target wasn't up to the job, or the measures applied were flawed.

Simulating a process can help to identify whether it will produce the desired target and to set the target itself. Simulation can reveal the second- and third-order consequences of forcing a process to yield a certain outcome (e.g., the equipment will have to run at 300 percent of capacity or never be down for maintenance.)

It can also help to identify flaws in a proposed process by showing how measures and the processes don't measure what they are thought to measure, how they measure incorrectly, or how they can be "gamed" by the people subject to measurement.

IMPROVING MANAGEMENT CONTROLS

One of the most powerful strategies for improving quality and productivity developed during the past fifty years has been innovation in management control. A now classic example from the automobile industry is the shift to just-in-time (JIT) systems. Previous theory suggested that to control suppliers, management should maintain its distance and play suppliers against one another. A customer should be careful not to become dependent on one or a small number of suppliers. JIT theory stood this principle on its head. It showed the advantages of extensive cooperation between customers and suppliers.

Simulating changes in the order in which work is done or management controls are applied can reveal the advantages and weaknesses of similar changes, whether they're large or small.

For example, as the workforce becomes better educated, and both equipment and IT quality improves, it's becoming more reasonable to consider changing the order of error correction. When is it better to ask forgiveness than permission? One of the benefits of workflow management systems is that they provide a real-time, 100-percent audit of each and every case as it progresses through an organization. This opens new possibilities for distributing authority as well as monitoring and correcting possible errors. As a principle, detecting mistakes and correcting them is thought to be more expensive than preventing them in the first place. This is the logic behind the Six Sigma movement. However, this principle isn't always true. For example, a mortgage lender that wants to maximize its return will do so by accepting a certain percentage of failed loans (i.e., errors).

So how should such a lender organize the loan authorization process? One option is to insist that an underwriter review all loans before authorization is given. However, this procedure could put the lender at a disadvantage to more nimble competitors. Alternatively, the lender might take an actuarial approach and analyze the characteristics of failed loans after the fact and use that information to qualify the next series of loans. It's a matter for empirical investigation whether preventing the first type of loan failure would be more profitable than preventing the second. Simulation can reveal not only the costs and benefits of alternatives but can also be used to investigate what changes in which processes produce the greatest benefits with the fewest risks.

COMPLIANCE AND
CONTINUOUS PROCESS IMPROVEMENT

This chapter identifies some of the uses of simulation for supporting the practice of continuous improvement. In addition, a central challenge of continuous process improvement (CPI) programs is to make them be actually "continuous." One of the disadvantages of using static business process analysis techniques and tools is that they encourage stepwise progression from one static state to another. This is caused by several factors. First, the burden of modifying and communicating static maps and documentation is substantial. Second, static documentation doesn't support easy, fast, inexpensive and low-risk testing of change ideas. Third, static documentation makes it difficult to anticipate second- and third-order effects and consequences that might be many steps away from the point of change. Fourth, static documentation doesn't enable easy measurement of what the benefits of change will be, nor easy identification of what else must change for the benefits to be harvested in a desirable form.

All these impediments increase the burden of change. Simulation not only reduces each substantially but provides two additional useful features: It makes audits of CPI and other process reviews much easier and more effective, and it enables "evergreen documentation," that is, maintaining the process record in digital form, typically as a Web site. By making the dynamic simulation repository the repository of ISO 9001:2000 or other required documentation, and by using the automatic publishing features of such tool sets, an organization can maintain its process descriptions as a continuously updated "intranet" site. There needn't be a lag between when a process change is on line and the availability of that description in the "official" process records.

Evergreen documentation combined with simulation capability can ease compliance quality management systems as well as audits by ensuring the following:

■ Only the current description of each job is available at the job location (e.g., via the company intranet)

- The process as documented is the process in action (because the simulation documentation, when it runs, produces the observed behavior).
- The dynamic walkthrough simulation enables speedy demonstration of the process as intended and exhaustively identifies all routes and outcomes.

CONTINUITY AND DISASTER RECOVERY PROCESSES

In the last few years, continuity and disaster-recovery planning have taken on a more important role and, increasingly, a government-mandated role. Typically, the first challenge after a major disruption is triage—i.e., how do we stop the bleeding and prevent any further damage? Second, are there workarounds to maintain viability while, third, repairs are made and full capability restored?

Dynamic simulation of the business line from end to end vastly speeds up the decision making required in all three of these analytic challenges. It allows the consequences, especially the second- and third-order consequences of alternative actions, to be anticipated immediately. So one can ask, for example, "If we lose 50 percent of our vaccine supply, but we stop service to our "C" class customers and serve all of our "A" class customers, which of our "B" class customers should we serve to minimize risks of further disruption?"

One might expect whole industries in critical areas such as medical vaccines or national power grids to develop enterprisewide dynamic simulation models, from raw materials to final application of finished goods and services.

A more mundane but also generally more productive use for this sort of analysis is planning and managing the lifecycle of a production or distribution system. Even without a disaster at hand, as time passes, questions arise concerning when to begin building a new facility and when to stop routine maintenance on the old and phase it out. Using simulation models to manage lifecycle planning can provide the framework for disaster-recovery planning and thereby greatly reduce the additional cost of such planning.

EFFECTIVE KNOWLEDGE MANAGEMENT

One of the biggest constraints in most organizations is that knowledge about "how we do things around here" is confined to very local settings. Managers and workers who are two layers apart (or sometimes only one layer, in this era of gold-collar knowledge workers) have little or no idea about the process the other uses to complete his or her tasks. Generally, it's safe to say that across departmental boundaries so little information about processes flows, that a manager in one department can make only the most general guesses about how a change in the processes of his department will affect the processes or products of any other department. The goal of enabling "all of us to know what each of us knows" about business processes is facilitated by dynamic business process simulation applications. The repository, process maps, and dynamic connectedness, when combined with tools to enable a management team to construct whatever perspective is required, make dynamic mapping a rich enough language to enable companies to be truly "learning organizations."

Such organizations use dynamic corporate modeling and its associated repository and publishing capabilities in the many ways shown in Figure 15.20.

Executives can call upon this approach to enhance their ability to think more deeply and thoroughly about what they're doing and why. Models can be used to persuade skeptics to buy in, but they can also encourage executives to consider the concerns and genuine challenges raised by those skeptics. By providing a safe and relatively low cost test environment, this approach enables executives to learn about a greater number of alternatives through exploration and trial and error.

Staff can be served by such an approach to corporate knowledge management and learning in multiple ways. Two stand out: (1) Such an approach can provide skill-building practice in a safe environment where the consequences of mistakes can be shown; and (2) error prevention can be learned. Not only employees but also customers and suppliers can be shown "how and why we do things this way."

In addition to these two uses, dynamic corporate modeling can provide managers with a means to identify what knowledge might be missing or need to be transferred from one place or team to another. It can facilitate the embedding of knowledge in workflow applications or its provision

Figure 15.20 Learning With Dynamic Corporate Modeling

- Executive development
  - ☐ Thinking about what we want to do
  - ☐ Achieving buy-in
  - ☐ Safely test hypotheses
- Staff training
  - ☐ Practice (building skills)
  - ☐ How and why we do things

in other on-demand modes by identifying what educational materials should be associated with each process.

PROCESSES FOR MANAGING IT INFRASTRUCTURE AND LARGE-SCALE APPLICATION PACKAGES

As noted in Figure 15.2, process modeling tools were invented by the IT industry to serve its own particular needs to understand user requirements and thereby guide the development of IT applications and infrastructure. That need is bigger and more complex than ever. Thus, when we consider the implications of dynamic simulation of business processes on the design, implementation, and maintenance of a company's IT application suite and infrastructure, we've come full circle. The IT era spawned the need for, and the development of, tool sets to fully describe business processes dynamically. To provide the infrastructure that integrating complex business processes now requires, these tools must be used to establish detailed requirements for all the infrastructure, including physical plant, locations, IT configuration, and so on. Figure 15.21 provides a schematic of the vast domain of knowledge that must be assembled and managed to operate a business from end to end, from strategy to tactics, from short term to long term.

Fortunately, CAD-based business process management systems suitable for the task are now available.

The progress of IT adoption and adaptation, beginning with office automation decades ago, has created the need for dynamic modeling as a core competency for business process management in the 21st century. It's also produced the tools to make such a business art possible.

CHAPTER SUMMARY

Because they "run" and thereby identify their consistency and the measures of their performance, dynamic process maps greatly reduce the effort and "touch time" needed to produce validated as-is models. For similar reasons, the process of building a consensus concerning the preferred to-be model is eased. Due to their dynamic nature, such maps quickly reveal the consequences of taking alternative actions.

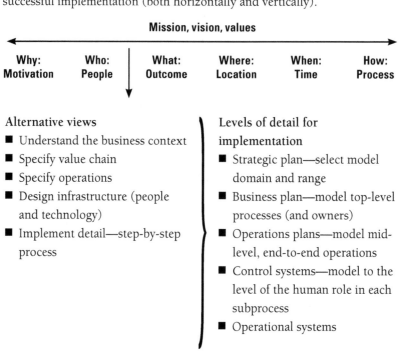

Figure 15.21 — Schematic of Necessary Business Knowledge

Dynamic corporate process models identify and track all elements critical for successful implementation (both horizontally and vertically).

Mission, vision, values

| Why: Motivation | Who: People | What: Outcome | Where: Location | When: Time | How: Process |

Alternative views
- Understand the business context
- Specify value chain
- Specify operations
- Design infrastructure (people and technology)
- Implement detail—step-by-step process

Levels of detail for implementation
- Strategic plan—select model domain and range
- Business plan—model top-level processes (and owners)
- Operations plans—model mid-level, end-to-end operations
- Control systems—model to the level of the human role in each subprocess
- Operational systems

Cheaper

Dynamic corporate modeling substantially reduces the cost of process management by reducing the amount of effort required to create and deploy process maps. Mistakes are expensive, but a mistake made in a test environment can be not only inexpensive but can actually produce positive value by pointing the way to an effective solution. Dynamic corporate modeling can help a company supply higher value for lower cost by moving error detection and correction from a change's implementation phase to the design phase. It reduces the risk and cost of experimenting with alternatives.

Better

Corporate modeling-based solutions to problems are better in two important ways. First, from an analytic standpoint, they're more verifiably correct and workable. They provide testable "proof of concept." But they're also better from a social or psychological standpoint because they enable more stakeholders to participate by contributing their knowledge and hypotheses. Because they produce behavior, simulations from such modeling efforts are powerfully persuasive to employees, customers, suppliers, and regulators.

Greater Customer Satisfaction

The ultimate measure of a process's contribution is the satisfaction of the customer who needs its output. This is true not only of the external customer but of each internal customer who depends on the output of the processes that precede his or her process. Dynamic corporate modeling can turn this chain of customers into a more satisfied team. It can facilitate at least three types of process improvement that boost customer satisfaction. First, such process management makes possible more tailoring of processes to meet more of the customers' requirements. Second, it can allow the customer to take a more active part in producing the desired service. Third, such modeling doesn't have to be limited to the organizational boundary but can extend to the domains of customers and suppliers. Therefore, in the same way that such modeling can optimize the design of companywide rather than department-specific solutions, tradeoffs made by and for the customer can be more easily identified, negotiated, designed, and implemented.

When desktop spreadsheets were introduced in the mid 1980s, the general reaction of most managers was, "Who needs these?" Yet, in fewer than ten years, the answer became "I do."

What line manager needs dynamic modeling of the processes for which he is responsible? Any manager who:

- Expects to continuously improve his or her processes while reducing the risk of testing alternatives
- Integrates his or her processes into a larger system
- Demonstrates to regulators and auditors that his or her practices match their requirements
- Educates employees as well as persuades them to commit to implementing changes

■ Believes that more effective communication, planning, and strategy is necessary
   to stay one step ahead of the competition

Note: The author gratefully acknowledges this chapter contribution by Victor C.
Walling Jr., Ph.D. For the past eight years, Walling has been investigating and applying
computer-based aids to the processes of business management and strategy implementation. During this time he co-founded Organizational Engineering, which helps organizations use computer-aided design technologies, especially simulation, to improve the
quality and effectiveness of management teams. He spent ten years as a senior strategy
consultant at SRI International's management consulting division, followed by six years
as head of IT application strategy for the Royal Dutch Shell Group in London and The
Hague, then ten years with Unilever in Rotterdam and London.

Along with a doctorate degree in innovation management and a master's in public policy analysis, both from Stanford, Walling has a master's degree in educational
psychology from the University of Washington. and a bachelor's degree from Seattle
University in philosophy. He can be reached by e-mail at *vic@organizationalengineering
.com*.

Appendices

Design Principles
for Process Redesign

As a general guideline, the following categories of principles should prove helpful:

■ Principles 1–16: use for work structure
■ Principles 17–19: use for information flow
■ Principles 20–30: use for design guides
■ Principles 31–37: use for organizing people
■ Principle 38: use for general guidance

See Chapter 10 for a more detailed discussion of each of these.

1. DESIGN THE PROCESS AROUND VALUE-ADDING ACTIVITIES

Know what the customer of the process needs, wants, requires, and desires. Any time you transform information or material into something the customer wants, you're performing a value-adding activity. Pull those steps out of your "as is" process and ask, "How can we do these value-adding steps in the most efficient and effective way possible?" In other words, try to create a process that is only value-adding steps.

As you answer the above question, try not to discuss who will do any particular activity or where the activity will be performed. If you combine the "what" of the activity with the "who" at this stage, it can kill getting to a creative, unique process solution.

2. WORK IS PERFORMED WHERE IT MAKES THE MOST SENSE

Once you have a great flow, it's time to figure out who should do what. Let your common sense be the guide. When you apply design principle No. 1, some work evaporates, some new work is created, and some work can move from one department to another.

3. PROVIDE A SINGLE POINT OF CONTACT FOR CUSTOMERS AND SUPPLIERS

A single point of contact can be a person, who might be a project manager, process consultant, or customer service representative. In addition, a single point of contact could be a data repository such as an intranet.

4. IF THE INPUTS COMING INTO THE PROCESS NATURALLY CLUSTER, CREATE A SEPARATE PROCESS FOR EACH CLUSTER

The inputs and outputs of a process can often vary by complexity, type, size, and so forth. So for some variations, the process might work smoothly, but for other variations, the process might be cumbersome and slow.

If your inputs naturally cluster, then a decision diamond should be placed at the front end of your process. The question in the diamond is, "What cluster is it?" The input cluster is then routed to the appropriate process.

5. ENSURE A CONTINUOUS FLOW OF THE "MAIN SEQUENCE"

In a manufacturing process, steps that directly add value to the customer, such as delivering supplies, building the product, and shipping it, constitute the main sequence. In lean terminology the main sequence is the value stream. It's through the value stream that your organization gets revenue. Don't let anything slow the main sequence.

6. REDUCE WAITING, MOVING, AND REWORK TIME

By using the process cycle time analysis sheet, you'll find those areas with the greatest amount of waiting, moving, and rework. Use a Pareto diagram and attack the greatest time-wasters first.

7. REDUCE SETUP AND CHANGEOVER TIMES

Setup is anything you have to do before performing the task at a particular step. Setup for manufacturing is configuring the equipment so processing can be done. Do this by performing all setup activities off-line, having machine parts and fixtures that automatically fit, or pre-work done ahead of time. In service organizations, setup might require looking for a file or scrolling through a computer screen before a person can actually do the work.

8. REDUCE BATCH SIZES

Batching causes wait time for the items at the bottom of the batch, and it causes inventory to build as it moves through your process. As you cut the size of the batch, you start creating a smoother flow through the process. Ultimately, a batch size of one is the ideal.

9. SUBSTITUTE PARALLEL PROCESSES FOR SEQUENTIAL PROCESSES

A good example is in new product development, where "concurrent engineering" is used rather than "sequential engineering." Where steps in a process can be done independently of one another, without having to be in sequence, consider parallel processing.

10. PERFORM PROCESS STEPS IN THEIR NATURAL ORDER

Sometimes you look at process steps and find the sequence needs reordering. Be sure to question the logic of one step preceding another.

11. REDUCE CHECKS AND REVIEWS

In traditional and involvement organizations, it's common to find processes with numerous reviews and checks. If a process operates at a six sigma level of quality (i.e., 3.4 defects per million), the need for review should be minimal or nonexistent.

Another aspect of multiple reviews is that it encourages poor quality at the initial step. However, if the worker and reviewer know there's only one review, first-pass quality suddenly improves. This might seem counterintuitive, but removing unnecessary reviews actually boosts quality.

12. PUSH DECISION-MAKING DOWN TO THE LOWEST REASONABLE LEVEL

Are managers and executives "signing off" on things they really don't know much about? If that's the case, push decision-making down to the lowest levels to where the work is actually being done. Eliminating unnecessary signoffs can dramatically decrease cycle time.

13. BUILD QUALITY IN TO REDUCE INSPECTION AND REWORK

Identify each step that's a cause of downstream rework and delay, and then brainstorm how to make the step perfect every time, or close to perfection. Use error-proofing techniques to make process steps error-free.

14. SIMPLIFY STEPS

What could be done to make the process far less complicated than it is today so that it could be tremendously faster? What steps, operations, or procedures could be greatly simplified?

15. ORGANIZE BY PROCESS

Instead of breaking a large cross-departmental process into departmental pieces, have all employees involved in a process under one manager with full responsibility to get it done, and fast.

16. CONSIDER HYBRID CENTRALIZED/DECENTRALIZED OPERATIONS

In some organizations it makes sense to have sales close to the customer but have a centralized accounting department. This would be an example of hybrid centralized/decentralized operations.

17. BRING DOWNSTREAM INFORMATION NEEDS UPSTREAM

When you're using the frustration lens, ask people at each step what frustrates them. When you hear, "It has missing, incomplete, or incorrect information," then this design principle should be considered.

If what's coming through the process is routine and not complex, then use training, check sheets, templates, etc. for the upstream person so that he or she captures what the downstream person needs.

But if what's coming through the process is of a complex and ever-changing nature, the downstream person must be brought upstream in a redesign to get information directly from the source.

18. CAPTURE INFORMATION ONCE AT THE SOURCE AND SHARE IT WIDELY

Look for data redundancy, re-keying, and reconciliation. Enterprise resource planning (ERP) software is designed to accomplish this principle. However, be sure you know your processes first before installing an ERP system.

19. SHARE ALL RELEVANT INFORMATION

Respect everyone's information needs. Hoarding information leads to mistakes and rework.

20. INVOLVE AS FEW PEOPLE AS POSSIBLE IN PERFORMING A PROCESS

Every handoff of work or information can be thought of as an opportunity for error.

21. REDESIGN THE PROCESS FIRST, THEN AUTOMATE IT

One of the worst things organizations do is to take the as-is flowchart and then lay information technology on top of it. It's crucial to first employ process design principles, benchmarking, best practices, and lean thinking prior to automating an as-is process. Otherwise, you might end up with a modestly faster but much more expensive and still ineffective process.

22. ENSURE 100-PERCENT QUALITY AT THE BEGINNING OF THE PROCESS

There are certain places in a process where an investment in time and money are warranted. The beginning of the process is one of those places. The time and money put in the front end to ensure quality more than pays for itself in terms of reviewing and rework.

23. INCREASE FLOW AND SPEED TO IDENTIFY BOTTLENECKS

Japanese manufacturers do this with processes to identify bottlenecks and then eliminate them. Oil refiners do this on their processes to increase production (called "de-bottlenecking"). In role-playing, practice, and simulation, a process is intentionally stressed to the breaking point. It's better to break it in a test than in real life.

24. ELIMINATE BOTTLENECKS

As a part of lean thinking, each step in a process should operate at "Takt" time, which is calculated by taking the total time available per day in seconds and dividing that by the demand rate per day. Those steps that are much slower than Takt time must be broken into smaller increments or else redesigned to achieve Takt time.

25. DESIGN FOR MANUFACTURABILITY AND SERVICEABILITY

This design principle is a variation on bringing downstream information upstream. Bring a manufacturing expert or a service technician upstream into the design meetings so that a complicated design can be easily manufactured and then serviced.

26. USE DESIGN FOR SIX SIGMA (DFSS)

DFSS is a systematic methodology for achieving world-class quality in product development and manufacturing.

27. INSTALL METRICS AND FEEDBACK TO FIND AND CORRECT PROBLEMS

If you can't measure it, you can't control it. If you can't control it, then you can't improve it.

28. FIND OPPORTUNITIES FOR CONTINUOUS IMPROVEMENT

Don't stop after one reduction in cycle time, even if it's a breakthrough. Continue to measure it, learn about it, and improve the process.

29. USE SIMULATION, PRACTICE, OR ROLE-PLAYING TO TEST NEW PROCESS DESIGNS

Computer simulation technology allows users to quickly try iterations of new processes and see how they work. A non-technological solution involves role-playing and practice. The purpose is to find out what works and what doesn't.

30. STANDARDIZE PROCESSES

Sometimes the root cause of high variation in output or results is five people doing the same process five different ways. When you have this kind of variation, it's extremely difficult, if not impossible, to improve the process. However, when people standardize on the same process, and variation occurs, it's much easier to find the root cause.

31. USE CO-LOCATED OR NETWORKED TEAMS FOR COMPLEX ISSUES

Complex problems require people to pour over information and data in real time. If the problems occur regularly, consider co-locating team members. If co-location doesn't make sense, then network the team so information can flow easily.

32. ASSIGN A PROCESS CONSULTANT FOR CROSS-FUNCTIONAL PROCESSES

Most organizations manage large processes by the pieces, with each department responsible for its piece. However, when you optimize on the pieces, you often sub-optimize the whole. Who's managing and monitoring the whole? One person must have oversight over these large cross-functional processes. This will move your organization to a matrix type management of work.

33. INVOLVE PROCESS WORKERS IN ANALYZING, DESIGNING, AND IMPLEMENTING IMPROVEMENTS

In traditional and some involvement organizations, day-to-day problem solving is done solely by supervisors and management. This is a mistake. People who work in the process often have the best ideas for fixing it.

34. FORM WORK CELLS FOR SPECIAL CASES OR EXCEPTIONS

Work cells perform very well with small lot sizes and complex products. This design principle is very similar to using teams for complexity.

35. USE MULTIFUNCTIONAL TEAMS

Assign teams full responsibility for cross-functional process improvement efforts.

36. USE MULTI-SKILLED EMPLOYEES

This eliminates the waiting and coordination time between steps by people with different skill sets. Multi-skilled employees create flexibility in your organization. As work fluctuates, bottlenecks naturally occur. The multi-skilled employees can go to the bottleneck and break it.

37. CREATE GENERALISTS INSTEAD OF MULTIPLE SPECIALISTS

Generalists do well as quality control checks, dealing with routine matters, being a single point of contact, and serving as project or process leaders.

38. EMPLOY MASS CUSTOMIZATION

Use a configurator to automatically turn custom customer requests into a bill of materials. Consider how Dell is able to mass-produce thousands of computers customized to each individual and ship out each order in less than a week.

Appendix B

Process Classification Framework

E xperience shows that benchmarking's potential to drive dramatic improvement lies squarely in making out-of-the-box comparisons and searching for insights not typically found within intra-industry paradigms. To enable this beneficial benchmarking, the APQC Process Classification Framework^{SM} (PCF) serves as a high-level, industry-neutral enterprise model that allows organizations to see their activities from a cross-industry process viewpoint.

Originally created in 1992 by APQC and a group of members, the framework has experienced more than a decade of creative use by hundreds of organizations worldwide. The PCF is supported by the Open Standards Benchmarking CollaborativeSM (OSBC) database and the Collaborative's advisory council of global industry leaders as an open standard. The PCF will continuously be enhanced as the OSBC database further develops definitions, processes, and measures related to process improvement. Please visit APQC's Web site periodically for updates. The PCF is available for organizations of all industries and sizes at no charge by visiting *www.apqc.org*.

The PCF represents a series of interrelated processes that are sociotechnical in nature, are business critical, and represent six major dimensions of the organization: knowledge communities/functions, processes, content, marketplaces, culture, and organizational structure.

The PCF enables organizations to understand their inner workings from a horizontal process viewpoint, rather than a vertical functional viewpoint. Although the PCF does not list all processes within a specific organization, every process listed in the framework is not present in every organization.

History

The Process Classification Framework was originally envisioned as a taxonomy of business processes during its initial design in 1991. That design involved more than 80 organizations with a strong interest in advancing the use of benchmarking in the United States and worldwide. This initial effort was undertaken with the collaboration of former firm Arthur Andersen.

In 2003 APQC initiated an effort to revise and update the PCF to reflect new business models and emerging dynamics. With a set of key members' guidance, the updated PCF was released in May 2004.

APQC would like to acknowledge the following organizations for their participation and help: the Boeing Co., Boehringer Ingelheim GmbH, BT Group plc, Ensco International Inc., Ford Motor Co., IBM Corp., Schlumberger Ltd., Solvay S.A, and the U.S. Navy. APQC would also like to acknowledge the other APQC members that have and continue to contribute to the ongoing development of the PCF.

TABLE OF CONTENTS

Interpreting the PCF

■ *Category:* The highest level within the PCF indicated by whole numbers (e.g., 8.0 and 9.0)
■ *Process Groups:* All PCF items with one decimal numbering (e.g., 8.1 and 9.1) are considered a process area.
■ *Process:* All PCF items with two decimal numbering (e.g., 8.1.1 and 9.1.2) are considered processes.
■ *Activity:* Items with three decimals (e.g., 8.3.1.1 and 9.1.1.1) are considered activities within a process.

Example:
Deliver Products and Services (Category) (4.0)
    Plan for and acquire necessary resources—supply chain planning (Process Group) (4.1)
        Manage demand for products and services (Process) (4.1.1)
            Develop baseline forecasts (Activity) (4.1.1.1)
                Collaborate with customers (Activity) (4.1.1.2)
                    Develop performance management structures and procedures (Task) (6.3.2.1.1)

OVERVIEW

OPERATING PROCESSES

1.0   Develop Vision and Strategy
2.0   Design and Develop Products and Services
3.0   Market and Sell Products and Services
4.0   Deliver Products and Services
5.0   Manage Customer Service

MANAGEMENT AND SUPPORT PROCESSES

6.0   Develop and Manage Human Capital
7.0   Manage Information Technology and Knowledge
8.0   Manage Financial Resources
9.0   Acquire, Construct, and Manage Property
10.0 Manage Environmental Health and Safety
11.0 Manage External Relationships
12.0 Manage Improvement and Change

1.0 Develop Vision and Strategy

1.1 Define the business concept and long-term vision

1.1.1 Assess the external environment

1.1.1.1 Analyze and understand competition

1.1.1.2 Identify economic trends

1.1.1.3 Identify political and regulatory issues

1.1.1.4 Assess new technology innovations

1.1.1.5 Understand demographics

1.1.1.6 Identify social and cultural changes

1.1.1.7 Understand ecological concerns

1.1.2 Survey market and determine customer needs and wants

1.1.2.1 Conduct qualitative/quantitative assessments

1.1.2.2 Capture and assess customer needs

1.1.3 Select relevant markets

1.1.4 Perform internal analysis

1.1.4.1 Analyze organizational characteristics

1.1.4.2 Baseline current processes

1.1.4.3 Analyze systems and technology

1.1.4.4 Analyze financial positions

1.1.4.5 Identify enterprise core competencies

1.1.5 Establish strategic vision

1.1.5.1 Align stakeholders around strategic vision

1.2 Develop business strategy

1.2.1 Develop overall mission statement

1.2.2 Evaluate strategic options

1.2.3 Develop and manage merger/acquisition/divestiture strategy

1.2.4 Develop enterprise-level brand strategy

1.2.5 Develop a knowledge management strategy

1.2.5.1 Identify knowledge management needs in all core functions

1.2.5.2 Develop a business case for managing knowledge in core functions

1.2.5.3 Identify corporate and business unit responsibilities for knowledge management activities

1.2.6 Design the organizational structure and relationships between organizational units

1.2.7 Develop and set organizational goals

1.2.8 Formulate business unit strategy

1.3 Manage strategic initiatives

1.3.1 Develop strategic initiatives

1.3.2 Evaluate strategic initiatives

1.3.3 Select strategic initiatives

1.3.4 Establish high-level measures

2.0 Design and Develop Products and Services

2.1 Design products and services

2.1.1 Develop strategy and concepts for new products and services

2.1.1.1 Research customer and market needs

2.1.1.2 Plan and develop cost and quality targets

2.1.1.3 Develop product life cycle and development timing targets

2.1.1.4 Research leading technology, components, and development requirements

        2.1.1.5 Integrate leading technology into product/service concept and components

    2.1.2 Generate new products and services, and evaluate and refine existing products and services

        2.1.2.1 Translate customer wants and needs into product/service ideas

        2.1.2.2 Generate new product/service ideas

        2.1.2.3 Evaluate existing products based on NPD strategy

        2.1.2.4 Identify enhancements/extensions to existing product and services

        2.1.2.5 Define product and service functionality

        2.1.2.6 Retire outdated products/services

        2.1.2.7 Identify and refine performance indicators

    2.1.3 Design, build, and evaluate products and services

        2.1.3.1 Assign resources to product/service project

        2.1.3.2 Prepare high-level business case and technical assessment

        2.1.3.3 Develop product/service design specifications

        2.1.3.4 Document design specifications

        2.1.3.5 Build prototypes

        2.1.3.6 Eliminate quality and reliability problems

        2.1.3.7 Conduct in-house product/service testing and evaluate feasibility

        2.1.3.8 Identify design/development performance indicators

        2.1.3.9 Collaborate design with suppliers and contract manufacturers

    2.1.4 Test market for new or revised products and services

        2.1.4.1 Prepare detailed market study

        2.1.4.2 Conduct customer tests and interviews

        2.1.4.3 Finalize product/service characteristics and business cases

        2.1.4.4 Finalize technical requirements

        2.1.4.5 Identify requirements for changes to manufacturing/delivery processes

    2.1.5 Prepare for production and marketplace introduction

        2.1.5.1 Develop and test prototype production and/or service delivery process

        2.1.5.2 Design and obtain necessary materials and equipment

2.1.5.3 Install and validate process or methodology

2.1.5.4 Introduce new product and/or service commercially

2.1.6 Support product manufacturing and service delivery

2.1.7 Support design and implementation of changes to manufacturing/ delivery process

    2.1.7.1 Monitor production runs

    2.1.7.2 Identify product/service design and configuration changes

    2.1.7.3 Capture feedback to "refine existing products and services" process

    2.1.7.4 Identify manufacturing/service delivery process performance indicators

3.0 Market and Sell Products and Services

3.1 Develop marketing, distribution, and channel strategy

    3.1.1 Understand consumer needs and predict customer purchasing behavior

    3.1.2 Identify market segments and target customers

    3.1.3 Define offering and positioning

    3.1.4 Define and manage channel strategy

3.2 Develop and manage customer strategy

    3.2.1 Develop customer management strategies

    3.2.2 Establish customer management goals

    3.2.3 Develop sales forecast

    3.2.4 Establish overall sales budgets

    3.2.5 Establish customer management metrics

    3.2.6 Prepare/Analyze/Evaluate customer management results

3.3 Manage advertising, pricing, and promotional activities

    3.3.1 Develop and manage advertising

        3.3.1.1 Define advertising objectives and strategy

        3.3.1.2 Define target audience

        3.3.1.3 Engage third-party advertising agency

        3.3.1.4 Develop advertising

    3.3.2 Develop and manage communication

        3.3.2.1 Develop media budget

        3.3.2.2 Develop media plan

        3.3.2.3 Execute media plan

3.3.3 Develop and manage placement and campaign management
3.3.4 Develop and manage pricing
    3.3.4.1 Develop volume/unit forecast and set price
    3.3.4.2 Execute pricing plan
    3.3.4.3 Evaluate pricing performance
    3.3.4.4 Refine pricing as needed
3.3.5 Develop and manage promotional activities
    3.3.5.1 Define direct-to-consumer promotional concepts
    3.3.5.2 Plan direct-to-consumer activities
    3.3.5.3 Test and execute direct-to-consumer promotional activities
    3.3.5.4 Prepare/analyze/evaluate direct-to consumer promotional performance metrics
    3.3.5.5 Refine direct-to-consumer promotional performance metrics
    3.3.5.6 Define trade-to-consumer promotional concepts
    3.3.5.7 Plan trade-to-consumer activities
    3.3.5.8 Test and execute trade-to-consumer promotional activities
    3.3.5.9 Prepare/analyze/evaluate trade-to-consumer promotional performance metrics
    3.3.5.10 Refine trade-to-consumer promotional performance metrics
3.3.6 Develop and manage packaging strategy
    3.3.6.1 Plan packaging strategy
    3.3.6.2 Test packaging options
    3.3.6.3 Execute packaging strategy
    3.3.6.4 Refine packaging
3.4 Manage sales partners and alliances
3.5 Manage sales opportunities and sales pipeline
    3.5.1 Identify and manage key customers and accounts
        3.5.1.1 Develop key customer plans
        3.5.1.2 Identify priority customers
        3.5.1.3 Establish budgets
        3.5.1.4 Develop sales/key account plan
        3.5.1.5 Schedule calls to customers
        3.5.1.6 Execute agreed to sales plan
        3.5.1.7 Prepare/analyze/evaluate sales results

3.6 Enter, process, and track orders—order management

    3.6.1 Accept and validate sales orders

    3.6.2 Collect and maintain customer account information

    3.6.3 Determine stock availability

    3.6.4 Determine logistics and transportation

    3.6.5 Enter orders into system

    3.6.6 Process back orders and updates

    3.6.7 Handle order inquiries including post-order fulfillment transactions

4.0 Deliver Products and Services

4.1 Plan for and acquire necessary resources—supply chain planning

    4.1.1 Manage demand for products and services

        4.1.1.1 Develop baseline forecasts

        4.1.1.2 Collaborate with customers

        4.1.1.3 Develop consensus forecast

        4.1.1.4 Allocate available to promise

    4.1.2 Create materials plan

        4.1.2.1 Create unconstrained plan

        4.1.2.2 Collaborate with supplier and contract manufacturers

        4.1.2.3 Identify critical materials and supplier capacity

        4.1.2.4 Generate constrained plan

    4.1.3 Schedule production

        4.1.3.1 Generate site level plan

        4.1.3.2 Manage work-in-progress inventory

        4.1.3.3 Collaborate with suppliers

        4.1.3.4 Generate and execute detail schedule

4.2 Procure materials and services

    4.2.1 Develop sourcing strategies

        4.2.1.1 Develop procurement plan

        4.2.1.2 Clarify purchasing requirements

        4.2.1.3 Match needs to supply capabilities

        4.2.1.4 Analyze company's spend profile

        4.2.1.5 Seek opportunities to improve efficiency and value

    4.2.2 Select suppliers and develop/maintain contracts

        4.2.2.1 Identify suppliers

4.2.2.2 Certify and validate suppliers

4.2.2.3 Negotiate contracts

4.2.2.4 Manage contracts

4.2.3 Order materials and services

4.2.3.1 Process/review requisitions

4.2.3.2 Approve requisitions

4.2.3.3 Solicit/track vendor quotes

4.2.3.4 Create/distribute purchase orders

4.2.3.5 Expedite orders and satisfy inquiries

4.2.3.6 Record receipt of goods

4.2.3.7 Research/resolve exceptions

4.2.4 Appraise and develop suppliers

4.2.4.1 Monitor/manage supplier information

4.2.4.2 Prepare/analyze spending and vendor performance

4.2.4.3 Support inventory/production processes

4.3 Produce/manufacture/deliver product

4.3.1 Schedule production

4.3.2 Produce product

4.3.3 Schedule and perform maintenance

4.4 Deliver product/service to customer

4.4.1 Confirm specific service requirements for individual customer

4.4.2 Identify and schedule resources to meet service requirements

4.4.3 Provide the service to specific customers

4.4.4 Ensure quality of service

4.5 Manage logistics and warehousing

4.5.1 Define logistics strategy

4.5.1.1 Translate customer service requirements into logistics requirements

4.5.1.2 Design logistics network

4.5.1.3 Communicate outsourcing needs

4.5.1.4 Develop and maintain delivery service policy

4.5.1.5 Optimize transportation schedules and costs

4.5.1.6 Define key performance measures

4.5.2 Plan inbound material flow

4.5.2.1 Plan inbound material receipts

4.5.2.2 Manage inbound material flow

4.5.2.3 Monitor inbound delivery performance

4.5.2.4 Manage flow of returned products

4.5.3 Operate warehousing

4.5.3.1 Track inventory deployment

4.5.3.2 Receive, inspect, and store inbound deliveries

4.5.3.3 Track product availability

4.5.3.4 Pick, pack, and ship product for delivery

4.5.3.5 Track inventory accuracy

4.5.3.6 Track third-party logistics storage and shipping performance

4.5.4 Operate outbound transportation

4.5.4.1 Plan, transport, and deliver outbound product

4.5.4.2 Track carrier delivery performance

4.5.4.3 Manage transportation fleet

4.5.4.4 Process and audit carrier invoices and documents

4.5.5 Manage returns: manage reverse logistics

4.5.5.1 Authorize and process returns

4.5.5.2 Perform reverse logistics

4.5.5.3 Perform salvage activities

4.5.5.4 Manage and process warranty claims

5.0 Manage Customer Service

5.1 Develop customer care/customer service strategy

5.2 Develop and manage customer profiles

5.3 Manage customer service transactions

5.3.1 Perform customer support

5.3.2 Obtain after-sale feedback

5.3.3 Respond to customer inquiries

5.3.3.1 Respond to information requests

5.3.3.2 Respond to billing inquiries

5.3.3.3 Respond to service inquiries

5.3.4 Manage customer complaints

5.3.5 Capture and assess customer feedback

5.3.5.1 Conduct qualitative/quantitative assessments

5.3.6 Measure customer satisfaction

5.3.6.1 Monitor satisfaction with products and services

5.3.6.2 Monitor satisfaction with complaint resolution

5.3.6.3 Monitor satisfaction with communication

5.3.6.4 Determine customer loyalty/lifetime value

5.4 Perform account management (i.e., service the relationship)

6.0 Develop and Manage Human Capital

6.1 Create and manage human resources (HR) planning, policy, and strategies

6.1.1 Manage/align/deliver HR strategy

6.1.1.1 Identify organizational strategic HR needs

6.1.1.2 Identify organizational tactical HR needs

6.1.1.3 Define HR and business function roles and accountability

6.1.1.4 Determine HR costs

6.1.2 Develop and implement HR plans

6.1.2.1 Develop work force plan

6.1.2.2 Develop compensation plan

6.1.2.3 Develop succession plan

6.1.2.4 Develop employee diversity plan

6.1.2.5 Develop other HR programs

6.1.2.6 Develop HR policies

6.1.2.7 Administer HR policies

6.1.2.8 Plan employee benefits

6.1.3 Monitor and update plans

6.1.3.1 Measure realization of objectives

6.1.3.2 Measure contribution to business strategy

6.1.3.3 Communicate plans and provide updates to stakeholders

6.1.3.4 Determine value added from HR function

6.1.3.5 Review and revise HR plans

6.2 Recruit, source, and select employees

6.2.1 Create and develop employee requisitions

6.2.1.1 Develop and open job requisition

6.2.1.2 Develop a job description

6.2.1.3 Post requisition

6.2.1.4 Manage internal/external job posting Web sites

6.2.1.5 Change/update requisition

6.2.1.6 Notify hiring manager

6.2.1.7 Manage requisition date

6.2.2 Recruit candidates

    6.2.2.1 Determine recruitment methods

    6.2.2.2 Perform recruiting activities/events

    6.2.2.3 Manage recruitment vendors

6.2.3 Screen and select candidates

    6.2.3.1 Identify and deploy candidate selection tools

    6.2.3.2 Interview candidates

    6.2.3.3 Test candidates

    6.2.3.4 Select and reject candidates

6.2.4 Manage preplacement verification

    6.2.4.1 Complete candidate background information

    6.2.4.2 Conduct background checks

    6.2.4.3 Recommend/not recommend candidate

6.2.5 Manage new hire/rehire

    6.2.5.1 Draw up and make offer

    6.2.5.2 Negotiate offer

    6.2.5.3 Hire candidate

6.2.6 Track candidates

    6.2.6.1 Create applicant record

    6.2.6.2 Manage/track applicant data

    6.2.6.3 Archive and retain records of non-hires

6.3 Develop and counsel employees

  6.3.1 Manage employee orientation and deployment

    6.3.1.1 Create/maintain employee induction program

    6.3.1.2 Introduce new employees to managers

    6.3.1.3 Introduce workplace

  6.3.2 Manage employee performance

    6.3.2.1 Define performance objectives

      6.3.2.1.1 Develop performance management structures and procedures

      6.3.2.1.2 Derive individual and team objectives from organizational goals

      6.3.2.1.3 Determine individual development objectives from job description/competence profile

      6.3.2.1.4 Communicate compensation system elements and philosophy

6.3.2.2 Review, appraise, and manage employee performance
    6.3.2.2.1 Perform coaching and mentoring
    6.3.2.2.2 Review employee objectives
    6.3.2.2.3 Measure performance against employee objectives
    6.3.2.2.4 Perform appraisal
6.3.2.3 Evaluate and review performance program
    6.3.2.3.1 Evaluate performance
    6.3.2.3.2 Review objectives
    6.3.2.3.3 Determine input for training plans
6.3.3 Manage employee relations
    6.3.3.1 Manage health and safety
    6.3.3.2 Manage labor relations
    6.3.3.3 Manage collective bargaining process
    6.3.3.4 Manage labor management partnerships
6.3.4 Manage employee development
    6.3.4.1 Develop competency management plans
        6.3.4.1.1 Define organizational and individual performance competency requirements
        6.3.4.1.2 Identify skills and competency gaps
        6.3.4.1.3 Develop plans to address skills gaps
        6.3.4.1.4 Define and align work outputs and metrics
    6.3.4.2 Develop employee career plans
        6.3.4.2.1 Develop career plan structure
        6.3.4.2.2 Develop performance management structures and procedures
        6.3.4.2.3 Derive individual and team objectives from organizational goals
        6.3.4.2.4 Determine individual development objectives from job description/competence profile
        6.3.4.2.5 Communicate compensation system elements and philosophy
    6.3.4.3 Manage employee skills development
6.3.5 Develop and train employees
    6.3.5.1 Align employee and organization development needs
    6.3.5.2 Develop functional/process competencies

6.3.5.3 Establish training needs by analysis of required and available skills

6.3.5.4 Develop, conduct, and manage employee and/or management training programs

  6.3.5.4.1 Reinforce training and development after delivery

  6.3.5.4.2 Evaluate training effectiveness

6.3.6 Manage employee talent

  6.3.6.1 Match resources to requirements

6.4 Reward and retain employees

6.4.1 Develop and manage reward, recognition, and motivation programs

  6.4.1.1 Develop salary/compensation structure and plan

  6.4.1.2 Develop benefits and reward plan

  6.4.1.3 Perform competitive analysis of benefit and rewards

  6.4.1.4 Identify compensation requirements based on financial benefits and HR policies

  6.4.1.5 Administer compensation and rewards to employees

  6.4.1.6 Award and motivate employees

6.4.2 Manage and administer benefits

  6.4.2.1 Deliver employee benefits program

    6.4.2.1.1 Retirement plans

    6.4.2.1.2 Insurance plans

    6.4.2.1.3 Medical plans

    6.4.2.1.4 Savings plans

  6.4.2.2 Administer benefit enrollment

  6.4.2.3 Process claims

  6.4.2.4 Perform benefit reconciliation

6.4.3 Manage employee assistance and retention

  6.4.3.1 Deliver programs to support work/life balance for employees

  6.4.3.2 Develop family support systems

  6.4.3.3 Review retention and motivation indicators

  6.4.3.4 Review compensation plan

6.4.4 Payroll administration

6.5 Redeploy and retire employees

6.5.1　Manage promotion and demotion process

6.5.2　Manage separation

6.5.3　Manage retirement

6.5.4　Manage leave of absence

6.5.5　Develop and implement employee outplacement

6.5.6　Manage deployment of personnel

6.5.7　Relocate employees and manage assignments

6.5.8　Manage employment reduction and retirement

6.5.9　Manage expatriates

6.5.10　Manage employee relocation process

6.6　Manage employee information

6.6.1　Manage reporting processes

6.6.2　Manage employee inquiry process

6.6.3　Manage and maintain employee data

6.6.4　Manage content

6.6.5　Manage HR information systems (HRIS)

6.6.6　Develop and manage employee metrics

6.6.7　Develop and manage time and attendance

6.6.8　Manage employee communication

6.6.8.1　Develop employee communication plan

6.6.8.2　Manage/collect employee suggestions

6.6.8.3　Manage employee grievances

6.6.8.4　Publish employee communications

7.0 Manage Information Technology and Knowledge

7.1　Plan for information system management

7.1.1　Understand information and knowledge needs of business and users

7.1.2　Define and administer service levels

7.1.3　Develop information management and knowledge management strategies

7.1.4　Derive information system requirements from business strategies

7.1.5　Define enterprise information system architectures

7.1.6　Plan and forecast information technologies/ methodologies

7.1.6.1　Conduct research

7.1.6.2　Manage IT offerings portfolio

7.1.7 Establish enterprise data standards

7.1.8 Establish information systems quality standards and controls

7.1.9 Establish information systems enterprise security standards and controls

7.1.10 Market IT offerings/capabilities

7.1.11 Develop and track IT plan

7.1.12 Manage projects

7.1.13 Manage IT supplier relationships

7.1.14 Manage IT customer satisfaction

7.2 Application development and maintenance

   7.2.1 Design, develop, and deploy enterprise information systems

      7.2.1.1 Conduct specific needs assessments and determine feasibility

      7.2.1.2 Develop information system architecture

      7.2.1.3 Design information system

      7.2.1.4 Acquire/develop information system

      7.2.1.5 Test, evaluate, and deploy information system

      7.2.1.6 Manage configuration of information system

   7.2.2 Manage information and content

      7.2.2.1 Develop and maintain enterprise information architecture

      7.2.2.2 Assign and maintain information ownership

      7.2.2.3 Develop and maintain a taxonomy

      7.2.2.4 Assign and maintain security levels required for each information type

      7.2.2.5 Develop and maintain information management standards, policies, and procedures

      7.2.2.6 Manage business records and documents

   7.2.3 Implement information systems security and controls

      7.2.3.1 Establish information system security strategies and levels

      7.2.3.2 Test, evaluate, and deploy information systems security and controls

7.3 Manage information technology infrastructure/data center operations

   7.3.1 Manage centralized information technology assets

   7.3.2 Deliver centralized operational services

   7.3.3 Deliver and manage distributed information technology assets

   7.3.4 Manage information technology network operations

      7.3.5 Ensure business continuity (i.e., disaster/emergency preparedness)

      7.3.6 Test, evaluate, and deploy information technology infrastructure security and controls

      7.3.7 Perform metering/billing

      7.3.8 Manage IT inventory and assets

      7.3.9 Provide operational support

  7.4 Support IT services

      7.4.1 Manage availability

      7.4.2 Manage facilities

      7.4.3 Manage backup/recovery

      7.4.4 Manage performance/capacity

      7.4.5 Manage incidents

      7.4.6 Manage problems

  7.5 Enable collaborative work

      7.5.1 Investigate specific needs of knowledge workers, project teams, and communities of practice

      7.5.2 Evaluate and select collaborative technologies

      7.5.3 Evaluate directory and expertise locator systems

      7.5.4 Define and assign roles to support collaborative work and content

  7.6 Implement new technologies using change management principles

      7.6.1 Plan change

      7.6.2 Administer change calendar

      7.6.3 Implement the change

8.0 Manage Financial Resources

  8.1 Perform planning and management accounting

      8.1.1 Perform planning/budgeting/forecasting

          8.1.1.1 Develop and maintain budget policies and procedures

          8.1.1.2 Prepare periodic budgets and plans

          8.1.1.3 Prepare periodic forecasts

      8.1.2 Perform cost accounting and control

          8.1.2.1 Perform inventory accounting

          8.1.2.2 Perform cost-of-sales analysis

          8.1.2.3 Perform product costing

          8.1.2.4 Perform variance analysis

          8.1.2.5 Report on profitability

8.1.3 Perform cost management

    8.1.3.1 Determine key cost drivers

    8.1.3.2 Measure cost drivers

    8.1.3.3 Determine critical activities

    8.1.3.4 Manage asset resource deployment and utilization

8.1.4 Evaluate and manage financial performance

    8.1.4.1 Assess customer and product profitability

    8.1.4.2 Evaluate new products

    8.1.4.3 Perform life cycle costing

    8.1.4.4 Optimize customer and product mix

    8.1.4.5 Track performance of new customer and product strategies

    8.1.4.6 Prepare activity-based performance measures

    8.1.4.7 Manage continuous cost improvement

8.2 Perform revenue accounting

8.2.1 Process customer credit

    8.2.1.1 Establish credit policies

    8.2.1.2 Analyze/approve new account applications

    8.2.1.3 Review existing accounts

    8.2.1.4 Produce credit/collection reports

8.2.2 Invoice customer

    8.2.2.1 Maintain customer/product master files

    8.2.2.2 Generate customer billing data

    8.2.2.3 Transmit billing data to customers

    8.2.2.4 Post receivable entries

    8.2.2.5 Resolve customer billing inquiries

8.2.3 Process accounts receivable (AR)

    8.2.3.1 Establish AR policies

    8.2.3.2 Receive/deposit customer payments

    8.2.3.3 Apply cash remittances

    8.2.3.4 Prepare AR reports

    8.2.3.5 Post AR activity to the general ledger

8.2.4 Manage and process collections

    8.2.4.1 Establish policies for delinquent accounts

    8.2.4.2 Analyze delinquent account balances

    8.2.4.3 Correspond/negotiate with delinquent accounts

8.2.4.4 Discuss account resolution with internal parties

8.2.4.5 Process adjustments/write-off balances

8.2.5 Manage and process adjustments/deductions

8.2.5.1 Establish policies/procedures for adjustments

8.2.5.2 Analyze adjustments

8.2.5.3 Correspond/negotiate with customer

8.2.5.4 Discuss resolution with internal parties

8.2.5.5 Prepare chargeback invoices

8.2.5.6 Process related entries

8.3 Perform general accounting and reporting

8.3.1 Manage policies and procedures

8.3.1.1 Negotiate service level agreements

8.3.1.2 Establish accounting policies

8.3.1.3 Set up and enforce approval limits

8.3.1.4 Establish common financial systems

8.3.2 Perform general accounting

8.3.2.1 Maintain chart of accounts

8.3.2.2 Process journal entries

8.3.2.3 Process allocations

8.3.2.4 Process period end adjustments (e.g., accruals and currency conversions, etc.)

8.3.2.5 Post and reconcile intercompany transactions

8.3.2.6 Reconcile general ledger accounts

8.3.2.7 Perform consolidations and process eliminations

8.3.2.8 Prepare trial balance

8.3.2.9 Prepare and post management adjustments

8.3.3 Perform fixed asset accounting

8.3.3.1 Establish fixed asset policies and procedures

8.3.3.2 Maintain fixed asset master data files

8.3.3.3 Process and record fixed asset additions and retires

8.3.3.4 Process and record fixed asset adjustments, enhancements, revaluations, and transfers

8.3.3.5 Process and record fixed asset maintenance and repair expenses

8.3.3.6 Calculate and record depreciation expense

8.3.3.7 Reconcile fixed asset ledger

8.3.3.8 Track fixed assets including physical inventory

8.3.3.9 Provide fixed asset data to support tax, statutory, and regulatory reporting

8.3.4 Perform financial reporting

8.3.4.1 Prepare business unit financial statements

8.3.4.2 Prepare consolidated financial statements

8.3.4.3 Perform business unit reporting/review management reports

8.3.4.4 Perform consolidated reporting/review of cost management reports

8.3.4.5 Prepare statements for board

8.3.4.6 Produce quarterly/annual filings and shareholder reports

8.3.4.7 Produce regulatory reports

8.4 Manage fixed assets

8.4.1 Perform capital planning and project approval

8.4.1.1 Develop capital investment policies and procedures

8.4.1.2 Develop and approve capital expenditure plans and budgets

8.4.1.3 Review and approve capital projects and fixed asset acquisitions

8.4.1.4 Perform justification for project approval

8.4.2 Perform capital project accounting

8.4.2.1 Set up projects

8.4.2.2 Record project related transactions

8.4.2.3 Monitor and track capital projects and budget spending

8.4.2.4 Close/capitalize projects

8.4.2.5 Measure financial returns on completed capital projects

8.5 Process payroll

8.5.1 Report time

8.5.1.1 Establish policies and procedures

8.5.1.2 Collect and record employee time information

8.5.1.3 Analyze and report paid and unpaid leave

8.5.1.4 Monitor regular overtime and other hours

8.5.1.5 Analyze and report employee utilization

8.5.2 Manage pay

8.5.2.1 Enter employee time into payroll system

8.5.2.2 Maintain and administer employee earnings information

8.5.2.3 Maintain and administer applicable deductions

8.5.2.4 Monitor changes in tax status of employees

8.5.2.5 Process and distribute payments

8.5.2.6 Process and distribute manual checks

8.5.2.7 Process end-of-period adjustments

8.5.2.8 Respond to employee payroll inquiries

8.5.3 Process taxes

8.5.3.1 Calculate and pay applicable payroll taxes

8.5.3.2 Produce and distribute employee annual tax statements

8.5.3.3 File regulatory payroll tax forms

8.6 Process accounts payable and expense reimbursements

8.6.1 Process accounts payable (AP)

8.6.1.1 Verify AP pay file with PO vendor master file

8.6.1.2 Maintain/manage electronic commerce

8.6.1.3 Audit invoices and key data into AP system

8.6.1.4 Approve payments

8.6.1.5 Process financial accruals and reversals

8.6.1.6 Process taxes

8.6.1.7 Research/resolve exceptions

8.6.1.8 Process payments

8.6.1.9 Respond to AP inquiries

8.6.1.10 Retain records

8.6.1.11 Adjust accounting records

8.6.2 Process expense reimbursements

8.6.2.1 Establish and communicate expense reimbursement policies and approval limits

8.6.2.2 Capture and report relevant tax data

8.6.2.3 Approve reimbursements and advances

8.6.2.4 Process reimbursements and advances

8.6.2.5 Manage personal accounts

8.7 Manage treasury operations

8.7.1 Develop treasury plan, policies, and procedures

8.7.2 Manage cash

8.7.2.1 Plan short-term cash

8.7.2.2 Manage cash balances

8.7.2.3 Manage cash equivalents

8.7.2.4 Manage cash receipts

8.7.2.5 Prepare cash forecast

8.7.2.6 Monitor credit

8.7.2.7 Monitor cash outflows

8.7.2.8 Report cash status

8.7.3 Reconcile bank accounts

8.7.4 Manage financial risks (exchange risk, liquidity, etc.)

8.8 Manage internal controls

8.8.1 Establish adequate internal control processes, including segregation of duties

8.8.2 Meet with internal and external auditors to discuss their assessments of internal controls

8.8.3 Assess the adequacy of internal controls over information systems and e-commerce

8.8.4 Create a process where employees can report suspected fraud in confidence

8.8.5 Create a formal process of investigating complaints

8.8.6 Recommend corrective action

8.8.7 Report audit results

8.9 Manage taxes

8.9.1 Develop tax strategy and plan

8.9.2 Process taxes

8.9.2.1 Perform tax planning/strategy

8.9.2.2 Prepare returns

8.9.2.3 Prepare foreign taxes

8.9.2.4 Calculate deferred taxes

8.9.2.5 Account for taxes

8.9.2.6 Monitor tax compliance

8.9.3 Address tax inquiries

8.9.4 Manage international funds/consolidation

8.9.4.1 Monitor international rates

8.9.4.2 Manage transactions

8.9.4.3 Hedge currency

8.9.4.4 Report results

9.0 Acquire, Construct, and Manage Property

9.1 Property design and construction

9.1.1 Develop facility strategy

9.1.2 Develop and construct sites

9.1.3 Plan facility

    9.1.3.1 Design facility

    9.1.3.2 Analyze budget

    9.1.3.3 Select property

    9.1.3.4 Negotiate terms

    9.1.3.5 Manage construction/building

    9.1.3.6 Dispose of old facility

9.1.4 Provide workspace and assets

    9.1.4.1 Acquire workspace and assets

    9.1.4.2 Change fit/form/function of workspace and assets

9.2 Maintain workplace and assets

    9.2.1 Move people and assets

        9.2.1.1 Relocate people

        9.2.1.2 Relocate material and tools

    9.2.2 Repair workplace and assets

    9.2.3 Provide preventative maintenance for workplace and assets

    9.2.4 Manage security

9.3 Dispose of workspace and assets

    9.3.1 Dispose of equipment

    9.3.2 Dispose of workspace

9.4 Manage physical risk

9.5 Manage capital asset

10.0 Manage Environmental Health and Safety

10.1 Determine health, safety, and environment impacts

    10.1.1 Evaluate environmental impact of products, services, and operations

    10.1.2 Conduct health and safety and environmental audits

10.2 Develop and execute health, safety, and environmental program

    10.2.1 Identify regulatory and stakeholder requirements

    10.2.2 Assess future risks and opportunities

    10.2.3 Create policy

    10.2.4 Record and manage environmental health and safety events

10.3 Train and educate employees

    10.3.1 Communicate issues to stakeholders and provide support

10.4 Monitor and manage health, safety, and environmental management program
    10.4.1 Manage environmental health and safety costs and benefits
    10.4.2 Measure and report environmental health and safety performance
        10.4.2.1 Implement emergency response program
        10.4.2.2 Implement pollution prevention program
    10.4.3 Provide employees with environmental health and safety support
10.5 Ensure compliance with regulations
    10.5.1 Monitor compliance
    10.5.2 Perform compliance audit
    10.5.3 Comply with regulatory stakeholders requirements
10.6 Manage remediation efforts
    10.6.1 Create remediation plans
    10.6.2 Contact and confer with experts
    10.6.3 Identify/dedicate resources
    10.6.4 Investigate legal aspects
    10.6.5 Investigate damage cause
    10.6.6 Amend or create policy

11.0 Manage External Relationships
11.1 Build investor relationships
    11.1.1 Plan, build, and manage lender relations
    11.1.2 Plan, build, and manage analyst relations
    11.1.3 Communicate with shareholders
11.2 Manage government and industry relationships
    11.2.1 Manage industry relations with government
    11.2.2 Manage relations with quasi-government bodies
    11.2.3 Manage relations with trade or industry groups
    11.2.4 Manage lobby activities
11.3 Manage relations with board of directors
    11.3.1 Report results
    11.3.2 Address audit
11.4 Manage legal and ethical issues
    11.4.1 Create ethics policies

11.4.2 Manage corporate governance policies

11.4.3 Develop and perform preventative law programs

11.4.4 Ensure compliance

11.4.5 Manage outside counsel

    11.4.5.1 Assess problem and determine work requirements

    11.4.5.2 Engage/retain outside counsel if necessary

    11.4.5.3 Receive strategy/budget

    11.4.5.4 Receive work product and manage/monitor case and work performed

    11.4.5.5 Process pay for legal services

    11.4.5.6 Track legal activity/performance

11.4.6 Protect intellectual property

    11.4.6.1 Manage copyrights and patents

    11.4.6.2 Maintain intellectual property rights and restrictions

    11.4.6.3 Administer licensing terms

    11.4.6.4 Administer options

11.4.7 Resolve disputes and litigations

11.4.8 Provide legal advice/counseling

11.4.9 Negotiate and document agreements/contracts

11.5 Manage public relations program

    11.5.1 Manage relations with global customers

    11.5.2 Manage relations with trade and industry groups

    11.5.3 Manage relations with global strategic suppliers

    11.5.4 Manage community relations

    11.5.5 Manage media relations

    11.5.6 Promote political stability

    11.5.7 Create press releases

12.0 Manage Improvement and Change

12.1 Measure organizational performance

    12.1.1 Create enterprise measurement systems model

    12.1.2 Measure process performance

    12.1.3 Measure product and service quality

    12.1.4 Measure cost of quality

    12.1.5 Measure costs

    12.1.6 Measure cycle time

12.1.7 Measure productivity

12.1.8 Measure impact on customers

12.2 Conduct process and functional performance assessments

  12.2.1 Conduct performance assessments based on external criteria

  12.2.2 Conduct performance assessments based on internal criteria

12.3 Conduct knowledge management assessments

  12.3.1 Evaluate existing knowledge management approaches

  12.3.2 Identify gaps and needs

  12.3.3 Enhance/modify existing knowledge management approaches

  12.3.4 Develop new knowledge management approaches

12.4 Benchmark performance

  12.4.1 Develop benchmarking capabilities

  12.4.2 Conduct process benchmarking

  12.4.3 Conduct competitive benchmarking

  12.4.4 Conduct gap analysis to understand the need for and the degree of change needed

  12.4.5 Establish need for change

  12.4.6 Implement corrective action

12.5 Manage change

  12.5.1 Plan for change

    12.5.1.1 Select a robust process improvement methodology

    12.5.1.2 Assess readiness for change

    12.5.1.3 Determine stakeholders

    12.5.1.4 Engage/identify champion

    12.5.1.5 Form design team

    12.5.1.6 Define scope

    12.5.1.7 Understand current state

    12.5.1.8 Define future state

    12.5.1.9 Conduct risk analysis

    12.5.1.10 Assess cultural issues

    12.5.1.12 Identify barriers to change

    12.5.1.13 Determine change enablers

    12.5.1.14 Identify resources and develop measures

  12.5.2 Design the change

    12.5.2.1 Assess connection to other initiatives

    12.5.2.2 Develop change management plans

    12.5.2.3 Develop training plan

    12.5.2.4 Develop communication plan

    12.5.2.5 Develop rewards/incentives plan

    12.5.2.6 Establish metrics

    12.5.2.7 Establish/clarify new roles

    12.5.2.8 Identify budget/roles

  12.5.3 Implement change

    12.5.3.1 Create commitment for improvement/change

    12.5.3.2 Re-engineer business processes and systems

    12.5.3.3 Support transition to new roles or exit strategies for incumbents

    12.5.3.4 Monitor change

  12.5.4 Sustain improvement

    12.5.4.1 Monitor improved process performance

    12.5.4.2 Capture and reuse lessons learned from change process

    12.5.4.3 Take corrective action as necessary

THE APQC PROCESS CLASSIFICATION FRAMEWORK LOOKING FORWARD

The APQC Process Classification Framework is an evolving model, which APQC will continue to enhance and improve regularly. Thus, APQC encourages comments, suggestions, and more importantly, the sharing of insights from having applied the APQC PCF within your organization. Share your suggestions and experiences with the PCF by e-mailing: *pcf_feedback@apqc.org.*

ABOUT APQC

An internationally recognized resource for process and performance improvement, APQC helps organizations adapt to rapidly changing environments, build new and better ways to work, and succeed in a competitive marketplace. With a focus on productivity, knowledge management, benchmarking, and quality improvement initiatives, APQC works with its member organizations to identify best practices, discover effective methods of improvement, broadly disseminate findings, and connect individuals with one another and the knowledge, training, and tools they need to succeed. Founded in 1977, APQC is a member-based nonprofit serving organizations around the world in all sectors of business, education, and government. APQC is also a proud winner of the 2003 and 2004 North American Most Admired Knowledge Enterprises (MAKE) awards. This award is based on a study by Teleos, a European-based research firm, and the KNOW network.

THE APQC PROCESS CLASSIFICATION FRAMEWORK
RIGHTS AND PERMISSIONS
©2004 APQC. ALL RIGHTS RESERVED.

APQC encourages the wide distribution, discussion, and use of the APQC Process Classification Framework as an open standard for classifying and defining processes. Therefore, APQC grants permission for using and copying the framework, as long as acknowledgement is made to the American Productivity & Quality Center. Please notify APQC about your use and application by directing your comments, suggestions, and questions to:

APQC
123 North Post Oak Lane, 3rd Floor
Houston, TX 77024-7797
800-776-9676 (phone)
+01-713-681-4020 (international)
+01-713-681-8578 (fax)
E-mail: *pcf_feedback@apqc.org*
Web site: *www.apqc.org*
Permission granted to photocopy for personal use. ©2004 APQC

Figure 7.5 Process Cycle Time Sheet

In the columns below, list the components of time for each process step.

Step No.	Processing time	Setup time	Wait time	Move time	Inspecting time	Rework time	Total time

Appendix D

Glossary

Activity flowchart: A chart depicting the individual activities of a process.

APQC: American Productivity and Quality Center

As-is flowchart: A flowchart that is an accurate representation of what is actually happening.

Benchmarking: Research that involves making comparisons between your organization and others that are similar. It's typically done between competitors or comparable organizations within one industry.

Best practices: Research that involves analyzing the best processes used within other organizations that are often in other industries.

BPR: Business process reengineering

Brain writing: A technique similar to brainstorming except that the ideas are written down instead of suggested out loud.

Business owner: An individual who is responsible for a specific process or set of processes that can both authorize and approve changes to standard business practices.

Check sheet: A form for gathering data that relate to uncovering both the frequency of problems and their root causes. Used to record types of defects, capture readings, or measure items along a continuum or scale.

Control: An action that self-corrects a process, like an automatic spell-checker or corrector.

Customer report card: A method of feedback and measurement about a process or service in which the customer (either internal or external) responds to the experience by assigning it a letter grade.

Error-proofing: A way of designing procedures so that it's difficult to create errors. Error proofing is done by identifying possible errors, determining a way to detect them, and selecting the type of action to be taken when one is detected.

Facilitator: An individual serving as a walking resource who can set the agenda and lead the team through all the process improvement steps.

Fishbone diagram: A visual display of the potential causes of a problem. Used when there are multiple causes for a problem, or when there's a lack of clarity about the different relationships between different causes.

Flow *kaizen*: A type of *kaizen* where strategic processes are improved in the value stream to give an overall system improvement.

FMEA: Failure mode and effects analysis

Four lenses of analysis: Frustration, quality, time, and cost.

Functional activity flowchart: Represents the middle level of process detail, and refers to job titles and activities or work performed by each individual.

IDC: Interdepartmental cooperation

Individual process *kaizen*: A type of *kaizen* where the team in the work unit improves individual processes within the unit.

Information technologist: An individual who is knowledgeable about technological resources.

Involvement organization: A style of management that gives workers the opportunity to input ideas.

***Kaizen*:** Japanese for "change for the better" or "improvement." A business philosophy of continuous cost reduction, reducing quality problems, and delivery-time reduction through rapid, team-based improvement activity.

***Kaizen* blitz:** A popular improvement technique that combines involvement with data analysis and process thinking.

Lean manufacturing: An initiative focused on eliminating all waste in manufacturing processes. Principles of lean include zero waiting time, zero inventory, scheduling (i.e., an internal customer "pull" instead of "push" system), batch to flow (i.e., cut batch sizes), line balancing and cutting actual process times.

Macro flowchart: Depicts from two to seven steps that comprise the critical elements of a process.

Matrix organization: A style of management where a process owner oversees the larger cross-functional processes of the company.

Maverick: A person placed on a process improvement team who comes from another department within the organization. As someone from outside the department, they bring fresh perspectives to the team.

Pareto diagram: A chart in which information is gathered on a horizontal line in descending order. Used when a problem can be broken down into categories, highlighting the vital few.

Process: Can be defined as either a group of activities that leads to some output or result, the means by which work gets done, or a mechanism to create and deliver value to a customer.

RPN: Risk priority number

Sensei: Japanese for "teacher." A *sensei* is an individual who is expert in applying lean techniques.

Six Sigma: Developed by Motorola, it's a methodology for improving process performance and boosting quality in industry. Literally, "six sigma" refers to the reduction of errors to six standard deviations from the mean value of a process output or task opportunities, i.e., about one error in 300,000 opportunities.

Shutdown: A procedure or device that blocks or shuts down the process when an error occurs. The automatic shutoff feature of a home iron is one example.

TQM: Total quality management

Traditional organization: A style of work management characterized by a hierarchy within departments that report to a president.

Traveler: A document attached to work that "travels" with it through each step, making it possible to calculate process, wait, and cycle times.

Value stream manager: An individual responsible for increasing the ratio of value to non-value and eliminating waste in the overall supply chain from start to finish; for defining a product family; and for ensuring that the value stream meets or exceeds customer requirements.

Warning: An alert to the person involved in the work that something is going wrong. For example, a control chart that shows that a process is "out of control." Warnings too often are ignored, so controls and shutdowns usually are preferable.

Index

ABOUT THE AUTHOR

Dan Madison is a principal at Value Creation Partners, an organizational consulting and training firm. He helps clients increase value through operational improvement, organizational redesign, leadership development, and strategic planning. He's been a consultant and university instructor for more than seventeen years and regularly teaches courses on analyzing and improving relations, leadership development, and process mapping and process management. He has an MBA in finance and is a chartered financial analyst.

You may reach him at:
Value Creation Partners
1207 Krona Lane
Concord, CA 94521
Tel: (925) 459-8755
Fax: (925) 459-0536
E-mail: *dan@valuecreationpartners.com*
Web: *www.valuecreationpartners.com*